FROM PAGE TO PERFORMANCE

Arnold Williams (1907-1992)

FROM PAGE TO PERFORMANCE

ESSAYS IN EARLY ENGLISH DRAMA

EDITED BY JOHN A. ALFORD

Michigan State University Press
East Lansing
1995

All Michigan State University Press books are produced on paper which
meets the requirements of American National Standard of Information
Sciences—Permanence of paper for printed materials ANSI Z39.48-1984.

Michigan State University Press
East Lansing, Michigan 48823-5202

02 01 00 99 98 97 96 95 1 2 3 4 5 6 7 8 9

Library of Congress Cataloging-in-Publication Data

From page to performance : essays in early English drama / edited by John A.
Alford.
  p.   cm.
  Includes bibliographical references and index.
  ISBN 0-87013-379-9
  1. English drama—Early modern and Elizabethan, 1500-1600—History
and criticism. 2. Mysteries and miracle plays, English—History and criticism. 3. English drama—17th century—History and criticism. 4. English
drama—To 1500—History and criticism. I. Alford, John A., 1938-
PR648.F76 1995
822.009—dc20
                                                    95-2384
                                                    CIP

PR
648
. F76
1995

In Memory of Arnold Williams

Contents

Abbreviations   ix

Introduction   1

1. The Mass as Performance Text
   T. P. Dolan   13

2. From *Mappa Mundi* to *Theatrum Mundi*:
   The World as Stage in Early English Drama
   Martin Stevens   25

3. Asleep Onstage
   David Bevington   51

4. Acting Mary: The Emotional Realism of the Mature Virgin
   in the N-Town Plays
   Alexandra F. Johnston   85

5. The Performance of Some Wakefield Master Plays on
   the University of Illinois Campus
   John B. Friedman   99

6. The Problem with Mrs. Noah: The Search for Performance
   Credibility in the Chester *Noah's Flood* Play
   William G. Marx   109

7. The Theaters of *Everyman*
   David Mills   127

vii

8. "My Name is Worship": Masquerading Vice in
    Medwall's *Nature*
    John A. Alford   151

9. Plays, Players, and Playwrights in Renaissance Oxford
    John R. Elliott, Jr.   179

10. English Chronicle Contexts for Shakespeare's Death
    of Richard II
    Lister M. Matheson   195

11. Family by Death: Stage Images in *Titus Andronicus* and
    The Winter's Tale
    Randal Robinson   221

12. Bearing "A Wary Eye": Ludic Vengeance and Doubtful
    Suicide in *Hamlet*
    Philip C. McGuire   235

    Contributors   255

    Index   259

Abbreviations

BL	British Library
ChR	*Chaucer Review*
CUL	Cambridge University Library
e.s.	extra series
EEDS	Early English Drama Society
EETS	Early English Text Society
EHR	*English Historical Review*
ELH	*English Literary History*
ELR	*English Literary Renaissance*
fol(s).	folio(s)
MED	*Middle English Dictionary*
MS(S)	manuscript(s)
MSR	Malone Society Reprint
N&Q	*Notes and Queries*
n.s.	new series
OED	*Oxford English Dictionary*
PL	J.-P. Migne. *Patrologiae Cursus Completus. Series Latina.* 221 vols.
PMLA	*Publications of the Modern Language Association of America*
REED	Records of Early English Drama (Toronto)
RES	*Review of English Studies*
S.D.	stage direction
s.s.	supplementary series
sc.	scene
ShQ	*Shakespeare Quarterly*

Introduction

I t is a truism that reading a dramatic script is like reading a musical score. Whatever impression may be conveyed by the printed page, the only measure of worth that matters ultimately is performance.

The point hardly needs stating in the case of modern drama. *The Importance of Being Ernest* or *A Streetcar Named Desire* are stock repertory because of their proven appeal as theater, and more people are likely to have seen these plays than to have read them. The reverse is true of our knowledge of earlier drama. Generally speaking, our *only* experience of a liturgical play like the Beauvais *Daniel*, or a Tudor morality like *Fulgens and Lucrece*, or even some of Shakespeare's plays, has come through books.

The *letteraturizzazione* of early drama—to borrow George Kennedy's term for the process undergone by another oral art, rhetoric, as it moved from the forum to the schoolroom[1]—has had profound consequences for criticism. Until recently it controlled our artistic judgments of these plays. Tucker Brooke's assessment of Merbury's *Marriage between Wit and Wisdom* (ca. 1579) provides a fair sample: "The poet has managed to get into the piece enough of irrelevant farce and melodramatic interest to make it tolerable reading."[2] Critics nowadays are less likely to speak in such terms. The fact that our knowledge of these older plays still comes primarily from reading continues to affect our critical judgments, of course, but the subtler challenges are now in the area of critical interpretation. The improper application of literary methods to dramatic works has resulted in interpretations that would be difficult or impossible to sustain in any actual performance.

The late Arnold Williams was especially sensitive to the confusion of literary and dramatic methodologies. One instance that came under his scrutiny was typological criticism. Williams readily conceded that

1

the cycle playwrights' *choices* of particular biblical stories might have
been determined by typology—a standard tool of medieval biblical
exegetes, who assumed, for example, that Abraham's sacrifice of Isaac
was intended to be a "type" or prefiguration of the sacrifice of Christ—
but he questioned how far this interpretative method could be pushed
within individual plays.

> [M]edieval drama . . . was produced in conditions almost strictly analo-
> gous to those governing a modern film or television program. There
> was no way by which anyone could experience the *Second Shepherds' Play*
> except by witnessing it. . . . The kind of typology such an audience
> could effectively absorb had to be simplified, common, obvious. It will
> not do to cite Irenaeus, Tertullian, Augustine, Aquinas. These are as
> remote to the medieval audience as are Robert Graves or Maud Bodkin
> to the television viewer of today, and remoter than Marx or Freud. . . . I
> am persuaded that most typologists forget this. They are suggesting
> meanings appropriate for literary texts but inappropriate for the
> stage.[3]

Williams was not opposed to typological interpretation as such. "If
any suggested typology is capable of representation on the stage, and
if it enhances and deepens the meaning of the piece, let us accept it"
(1968, 681). From his own experience, however, he was convinced
that more often than not "the use of typology produces bad theater"
(683). In drama the ultimate test of meaning, as of artistic value, is
performance.

For Williams, therefore, the modern production of medieval
drama was, among other things, a research tool, a form of inquiry no
less important than the study of its cultural context and history; and
much of his career was given to promoting the performance of these
old plays. His classes in medieval drama at Michigan State University,
where he taught from 1939 until 1974, often involved the blocking
and acting out of scenes, and sometimes culminated in full-scale productions open to the public. A few of these (*Mankind* and the
Wakefield *Second Shepherds' Play*), directed by his student William
Marx, were presented before even wider audiences at annual meetings of the International Congress on Medieval Studies at Western
Michigan University (Kalamazoo). It was also Williams's thoughts on
the value of performance, delivered at a meeting of the Modern
Language Association in 1965, that inspired John Leyerle to organize
his first graduate seminar at the University of Toronto around the
production of a medieval play—the beginning, as it turned out, of the
Poculi Ludique Societas, for many years the most active medieval and

Renaissance play group in North America. When the British Broadcasting Corporation decided to make its performances of *The First Stage (English Drama from its Beginnings to the 1580s)* available on phonograph record, it was to Williams that the publisher turned for the program notes.[4] He was the ideal choice, not only because he had long campaigned for reviving "the first stage" through performance, but also because he was uniquely capable of illuminating the performance aspects of these early plays in simple and direct language.[5] In short, it can be said that Williams, as much as anyone else in modern times, helped to bring early English drama back to life.

The subject of this book, written expressly to recognize Arnold Williams's contribution to our understanding of early English drama, is, most appropriately, dramatic performance. All twelve essays— whether focused mainly on dramatic texts or on actual productions, both early and modern—are bound by a keen awareness of the difference between the two, of the pitfalls that lie in the way (as Williams so often reminded us) from page to performance.

In the first essay T. P. Dolan argues for a correlation between lay literacy and clerical approaches to the Mass as a "performance text." As congregations were gradually shut out from an understanding of the Liturgy by their ignorance of Latin, many priests compensated by trying to make the Mass more dramatic. In this they were guided primarily by the typological interpretation of Amalarius of Metz (d. 850), who connected each stage of the Mass with an event from the last days of Christ. Like Williams, Dolan is concerned with how and to what extent such typologies could be communicated by performance. Drawing upon the text of the York Rite, as found in the vernacular *Lay Folks Mass-Book,* he attempts "to come to some conclusions as to the degree of passivity or activity experienced by members of the congregation at Mass."

In his study of the convention of "world as stage," Martin Stevens examines the typology of performance itself. The convention is best known, as he observes, from Shakespeare's *As You Like It*—

> All the world's a stage,
> And all the men and women merely players—

but Shakespeare inherited the idea from medieval dramatic tradition. A key element in the formation of that tradition was the medieval *mappa mundi.* Pointing to such examples as the Hereford and Ebstorf maps, which show the known world contracted within a circle, Stevens argues that early dramatists were similarly disposed to create stages that replicated the world. "The idea of the *mappa mundi* can be inscribed onto a dedicated theatrical space, such as the stage of *The Castle of Perseverance,* or it can serve as a superimposition to convert an entire city into a stage as happened at York and at Chester." During the Renaissance, notably in the plays of Shakespeare, the medieval idea of the *theatrum mundi* is "brought into critical, metatheatrical play."

Using a different example, David Bevington argues along similar lines. Like the convention of the world as stage, that of sleeping onstage "is a theatrical motif that seems to connect Tudor and Stuart English drama with medieval drama"; it too "undergoes considerable change over time," until it too is transformed into a metatheatrical image, "consciously connected by Renaissance dramatists with the very business of writing and acting plays." Bevington traces the changing metaphorical significance of the convention over a span of nearly 500 years, from its earliest appearance in twelfth-century plays like the Fleury *Herod* until its decline in the seventeenth century.

While the first three essays are concerned with the realization of metaphor in performance—with the Passion played out in the parts of the Mass, with the world as stage, with sleep as "a theatrical signifier" of various ideas—the next three essays explore the usefulness of modern performance as a critical tool. Alexandra F. Johnston's choice of words in describing the Toronto *Poculi Ludique Societas* sets the theme: "The group has passed through many phases . . . but it remains at the center of much of what we now *know* about early drama" (italics added). Johnston's own experience of acting Mary in the N-Town cycle led her to a deeper appreciation of the "emotional realism" of this character. "If you have never been called on to act this role," she stresses, it is easy to pass over the Virgin's late-in-life speeches as "painful, but formulaic." As Johnston discovered, they are anything but formulaic in their power to evoke an emotional response. The effect must have been even greater in the fifteenth century. "The portrayal of the Virgin . . . as a mature woman whose life experience paralleled that of many members of the audience," she concludes, "is yet another way that women's spiritual needs found empathetic expression."

John B. Friedman's account of several performances at the University of Illinois provides a different slant on the issue of "emotional realism." For example, his use of cast members' children as the victims in the Chester *Massacre of the Innocents* proved unacceptable to the audience, "for whom the line between drama and reality had already been weakened and threatened by their familiarity with the actors." It was necessary to substitute dolls. Friedman's experience helped to illuminate, for him, three characteristics of the cycle plays emphasized by his mentor Williams: "their improvisatory and puppet-show-like qualities, their incorporation of popular and secular elements, and the fact that the actors playing divine or sometimes diabolical roles were usually ordinary townspeople well-known to the audiences." These characteristics guided Friedman's productions, in particular, of the Wakefield *Noah*. "As each new class of students came to realize," he reports," the experience of play production brought a degree of textual understanding and awareness of staging problems that no amount of classroom analysis of the text could equal."

Read in conjunction with Friedman's piece, William G. Marx's account of his direction of the Chester *Noah's Flood* provides an excellent illustration of how the same narrative can be made to yield, in the hands of different directors, vastly different results. Friedman's production of the Wakefield *Noah* played up the shrewishness of Noah's wife "for comic and satirical purposes"; in Marx's opinion her very appeal as "*the* archetypal shrewish wife" poses a threat to the story's basic message of reconciliation. Her character is a potential distraction. "To give Mrs. Noah a human character and to integrate her role into the dramatic progress of the *whole* play," Marx suggests, "directors need to help their actors preserve Mrs. Noah's feisty spirit and comic action, while they bring that spirit and action to the service of higher—in fact, transforming and transcending—purposes."

The creation of a new dramatic genre in the late Middle Ages, the morality play, both complicated and expanded the expressive possibilities of theatrical performance. Complications arose from the fact that many of the allegorical devices native to literature were not readily adaptable to the stage; for example, to give substantive form to certain abstractions, such as Anima (soul), was to betray or contradict their very essence. On the other hand, conventions that had developed as part of dramatic tradition, such as the metaphor of "the world as stage," were vastly enriched by their union with allegory.

When the idea of the world as stage is brought within the allegorical mode of a morality play such as *Everyman*, its tendency, as David Mills shows, is to replicate itself in a series of variations. The *theatrum mundi* unlooses a plenitude of "theaters." It is this metaphorical energy in *Everyman* that largely explains how a work probably "intended for private reading, not for theatrical performance" has paradoxically become one of the most popular and frequently performed of all medieval plays. Initially the stage opens out upon the cosmos: God is represented as the "spectator of a play of his own creation." The focus is then narrowed to "the theater of the world."

Whereas the God of the cycles constructs the city in which the cycle is
performed as the world, in *Everyman* specific allusions to *worldly prosperyte*
and *worldly ryches* characterize a more restricted society, one that is
wealthier and materialistic. . . . What is evidently a nobleman's hall [the
implied setting] thus becomes a metaphor of the world, its ostensible
security the illusory materialism that is the prime initial target of the play.

As Everyman turns from Goods to Good Deeds, from the material to
the spiritual, the acting space shrinks further "from worldly society to
the inner world of the mind." At the same time the allegorical mode
shifts. Unlike Goods and those other fair-weather friends (Fellowship,
Kindred, and Cousin), Good Deeds "exists" only in Everyman's past,
that is, in "the theater of memory." Further allegorical shifts redesig-
nate the acting space as "the theater of salvation" and finally, as the
grave-bound protagonist recalls the Strength and Beauty of his youth,
"the theater of the body." In short, Mills concludes, "*Everyman*'s
appeal and power result in large measure from the accommodation
of familiar elements of performance to its metaphoric strategy, redesignating its acting spaces and drawing upon a variety of dramatic and
allegorical modes."

The morality's assimilation of another important convention, pseu-
donymous vice, proved more difficult. Although it had long been a
familiar part of literary allegory, dating back to Prudentius's
Psychomachia (late fifth century), the topos was not translated into dramatic form until Henry Medwall's *Nature* (ca. 1500). Its essential liter-
ariness impeded the process. "Reading a text and watching a play are
very different kinds of experience," John A. Alford observes, "and
until an adequate *dramatic* rhetoric had been developed the figure of
masquerading vice could not express itself." That rhetoric, as formulated by Medwall, is both verbal and visual. The vices' characteristic
use of pseudonyms (Pride: "My name is Worship") is extended in a
variety of speech habits (sophistry, mistranslation, slips of the tongue,
laughter) and visual signs (principally costume). In *Nature*, then, the
masquerade of vice functions as far more than clever convention. "It
is an emblem of the psychological matrix out of which the entire play
develops." The play's protagonist, Man, believes that Pride is Worship
because he *wants* to believe it. The vices are not autonomous persons.
"Pride and his confederates are only the projections of Man's will;
and their 'disguises' merely his own rationalizations." After Medwall's
successful translation of masquerading vice from page to performance, the figure came to dominate the sixteenth-century morality—
not only because it distilled a complete psychology of sin but also
because it proved to be excellent theater.

Medwall's transformation of the morality play probably helped to keep it alive for another hundred years. Even after it had run its course, however, the stage career of its popular villain continued to prosper. Masquerading vice did not fade with the dramatic vehicle that had made him a star. He simply *evolved*—into Shakespeare's Iago, Richard III, and Sir John Falstaff. Although other elements of the morality tradition also survived in various forms, strictly allegorical drama died a lingering death in academia. The *bellum intestinum* was reduced to the *bellum grammaticale*—the latter actually the name of an extremely popular interlude in which the parts of speech do battle with one another, performed, as John R. Elliott, Jr. notes in the next essay, at Oxford in 1581.

Academic drama was far more than a shelter for effete dramatic forms, however, and Elliott offers a fascinating glimpse of a vital, innovative tradition in Renaissance Oxford. Play production was "quasi-curricular," regulated and supported financially by the colleges. Though university officials were unfriendly toward itinerant players, their encouragement of student performances "reflected the humanist conception of the practical value that drama was thought to have in the training of young men for public life." Elliott describes several performances at both the college and university levels. The former he illustrates from an anthology of play-texts called *The Christmas Prince*, "commemorating the performance of eight different plays by the students of St. John's over the Christmas vacation of 1607-8, on a scale to match the revels of the Inns of Court in London, on which they were clearly modeled." Even more ambitious were the performances mounted by the university as a whole. These took place during royal visits. Elliott describes the performances arranged for the visits of Elizabeth I in 1566 and 1592; of James I in 1605; and of Charles I in 1636. Most striking to the modern observer, perhaps, is the level of rowdiness, destruction, and even violence associated with such events—in this respect the forerunners of today's soccer matches.

Finally, our study of performance, like many other studies of early English drama, culminates in Shakespeare. Countering Derek Traversi's description of the death of the king in *Richard II* as "no more than a pedestrian piece of melodramatic writing," Lister M. Matheson argues that "a consideration of Shakespeare's sources shows that the manner of Richard's death represents a choice among conflicting current accounts and that the language has been carefully constructed." According to Shakespeare's main sources, the chronicles of Hall and Holinshed, the commonly accepted view was that Richard had died of forced starvation. Yet Shakespeare chose to dramatize his death as the result of a blow from a poleax by Sir Piers de Exton. There can be no doubt about which method lends itself better to performance. But there is a generic consideration as well. If Shakespeare "has deliberately chosen the most colorful (and melodramatic) but not the commonly accepted account," Matheson points out, "he would be asserting quite categorically that *Richard II* is a *tragedie*, not a chronicle play." In fact, Matheson goes on to note, the melodramatic version actually became the accepted one over the course of the sixteenth century.

The visual aspects of performance are the focus of Randal Robinson's essay. By "reading the stage images" of *Titus Andronicus* and *The Winter's Tale*, he argues, we can find connections between the two "that reside deeper than words." Provisionally treating the plays as dumb shows, Robinson offers up haunting and disturbing descriptions of their parallel action. "Significant messages wait in such visual links," he claims, "emotionally charged fantasies . . . of killing the infant and setting the infant free." The principal difference between the two plays is that Leontes "makes a kind of progress that modern therapists would associate with health," whereas Titus "makes no essential changes." Compared to *The Winter's Tale, Titus Andronicus* is a nightmare, but one whose visual impact forces us to confront our own deepest, communal fears.

No less crucial to interpretation is the visual imagery of *Hamlet,* but, as Philip C. McGuire shows, the text offers little guidance at the most critical moments. That Hamlet kills Laertes and Claudius is certain. But how? Does he wound Laertes with the same agility and grace with which he scored his earlier touches (as in Olivier's 1948 film)? Or does the fencing match degenerate into a brawl (as in Zeffirelli's 1990 film)? Does he force Claudius to drink from the poisoned cup (as in most productions) or not (as in Peter Hall's 1965 production for the Royal Shakespeare Company and in Trevor Nunn's for the same company five years later)? Does he stab Claudius cooly, "tempering passion by discretion"? Or does he run him through in a fury? How many times? In what parts of the body? The answers to such questions, which the text leaves open, must necessarily be provided in performance. McGuire suggests that the interpretative problems raised by these deaths are anticipated in Shakespeare's handling of Ophelia's death. Although the text specifically addresses the manner of her death, it does so in a way that is calculated to create uncertainty. Gertrude describes Ophelia's death as a suicide, but the priest officiating at her funeral declares, "Her death was doubtful." Moreover, our own judgment is made inescapably "doubtful," McGuire points out, by a factor easily overlooked in reading: we "do not see her death performed." So whether we see the act performed (the deaths of Laertes, Claudius, Gertrude, Hamlet) or hear it reported (the death of Ophelia), the play anticipates and allows for diverse opinion. "*Hamlet* is profoundly concerned with the specific judgments and interpretations one comes to," McGuire concludes, "but it is also concerned, at least equally, with the processes by which they are reached."

McGuire's subtle analysis of the grounds of meaning in *Hamlet* is a fitting conclusion to the collection as a whole. It confronts directly the unifying assumption that dramatic meaning is realized only in performance. *Which* Hamlet emerges from the countless possibilities implicit in the text depends on the director, the actor, the audience, the setting, the occasion. The same is true of pre-Shakespearean drama. John B. Friedman, guided by medieval convention and his sense of the "puppet-like" style of medieval acting, chose to play Mrs. Noah as the archetypal shrew; while William G. Marx, clearly influenced by the modern methods of Constantin Stanislavski, sought to realize her character as a function of the play's larger purpose. One can argue at length about which approach is more appropriate, but ultimately the issue will be decided in the theater. The "meaning" of any play, medieval or modern, is whatever meaning performance will sustain. Despite the original anti-Reformation intent of *Everyman,* "a topicality that is lost in a modern revival," David Mills reminds us of the power of performance to awaken other meanings in this play; and Alexandra F. Johnston confirms that her own "experience of acting Mary" brought life to lines that had earlier seemed merely formulaic. Performance is more than simply a vehicle of meaning. It is also, as Arnold Williams insisted repeatedly, an instrument for exploring and discovering meaning. What a play means or can mean is not clear until it is actually performed.

This view of performance is hardly modern. Behind the church's condemnation of Amalarius of Metz's allegorization of the Mass, and of those clergy who treated it as "a performance text," there lay the fear of an uncontrollable proliferation of meanings. Protecting the mystery required limiting the participation of the laity. Dolan provides ample evidence of the "sense of separation between the action on the altar and the experience of the parishioners." While the priest silently mumbled the prayers in Latin, his back turned, the members of the congregation were largely "left to their own devices." By contrast dramatic performances were participatory affairs. The "sense of separation" was slight. Often players and playgoers occupied the same space, and the latter might find themselves not only placed in the midst of the action but also transformed on the spot into *dramatis personae.* Mills points out that *Everyman* "assigns a role to the audience in the manner of the cycle plays where, as here, the literal gaze of the actor-God reconstitutes the audience as the totality of humankind." God's command to Death at the beginning of the play, "Go thou to Eueryman," seems to lack a specific referent. "Everyman is Anyman among the audience gathered in the space before God, and the actor Death might draw any one of them into the play, just as Death might strike anyone." This "easy interchange of actor and spectator" characterizes other hall interludes as well— Mills cites Medwall's *Fulgens and Lucrece,* Alford adds *The Trial of Treasure* and *The Contention between Liberality and Prodigality,* and Elliott notes Queen Elizabeth's practice of "interrupting the actors and speaking back to them," by no means a purely royal prerogative.

Medieval and Renaissance playwrights not only brought the audience into the performance, they also called attention to the performance as an object in itself. They did so by means of certain metatheatrical devices, that is, conventions that invited the audience to contemplate the nature of the medium and hence the whole problem of dramatic meaning.[6] As the convention of sleeping onstage became increasingly metatheatrical, Bevington observes, it also became "an apt vehicle for explorations of . . . indeterminacy of meaning." The same thing happened, Alford notes, when the literary convention of masquerading vice was relocated within an art form that was itself a masquerade: the figure served unavoidably as a commentary on the essential dramatic act of impersonation, and the figure's habitual abuse of language also called into question the verbal medium of which it was now a part. But the definitive example, traced by Stevens from its origin until it was "brought into critical, metatheatrical play" during the Renaissance, is the world as stage. The two became "poetically interchangeable subjects." The stage is a figure of the world, and, conversely, "the discourse of the plays themselves reinforced for the audience that the world as imagined by the playwright is indeed a stage." The hope implicit in this merging of life and performance partly explains the imaginative appeal of the convention in Shakespeare's time. For experienced playgoers, both then and now, the sour determinism of Jacques's famous speech—

> All the world's a stage,
> And all the men and women merely players—

is answered by the acquired knowledge that meaning is in the performance and that each part can be played in many ways.

Notes

1. "*Letteraturizzazione* is the tendency of rhetoric to shift its focus from persuasion to narration, from civic to personal contexts, and from discourse to literature, including poetry" (George Kennedy, *Classical Rhetoric and Its Christian and Secular Tradition from Ancient to Modern Times* [Chapel Hill: University of North Carolina Press, 1980], 5).
2. Tucker Brooke, *The Tudor Drama* (Boston: Houghton Mifflin, 1911), 77.
3. Arnold Williams, "Typology and the Cycle Plays: Some Criteria," *Speculum* 43 (1968): 679-80.
4. The boxed set of five records comprises BBC performances (directed by John Barton) of the following plays: *The Creation and Fall* (a composite based on Norwich, Chester, York, Wakefield, and N-Town), *Abraham and Isaac* (Brome, Chester, and Wakefield), *Noah's Flood* (Newcastle, Chester, and Wakefield), *The Nativity* (Wakefield), *The Betrayal, Trial, and Crucifixion* (York, Wakefield), and *The Resurrection* (York). The series also includes other boxed sets of later plays, such as *The Castle of Perseverance, Everyman, Fulgens and Lucrece, Hickscorner, Ralph Roister Doister, Gorboduc,* and *The Spanish Tragedy*; in all 27 plays (New York: Dover Publications, 1970).
5. Williams's talent for finding a simple, often homely, means of explaining complex phenomena is seen again and again in his scholarly writings. Of typology as metaphor, for example, he writes: "Any metaphor involves a transference, a fact which was brought home to me most forcibly in a recent visit to Greece, where the moving vans are labelled metaforai, 'metaphors'" ("Typology and the Cycle Plays," 679). Years before O. B. Hardison launched his elaborate argument against the evolutionary theory of dramatic development (*Christian Rite and Christian Drama*), Williams offered a simple analogy as refutation: "How perilous it is to deal with problems of chronology as though they were problems of logic will appear if we take the 'evolution' of some familiar device. An archaeologist of 3100 A.D., having dug up several refrigerators, might well arrange them in this order: simple wooden boxes for ice, more elaborate metal boxes for ice, metal boxes for mechanical refrigeration. But those who lived through the period when the mechanical refrigerator replaced the ice box know better. The right order is: wooden boxes for ice, mechanical refrigerators, metal boxes for ice. The makers of wooden ice boxes, suffering from the competition of the mechanical boxes, redesigned their product in metal" (*The Drama of Medieval England* [East Lansing: Michigan State University Press, 1961], 12).
6. The presence of such devices at an early stage in the history of the drama has led scholars recently to re-evaluate the sophistication of the playwrights and their audiences. Pamela King's assessment of the five surviving medieval moralities typifies current opinion: "Each play, far from representing a beginning, demonstrates an allusive, self-conscious theatricality. The texts show a variety of ways in which their authors manipulated the boundary between the play world and the real world, often

addressing the audience directly and using the varied communication codes of the theatre to draw them into the action of the play. The assumption within the texts of audiences sufficiently competent and experienced in the workings of theatre to comply with such strictly metatheatrical devices again seems to bear witness to the maturity of the form" (*The Cambridge Companion to Medieval English Theatre*, ed. Richard Beadle [Cambridge: Cambridge University Press, 1994], 262).

The Mass as Performance Text

T. P. Dolan

Some ministers of religion who have seized on the dramatic possibilities of conducting services in order to win over the hearts and minds of their parishioners have attracted criticism. For instance, in a poem entitled "In Church" Thomas Hardy writes about a preacher who is seen by one of his parishioners after he has gone into the vestry after a service:

> The door swings softly ajar meanwhile,
> And a pupil of his in the Bible class,
> Who adores him as one without gloss or guile,
> Sees her idol stand with a satisfied smile
> And re-enact at the vestry-glass
> Each pulpit gesture in deft dumb-show
> That had moved the congregation so.[1]

It is obvious that the poet disapproves of the histrionics of this preacher who seemed so natural and unartificial to the congregation when he was in the pulpit. Even so, the preacher himself saw nothing wrong with using dramatic gestures in order to move his congregation. This preacher had a script, and he made it interesting by acting it out because the message of his sermon was apparently not lively enough to maintain his congregation's attention. The church's teachings were repeated so often that they had ceased to be effective without some attempt at dramatic representation. Hardy's clergyman was a contemporary Protestant, but the basis of this kind of criticism has a very long history in the Liturgy of the Christian church. Centuries earlier, as we shall see, commentators had voiced their disapproval of priests who performed the Liturgy as if they were actors who had rehearsed their scripts like Hardy's preacher. The danger lay in the

13

possibility that the pleasure experienced by the laity in witnessing such theatricality would lessen or remove the spiritual benefit of attending a prescribed service of the church.

In this essay I wish to examine the implications of a remark made long ago by E. K. Chambers: "At least from the fourth century, the central and most solemn rite of [Christian] worship was the Mass, an essentially dramatic commemoration of one of the most critical moments in the life of the Founder."[2] Much discussion has centered on Chambers's phrase "essentially dramatic." Karl Young, for example, insisted that the Mass could not be considered "dramatic" unless it involved impersonation by the priest.[3] O. B. Hardison's use of the word was less rigid. "That the service . . . is dramatic cannot be doubted," he said. "The nature and, as it might be called, the tonality of the drama is another matter."[4] On "the nature . . . of the drama" critics still do not agree. As David Bevington observes, "The dividing line between the liturgy itself and liturgical drama is exasperatingly hard to locate."[5] My purpose here is not to reopen, much less to settle, the question of whether the Mass is rightly described as "essentially dramatic." I am more interested in early views of the Mass as a performance text and in the changing nature of the roles played by the celebrant and by the congregation itself. If the medieval Mass was not drama, the way in which it was performed was sufficiently *like drama* to elicit concern and even condemnation in some quarters.

"The Sacrifice of the Mass," as it is properly called, is a "representation and renewal of the offering made on Calvary."[6] It is an unbloody acting out of Christ's sacrifice of himself at the Crucifixion, as defined at the Council of Trent: "Et quoniam in divino hoc sacrificio, quod in Missa peragitur, idem ille Christus continetur et incruente immolatur."[7] The Mass was celebrated as a public act by a priest with a congregation as audience, most of whom would not have understood the words since they were originally in Greek, and even when the Mass was translated into Latin some time during the third century,[8] the congregation's apprehension of the actual words may not have been very great. What they experienced was a spectacle in which the actions of the celebrant symbolically demonstrated the story of the Last Supper. Even so, it appears that members of the congregation were able to understand the words spoken by the priest to a certain extent up to about the eighth and ninth centuries. During that period it became the practice for priests to say many of the prayers in silence, which left the congregations to their own devices except when they heard the priest declaiming the words of the canon of the Mass aloud. After then it appears that the laity no longer understood most of the Latin of the prayers.[9]

The reduced active participation of the laity led to some attempts to excite their interest by dramatizing the proceedings. The most famous of these was devised by Amalarius of Metz (780?-850).[10] In book 3 of his *De Officiis Libri IV* Amalarius relates the various parts of the Mass to incidents in Christ's life and by so doing presents the celebrant's role as an allegorical reenactment of events in the life of the Savior. For instance, in dealing with the greeting *Pax vobiscum* or *Dominus vobiscum*, Amalarius gives a series of citations from the Bible to explain its significance, among them a reference to the salutation which Christ gave to his disciples before the Resurrection: "Sic et Christus antequam ascenderet in coelum benedicit eos, sicut scriptum est in Evangelio Lucae: *Eduxit autem eos foras in Bethaniam; et elevatis manibus suis, benedixit eis* (Luc. XXIV)" (*PL* 105: 1116). Later he uses this same quotation from Luke to explain the dramatic circumstances of the last blessing in the Mass, after the rites have been concluded: "Etenim Dominus ant ascensionem in coelos duxit discipulis in Bethaniam, ibique benedixit eos, et ascendit in coelum (Luc. ult.). Hunc morem tenet sacerdos, ut post omnia sacramenta consummata, benedicat populo, atque salutet" (*PL* 105: 1155).

The attempts that Amalarius made to inform the laity of the significance of the Liturgy of the Mass were regarded as unorthodox, and the work was hereticated by the Council of Quiercy in 838.[11] Even so, despite reservations about this and other attempts to render the Mass more appealing to the laity, who otherwise would not have known what was going on at the altar, there seems to have been a fashion for priests of a histrionic bent to dramatize the Liturgy. Aelred of Rievaulx (1109-67) was so incensed by the theatrical antics of some priests that in a lively chapter in his *Speculum Charitatis* he describes them almost as if they were modern opera singers and complains that they sang the services with strangulated voices (sometimes resembling the neighing of horses or women's voices), accompanied by twisting and turning their bodies:

Nunc vox stringitur, nunc frangitur, nunc impingitur, nunc diffusiori sonitu dilatatur. Aliquando, quod pudet dicere, in equinos hinnitus cogitur; aliquando virili vigore deposito, in feminieae vocis gracilitates acuitur, nonnumquam artificia quadam circumvolutione torquetur et retorquetur. (*PL* 195: 571)

Such was the histrionic way they moved their bodies, even their lips and shoulders, he continues, that you would think you were at the theater, not at church: "ut eos non ad oratorium, sed at theatrum, nec ad orandum, sed ad spectandum aestimes convenisse." These priests, he claims, had no sense of the awe necessary for celebrating the mystery of the consecration of the bread and wine into the Body and Blood of Christ. What is interesting is that he identifies the fact that the laity are being presented with a spectacle, similar to the experience of a theatrical performance—an obvious result of the tendency of the "orthodox" clergy to exclude them from actively participating in the Liturgy. Some concessions, however, seem to have been made in the twelfth century when, for the first time, the Host was elevated at the consecration in the Mass and both celebrant and people knelt down.[12] At least then, at the most dramatic part of the Mass, the laity were able to know and join in what was happening.

The reason that this appears to be such a dramatic event in the Mass is that the elevation of the Host is the central act of the canon, although all of the canon was said silently. It is unlikely that the laity in England ever knew enough Latin in the early stages of their Christian history to join in with the prayers of the celebrant. This part of the service was always nonparticipatory. By contrast, in the Gallican rite, the members of the congregation were originally expected to join in, but later their understanding of the Latin was lost.[13] It may be assumed, then, that the congregations in England had little part to play in the recitation of the prayers of the Mass by the priest. Even so, examination of a text of the Mass will furnish some indication of the way a Mass was performed and of what the congregation was able to witness of the narrative stages in its development, because it was designed as "a memorial of the Passion, Resurrection and Ascension of our Lord—that is, of the sacrifice whereby he redeemed us."[14] In other words, the Mass was a dramatization of the biblical narrative of the most important events of Christ's final period on this earth.

The text of the Mass on which the following discussion is based comes from the York Rite and was designed to be said on Trinity Sunday.[15] It is a good representative of the type of Mass attended by parishioners of the diocese of York, and also of other types of Masses, because the basic format of the liturgical sacrifice (excluding the prayers) was fixed from about the beginning of the thirteenth century. Indeed, apart from major changes, such as the genuflection at the elevation of the Host, the medieval plan of the Mass did not differ substantially from that constructed during the reign of Pope Gregory the Great (590-604).[16] This form lasted long after the medieval period, as comparison with the Mass text used up to the modern era shows.[17] There was some variation in the placing of some prayers before the canon of the Mass (e.g., the *Gloria* and the *Kyrie Eleison*), but the basic action was established.

In the York Rite, the congregation sees the priest wash his hands and hears him intone a series of prayers before going to the altar, preceded by his ministers in order. He then says the *Confiteor,* in which he confesses that he has sinned. The ministers and congregation then make their confession as participants in the sacrifice of the Mass, and the priest asks God to grant them absolution and remission of all their sins. The congregation acknowledges his prayer with "Amen."

After the confessions, the York Rite rubric instructs the priest to walk up the steps to the altar and say a prayer comprising quotations from the Psalms, after which he says "Dominus Vobiscum" (The Lord be with you), to which the congregation replies, "Et cum spiritu tuo" (And with thy spirit). The priest then alters the stance of his body and bows to the altar, asks God to take our iniquities away from us, and ends with the traditional concluding formula "Per Dominum nostrum . . ." (Through Our Lord), a formula that is used throughout the service to signal the end of a set piece of praying and which keeps the congregation informed of the evolution of the action.

The priest then stands upright again, makes the sign of the cross on himself, and moves to the right side of the altar to say the office of that feast day. There is more action then because he is instructed to incense the altar as a mark of honor to God.

The actions performed during the celebration of the Mass were invested, as we have seen, with the allegorical meanings of Amalarius of Metz and other commentators. Indeed, Amalarius started a trend,[18] one that became so important that the list of possible allegorical interpretations was always being extended. For instance, the raising of the Host at the consecration was said to suggest the raising of Christ on the cross, just as the taking down of his body was represented by the lowering of the Host after the words of consecration. As far as we can tell, priests saying Mass were to a varying extent familiar with the relationship between their actions on the altar and the narrative of Christ's sufferings, death, resurrection, and ascension into heaven.[19] Presumably the lay members of the congregations were also at least superficially aware of the significance of what was happening on the altar, but this is to regard the laity's experience of going to Mass in intellectual terms. It would be more enlightening to try to envisage how the members of the congregation would experience the controlled dramatic energy inherent in the celebration of a blood sacrifice involving the miracle of transubstantiation.

The text of the Mass was not fixed in its entirety until the publication of the *Missale Romanum,* authorized by Pope Pius V in July 1570 after the deliberations of the Council of Trent.[20] The text contained in this missal became the standard version throughout the Western church. In many ways, however, its main effect was to remove local variations that had become attached to the standard text, the main ingredients of which had become well established by the sixteenth century, especially the canon of the Mass, which by the end of the sixth century already resembled the Tridentine Canon.[21]

Using the version of *The Lay Folks Mass-Book* edited by Simmons from British Library Royal MS 17 B xvii (dated ca. 1375),[22] the *Ordo Missae In Festo Sanctae Trinitatis Secundum Usum Matris Ecclesiae Eboracensis*, edited by Simmons from MS York Minster Library xvi.A.9 (dated ca. 1425),[23] and the *Ordo Missae* from the Tridentine text of the Mass,[24] we shall be able to come to some conclusions as to the degree of passivity or activity experienced by members of the congregation at Mass. Certainly the clergy seem to have been anxious to increase the laity's awareness of what was happening, but our concern is with what a parishioner would see and hear, whether or not he or she had been instructed in the allegorical meanings of the celebrant's movements. If members of the congregation had little or no idea of the meditations they should be saying as the Mass progressed, they would have no experience of having been at a church service except for the sounds and actions produced by the celebrant and his assistants at the altar. According to Eamon Duffy's reading of the evidence from the fourteenth century and onward, the individual members of the congregations were virtually left to their own devices to say well-known prayers such as the Our Father and the Glory Be to coincide with, but rarely to duplicate, the stages of the narrative being enacted by the celebrant on the altar.[25] This growing sense of separation between the action on the altar and the experience of the parishioners is corroborated in a story relayed by Simmons of the young princess (later queen) Mary who questions her tutor about the correct way to attend Mass: should she go "nat to pray at masse, but rather onely to here and harken?" Her tutor tells her that she "shall thynk to the mystery of the masse and shall herken the wordes that they preest say."[26] In other words, she was expected to look at what the priest was doing, listen to the Latin prayers, and passively participate in the ritual by meditating appropriate thoughts, stimulated by the gestures of the priest as he enacted the narrative of Christ's suffering, death, and resurrection.

Before we investigate the text of the Mass, we should consider how much of the Latin a typical parishioner would be expected to understand, because some of the most important prayers were said out loud by the priest in a clear voice such as the whole church would hear. The instructions in *The Lay Folks Mass-Book* make this clear:

> when the preste saies he, or if he singe,
> to him thou gyue gode herknynge;
> when the preste praies in priuete,
> tyhme of prayere is then to the.[27]

It appears that some members of the congregation could understand at least the major prayers in Latin (e.g., the *Pater Noster*). According to M. T. Clanchy, writing of the period 1066-1307, which takes in the time when *The Lay Folks Mass-Book* was written,[28] "The suggestion that some peasants were acquainted with Latin is not implausible when the role of the church in village life is considered. . . . As it was, most people probably did not find this minimal amount of Latin overwhelmingly difficult because they heard these texts recited whenever they went to church."[29] When the laity were not participating in reciting the prayers out loud there should be no "ianglyng" (1879, 4/22), says the author of *The Lay Folks Mass-Book*, Dan Jeremy. The only noise was that made by the celebrant, other than the bell at the consecration (38/401).[30]

At the beginning of the ceremony, the parishioners see the priest put on his vestments, except for the chasuble, and come to the altar with his attendant ministers. There he takes the chasuble, which had been placed in readiness on the altar, and puts it on. Now, fully vested, he faces the altar, with his back to the congregation, because all prayers had to be directed toward the east.[31] This means that throughout the service—unless, as at Low Masses, the parishioners could move up close to the altar—their experience of the action was limited to viewing the movements, gestures, and genuflections of the celebrant from behind. All the parishioners kneel, but the celebrant remains standing, holding up both his hands to God. He makes his confession and the laity then make theirs with their hands joined. After this, they stand up, while the priest moves to pray from the missal at the epistle side of the altar (stage-left).

The congregation remains standing till the *Gloria* has been said by the priest in Latin and by them in English. The priest then moves the missal to the other side of the altar (stage-right), the people stand up again, the priest makes the sign of the cross on the book with his thumb, then on his face, and the Gospel is intoned (16/153-59). Dan Jeremy does not want the laity to be emotionally passive during the reading of the Gospel but wants them "to haue ful mikel drede" (16/167), which enforces the dramatic quality of the experience, and to make a flourishing sign of the cross on themselves both at the beginning and at the end of the reading of the Gospel. The second sign of the cross is made differently from the first, because the parish-

ioners are told to make the sign on their hands and then kiss it
(18/196).[32] Repeatedly making the sign of the cross here, and elsewhere throughout the Mass, helps to focus the minds of the congregation on the central purpose of the Liturgy, which is to
commemorate the biblical narrative of Christ's Crucifixion.

The priest then says the *Credo*, and the congregation joins in this
asseveration of faith by saying the words of the Creed to themselves in
English. Next comes the offertory procession, and those parishioners
who wish to make an offering process to the altar and do so. They
become part of the action. In terms of dramatic experience, this
movement between the body of the church and the altar temporarily
changes the atmosphere in the service and, through its novelty,
refreshes the interest of the participants.

After the people who have made their offerings return to their
places, the rite of the Mass continues with more action on the altar
when the priest washes his hands at the *Lavabo* with the congregation
standing. After the washing, the people see the priest bow to the altar
and turn around to face them with a prayer. At this point, they are
enjoined to strike their breast and to respond out loud to the priest's
request for their prayers (24/248). The priest turns back to the altar,
and while he says the next prayers silently, members of the congregation kneel and say their own prayers with the dramatic gesture of
holding up both their hands (26/284). They then say the *Pater Noster*
(26/298-99).

After these prayers the congregation sees the priest move to the
middle of the altar and stand up. The priest signals the end of the
first part of the Mass by intoning out loud "Per omnia saecula saeculorum," to which the answer is "Amen," then "Dominus Vobiscum"
(Response: "Et cum spiritu tuo"), then "Sursum corda" (Response:
"Habemus ad Dominum"). After completing the saying of the preface, they hear the priest say three times, "Sanctus, Sanctus, Sanctus"
and then "Dominus Deus Sabaoth. Pleni sunt caeli, et terra gloria tua.
Hosanna in excelsis. Benedictus qui venit in nomine Domini.
Hosanna in excelsis." The dramatic repetition of "Sanctus" and
"Hosanna in excelsis" signals a break in the performance of the rite,
rather like the change from one act to another in a play, because the
next section of the Mass, the canon, rises in intensity to the climax of
the consecration.

Members of the congregation kneel and see the priest, still with his
back to them, begin the canon. He continues silently, and they qui-
etly pray and meditate in preparation for the miracle of transubstantiation, when the substance of the bread is converted into the Body of
Christ and the substance of the wine is converted into his Blood,

while the accidents of bread and wine remain the same. There is no action to be seen on the altar from the congregation's point of view until its attention is called back to the progress of the Liturgy by the ringing of a bell, which signals that the elevation of the Host is about to be performed (38/401), the most dramatic moment in the whole Mass.

The parishioners are kneeling and they raise up their hands (38/405). They see the Host raised up by the celebrant.[33] This is a most theatrical moment. Its importance has been carefully prepared for, first by a period of silence, then the bell, then the elevation, which caused great excitement among the congregation. The Host, which had been kept from its gaze throughout the Mass but now miraculously changed in substance by the words of consecration ("Hoc est enim corpus meum"), is raised aloft for all to see—the body of the man who was betrayed, scourged, put to death on the cross (an event symbolized repeatedly during the service by making the sign of the cross), and then divinely raised to life. After the high drama of the consecration and elevation of the Host, silence falls again, with a series of prayers, until the priest breaks this lengthy silence by saying out loud ("on hight" 44/482) "per omnia saecula saeculorum," after saying to himself the beautiful concluding prayer "Per ipsum, et cum ipso, et in ipso est tibi Deo Patri omnipotenti in unitate Spritus Sancti omnis honor et gloria."[34] After the "Amen," which finishes this quiet section of the Liturgy, the members of the congregation are enjoined to stand up for the *Pater Noster*, which the priest says in a loud voice. Parishioners are told to hold themselves still ("hold the stille" 46/487) during this prayer so that they may savor every word. The construction of the prayer itself is designed to create maximum dramatic and rhetorical effect with its balanced clauses, repetitions, and wordplay, which the celebrant is forced by the structure to express:

Pater *noster*, qui es in coelis, sanctificetur nomen *tuum.*
Adveniat regnum *tuum.*
Fiat voluntas *tua,*
   sicut in coelo, *sic in* terra.
Panem *nostrum* quotidianum da *nobis* hodie:
   et *dimitte* nobis *debita nostra*, sicut ut nos *dimittimus debitoribus nostris*:
et ne *nos* inducas in tentationem,
Sed libera *nos* a malo. Amen.[35]

The parishioners listen as far as the "tentationem" and then answer, "Sed libera nos a malo. Amen" (46/488-89). They remain standing as the celebrant breaks the Host, accompanied by silent prayers, until he intones, "Agnus Dei, qui tollis peccata mundi, miserere nobis. Agnus dei, qui tollis peccata mundi, miserere nobis. Agnus dei, qui tollis peccata mundi, dona nobis pacem" (112/21-23), after which he kisses the altar, and the congregation kneels down, and remains so until after the celebrant has washed his hands.[36]

This version of the Mass does not include guidance about the receiving of Holy Communion, and so it proceeds quickly to its conclusion. The clerk takes the missal to the south side of the altar (stage-left), and the priest says the concluding words of the Mass: "Ite, missa est" (Go—it is the dismissal)[37] or "Benedicamus Domino." After the parishioners hear these words of dismissal they are free to leave the church (58/609).

Attendance at a medieval Mass, such as the one we have just considered, was a dramatic experience for the laity. They were spectators at an event that involved the exchange of prayers (some silent, some expressed aloud), the enactment of ritual gestures (vesting, bowings, genuflections, movement around the altar, turnings to the congregation, walking around the altar space, raising the hands, elevating the bread), and participation in the dialogue at certain stages of the Liturgy. The atmosphere during the service was carefully orchestrated to suggest the important moments of the commemorated narrative of Christ's life, especially before and after the consecration with the lengthy silence, the ringing of the bell, the elevation of the Host, then more silence. Obviously, the Mass was not as dramatically effective as the religious drama that evolved after *The Lay Folks Mass-Book* was written, but it included the essential elements that furnished celebrants with the opportunity and indeed the excuse to impersonate and perform the biblical narrative of the eucharistic sacrifice. Amalarius of Metz and commentators like him recognized the dramatic potential of the Liturgy, but it should be acknowledged that the traditional text of the Mass as it stood lent itself to dramatic performance without necessarily having to rely on complicated interpretations and directions such as Amalarius proposed.[38]

Notes

1. *The Variorum Edition of the Complete Poems of Thomas Hardy*, ed. James Gibson (London: Macmillan, 1971), 416-17.
2. E. K. Chambers, *The Medieval Stage* (Oxford: Oxford University Press, 1903), 2:3.
3. This is the premise of Karl Young's classic study of the liturgical beginnings of medieval drama, *The Drama of the Medieval Church*, 2 vols. (London: Oxford University Press, 1933).

4. O. B. Hardison, Jr., *Christian Rite and Christian Drama in the Middle Ages* (Baltimore: Johns Hopkins, 1965), 77.

5. David Bevington, *Medieval Drama* (Boston: Houghton Mifflin, 1975), 7. For examples of the partial re-enactment of the Mass in plays on the medieval stage see Lynette R. Muir, "The Mass on the Medieval Stage," in *Drama in the Middle Ages, Comparative and Critical Essays*, Second Series, ed. Clifford Davidson and John H. Stroupe (New York: AMS Press, 1991), 223-29.

6. *The Catholic Encyclopaedic Dictionary*, Donald Attwater, gen. ed. (London: Waverley, 1930).

7. Council of Trent, Session XXII, cap. 2; see *Enchiridion Symbolorum*, ed. H. Denzinger and C. Bannwart (Freiburg: Herder, 1927), 312.

8. See J. A. Jungmann, *The Early Liturgy to the Time of Gregory the Great*, trans. F. A. Brunner (London: Darton, Longman, Todd, 1966), 288.

9. See J. A. Jungmann, *Public Worship*, trans. Clifford Howell (London: Burns and Oates, 1965), 95.

10. A full discussion of Amalarius's allegorization of the Mass, and its place in the development of medieval drama, will be found in Hardison, *Christian Rite and Christian Drama in the Middle Ages*, 35-79.

11. See John Wesley Harris, *Medieval Theatre in Context, An Introduction* (London: Routledge, 1992), 26. For a brief summary of Amalarius's proposals see Jungmann, *Public Worship*, 95-96.

12. See Jungmann, *Public Worship*, 96.

13. See *The Lay Folks Mass-Book*, ed. T. F. Simmons, EETS 71 (Oxford: Trübner, 1879), xix.

14. Jungmann, *Public Worship*, 103.

15. The text appears in Simmons's edition of *The Lay Folks Mass-Book*, 90-117. For the origins, development, and use of the rite, see A. A. King, *Liturgies of the Past* (London: Longman, 1959), 326-47.

16. See Jungmann, *The Early Liturgy*, 298-99.

17. See *Missale Romanum Ex Decreto Sacrosancti Concilii Tridentini Restitutum S. Pii V Pontificis Maximi Jussu Editum Aliorum Pontificum Cura Recognitum A Pio X Reformatum et Benedicti XV Auctoritate Vulgatum* (Mechelen: Dessain, 1947), 214-19, 298-309.

18. Jungmann, *The Mass of the Roman Rite, Its Origins and Development*, trans. F. A. Brunner, rev. C. K. Riepe (New York: Benziger, 1959), 69.

19. Ibid., 82.

20. *Missale Romanum*. See also *The Catholic Encyclopedia* (New York: Appleton, 1910), s.v. "Mass," 9: 798, and Jungmann, *The Mass*, 103-5.

21. Jungmann, *The Early Liturgy*, 298.

22. Cited and edited as Text 'B,' by Simmons, 2-60.

23. Ibid., 90-117.

24. *Missale Romanum*, 214-309.

25. Eamon Duffy, *The Stripping of the Altars: Traditional Religion in England, c. 1400-c. 1500* (New Haven: Yale University Press, 1992).

26. Simmons, *The Lay Folks Mass-Book*, 158.

27. Lines 27-30, with thorn rendered as "th" and abbreviations expanded.

28. The work was written by a priest called Jeremy (see Simmons, *The Lay Folks Mass-Book,* Introduction, xxi), who was a friend of Archbishop Thurston of York (d. 1140).

29. M. T. Clanchy, *From Memory to Written Record: England, 1066-1307* (Cambridge: Harvard University Press, 1979), 188-89.

30. Citations of the *Lay Folks Mass-Book* are by page/line number.

31. Jungmann, *The Mass of the Roman Rite,* 181-82.

32. On this ritual, see *The Lay Folks Mass-Book,* 220.

33. The raising of the Host dates from the twelfth century (Duffy, *The Stripping of the Altars,* 95-96). The raising of the chalice was not introduced until long afterward: "Even in the sixteenth century the elevation of the chalice had not yet become a universal custom" (Jungmann, *Public Worship,* 133).

34. Quoted from the text of the Canon of the Mass as used in the diocese of York, ed. Simmons, *The Lay Folks Mass-Book,* 110/21-23. The formula is unaltered in the *Missale Romanum,* 301.

35. Ibid., 110/28-34. I have italicized the words that supply the rhetorical effect.

36. This is a very early reference to this act of cleansing, which did not become established in the Western church until the thirteenth century, some time after Dan Jeremy wrote his original *Mass-Book;* see Simmons, *The Lay Folks Mass-Book,* 303.

37. See Jungmann, *Public Worship,* 147-48. The medieval Mass ends here. The reading of the Gospel of John (1:1-14) was not attached to the end of the Mass until the sixteenth century, when it was given what became its traditional place at the end of the service in the *Missale Romanum* of Pius V.

38. I wish to thank my colleague Alan Fletcher for his advice and help.

From Mappa Mundi *to* Theatrum Mundi: *The World as Stage in Early English Drama*

Martin Stevens

The continuity of the native dramatic tradition from its popular roots to the drama of Shakespeare has been given less theoretical attention over the years than the subject commands. In part, I believe, the problem has resulted from the narrow periodization and specialization that has drawn hard and fast boundaries between the culture of the Middle Ages and the Renaissance in England.[1] In part, it results from the widespread tendency to associate Shakespeare with high culture and medieval drama with low culture, an estimate that is surely out of touch with the temperament of postmodern criticism. In this essay I propose to examine an iconographic referent which, I shall argue, played a central role in the development of the English stage. It is my contention that the native dramatic tradition, which finds its full expression in Shakespeare, created a stage that replicated the world. This stage reflects the medieval Noachic map or, as it came to be known, the "T-O" map, and it is grounded in a theological, mythical and historical reading of the world as the basis of a new Western dramaturgy that represents even today a significant strand in the conceptualization of the stage and the screen.

To draw the implied connection between the ideational design of the popular medieval outdoor stage and the Elizabethan playhouse, we need at the outset to depart from an objective, positivistic reconstruction and developmental study of the two stages. My argument does not require that Shakespeare was personally familiar with the design of the medieval popular stage or that he actually witnessed the performance of a Corpus Christi play,[2] though I believe that he had seen cycle plays in his youth and early adulthood. In so arguing, I do not disparage or in any way dismiss the very valuable work done by theater historians, especially that of Glynne Wickham, in tracing the design of the playhouse to the *platea-sedes* stage design of the popular drama.[3] To the contrary, the central argument advanced by Wickham is invaluable for our understanding of the continuity in the design and function of staging practices. For the sake of the argument advanced here, however, it is even more important that we recognize the pervasive influence of what Brian Stock has called the "operative cultural memory" of a given civilization.[4] Could the later sixteenth century have forgotten the whole textual reference system and the cultural practices that controlled English society in the first half of the century? Is it insignificant that the public clamored for the continuation of religious festival plays for many years after the accession of Queen Elizabeth and the archdiocesan prohibition against the Corpus Christi cycles?[5] In recent years, as Stock has argued, the Middle Ages have become more and more remote. Like primitive cultures that exist elsewhere, they have become the subject of anthropological study, and the Middle Ages themselves have become the focus of studies in "alterity." This new orientation, however fruitful it may be in reclaiming what intervening epistemes may have defamiliarized, does not serve the student of the early English drama, which ought to take for its subject the continuous history of the popular stage from the time of its formation.

●　　●　　●

To gain a better understanding of the urban festival drama of the late Middle Ages and especially of the Corpus Christi play, I propose to examine the cultural matrix that gave shape to the city as stage. The performance space that the civic structure appropriated for its play was, in fact, a *theatrum mundi*,[6] the quintessential "theater in the round." One of the earliest uses in the English language of the word *theatre* referring to a place of performance occurs in Chaucer's *Knight's Tale*, describing the amphitheater that Theseus builds to accommodate the lists between Palamon and Arcite (see *OED*, s.v. Theatre, I.b.). This theater is notable for its resemblance to the architectural plan of the medieval city, and in Chaucer's tale it serves as a cosmic stage[7] wherein the gods are at war:

> swich a noble *theatre* as it was
> I dar wel seyen in this *world* ther nas.
> The circuit a myle was aboute,
> *Walled of stoon, and dyched al withoute.*
> Round was the shap, in manere of compas,
> Ful of degrees, the heighte of sixty pas,

> That whan a man was set on o degree,
> He letted nat his felawe for to see. (I.1885-92; emphasis added)[8]

As we shall see shortly, this model of the *theatrum mundi* is designed in the shape of the *mappa mundi*. It can serve, for now, as a reference point to define the two principal sites that served as the outdoor festival stage for the late medieval popular drama: the *entire* city or a central open space, most commonly the marketplace. The first of these models was employed by Corpus Christi productions that relied on the processional performance of plays on pageant wagons, as at York; the second presented the "fixed drama" on a specially designated and converted theatrical space such as the Weinmarkt at Lucerne. While these two types of stages differ in their basic mode of performance, they both reflect the ideology of one overarching cultural inscription, and both are ritual designs in which the suppressed desires of ordinary life are transformed by the imagination into the mood of holiday. In what follows, my primary visual evidence will come from maps, dramatic diagrams, paintings, and the archaeological remains of several cities in England and on the Continent.

It should be clear that my interest here does not lie so much with the actual staging details as with the idea of performance in public theaters. I propose to speak, as Victor Turner did so often, in the *subjunctive* rather than the *indicative* mood. The medieval public, open-air, holiday play, whether at Shrovetide, Hock Tuesday, Corpus Christi Day, Midsummer Day, or Christmas, was in the broadest terms a cultural performance, one that embraced its social setting and constituted "a threshold between sacred living and secular living."[9] Turner refers to the festival play as a "liminal" (i.e., marginal) event, a "social process," at a time when mainstream society generates cultural performances that are an inversion of quotidian life and that are often marked by taboo (1987, 24-25). Corpus Christi dramas are pure examples of such performances. Their central subject is the Incarnation, their mystery is Christ's Resurrection, and their climactic moment occurs when the community enacts the most formidable of all taboos, the killing of its god. What in fact makes the Corpus Christi play the liminal public event of its time is its timelessness—its transfer through anachronism of the central ritual event, the Passion, to the here and now, so that the community becomes fully implicated in the source of its spiritual history. The torturers of Jesus are ordinary carpenters, the instruments of the Passion are tools produced in the workshop of such guilds as the pinners and the carpenters, the crowd at Calvary is the audience, and sacramental history is relived in a topsy-turvy, upside-down world which transforms the quotidian "N-town" into both the earthly and the heavenly city. The marketplace (whether in a fixed or a processional performance) is the center of the urban stage, just as Jerusalem is the center of the world; the ritual enactment transforms the ordinary city into the *theatrum mundi.* To understand how it does so, we need now to examine the typical plan of the *mappa mundi,* which for our purposes is well exemplified by two world maps executed in medieval England: the first is the celebrated Hereford map; the second is the widely known stage plan of *The Castle of Perseverance.*

•   •   •

Maps constitute one of the more interesting examples of the relation between discursive practices and material reality. In a world constructed by the objectivism of the Enlightenment, the value of a map is related directly to its "accuracy" in representing the physical and political terrain that it delineates. It is not entirely relevant here to ask whether such accuracy can ever be attained, but it is of some interest to recall the slogan of the school of General Semantics (associated with Alfred Korzybski's *Science and Sanity*[10]): "the map is not the territory." To gain an understanding of a medieval map, let us review the most famous map that survives from medieval England, the Hereford map (see fig. 1). Like all medieval maps, it is a cultural inscription, a discursive plan of the universe as rendered by history, philosophy, Scripture, folklore, and travel accounts. Dating to the late thirteenth century, it was first installed perhaps as an altarpiece at Hereford Cathedral.[11] It is a large map (5 feet 3 inches high by 4 feet 6 inches wide), hence potentially visible to the entire congregation, drawn on vellum and delineating a circular world. In its configuration it resembles other surviving world maps of the period, such as the Ebstorf map in Germany (see fig. 2), and it is usually associated with the so-called T-O map. T-O stands for *orbis terrarum* but also represents two essential configurations. First there is the "O" of its circumference, a body of water known as the *circumfluent,* which is the ocean and which outlines the three continents of Asia, Europe, and Africa that form its inner land mass. Second there is the "T" design that delineates two boundaries. The crossbar of the T is the diameter of the circle separating the upper hemisphere, or the east (i.e., Asia), from the lower hemisphere, which contains the land mass of the north (Europe; see fig. 3) and the south (Africa; see fig. 4). The ascender of the T, which forms the lower radius of the circle, divides the north and the south into roughly equal quarters. Asia occupies the east, which essentially represents the biblical territory of the ancient world and is thus a historical/scriptural/literary construction.

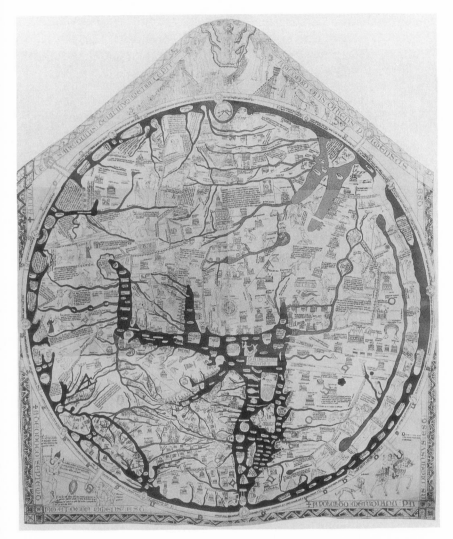

Figure 1. The Hereford Map (late thirteenth century)

Jerusalem, in the form of a castellated city, is in Asia (see fig. 5), but it marks the dead center of the world and is something of a microcosm of its larger context. At the very top, overlooking the Terrestrial Paradise, which is represented as an island surrounded by a wall, is the seated figure of *Christus Triumphans* of the Last Judgment (see fig. 6), a figure found repeatedly on the tympana of medieval cathedrals. The north (extending to the west) is Europe, a part of the contemporary and immediate world, which to some extent reflects the observations of

Figure 2. Ebstorf Map

actual travelers. It is separated from Asia by the Don River, the left half
of the T crossbar, and from Africa by the ascender of the T which
marks the Mediterranean Sea (see fig. 6). Africa is the southern region;
it is separated from Asia by the other great river, the right crossbar section of the T, the Nile (see fig. 4). Africa is essentially the land of myth,
folklore, and the marginal, including such humanoid figures as the
Androgini (having the genitals of both sexes), the *Blemmyae* (headless
men with faces on their chests), or the *Cynocephali* (dogheaded men).[12]

Figure 3. The Hereford Map (detail of Europe)

The Straits of Gibraltar are the *terminus* of both Europe and Africa at the western extremity of the land mass, or the bottom tip of the T. This is the traditional boundary between the known and the unknown world. The latter is, of course, uncharted, and it was not known how far it might have extended.

Recent research has given us a better idea of how the world map of Hereford and its analogues served as a guiding metanarrative to the *imago mundi* that governed the architectural program of the medieval

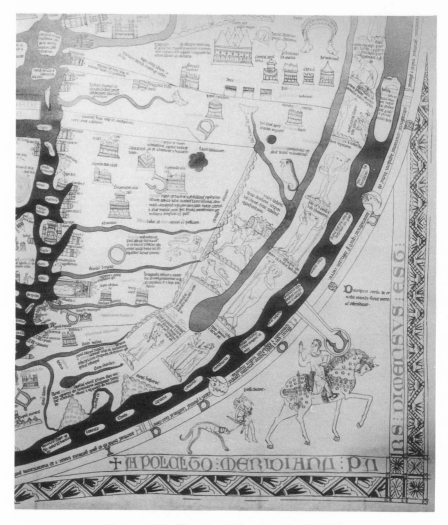

Figure 4. The Hereford Map (detail of Africa)

cathedral. Relating a now lost *mappa mundi* in the Church of Saint
Silvain at Chalivoy-Milon in France to a recently reconstituted mural
painting, Marcia Kupfer argues persuasively that "cartographic
imagery functioned symbolically to locate the church building within
a sacred or cosmological scheme."[13] On the basis of reliable descriptions of the Chalivoy map, which was a wall mural, and in relation to
the mural painting, Kupfer shows that the map gave emphasis to the
location of the apse as a sacred space in the east and the nave as the

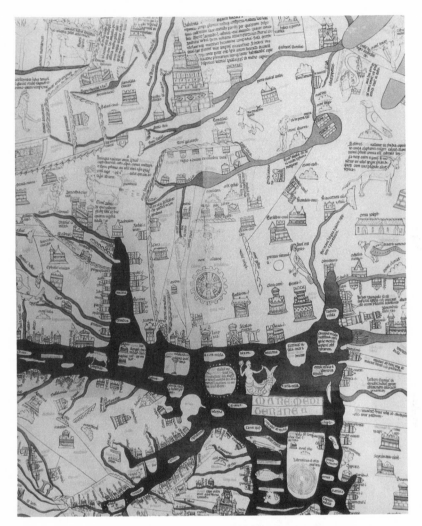

Figure 5. The Hereford Map (detail of Asia)

site of the post-lapsarian world in the west. In other words, the huge map served as a cosmographical index to the architecture of the church.

For our immediate purpose the most important relationship between the map and the configuration of the stage—whether it be the whole city, just its marketplace, or a special theater built for the performance of plays—is its circular (or as in Renaissance London, sometimes hexagonal) form, with the east as the zone of heaven,

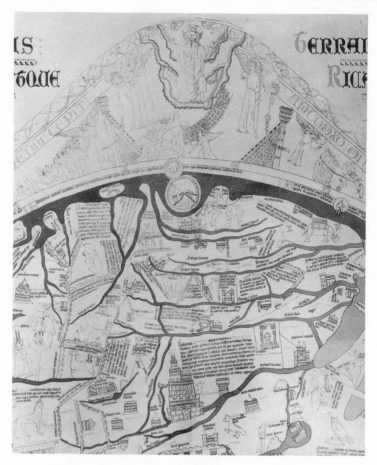

Figure 6. The Hereford Map (detail of Terrestrial Paradise)

usually at the top, and Jerusalem at dead center. I mean to suggest
that the world as shown in the *mappa mundi* was the controlling
image that performers and spectators alike implicitly carried with
them to shape their idea of the traditional overall outdoor stage for
the performance of religious plays. The very same picture that dominated their perception of the cathedral served as a mental
palimpsest over the historic and ubiquitous circular city walls and the
moat that usually surrounded them.

   A plan very similar in general outline to the Hereford map is the
most famous of all English stage drawings surviving from the Middle
Ages. This is the plan of *The Castle of Perseverance* stage, preserved in
the Macro manuscript of the early fifteenth century (see fig. 7). As
noted by others previously,[14] the map and the stage plan are indeed

very similar. Although the east is not at the top of the plan, it is the locus of the heaven pageant, where God sits throughout the unfolding of the life of Mankind (*Humanum Genus*), which is the subject of the play. He occupies the same commanding throne as *Christus Triumphans* at the apex of the map. The other compass points make interesting though not always direct associations with the map.[15] The south, at the top, is the scaffold of *Caro* (Flesh), hence it features the fleshly sins of lechery, gluttony, and sloth—sins of indulgence which are spawned by the heat of the sun and suggest the marginal world of Africa. The west is the scaffold of *Mundus* (the World), i.e., the gateway from the known to the unknown, or Gibraltar, which is labeled "*terminus europe*" and "*terminus Affrice*" on the Hereford map. It is also the region that extends upward to the most immediately known world, that of Europe. "The far recesses of the north," as we are told by Isaiah 14:13, constitute the traditional region of the Devil. The association of the north with hell is in fact a commonplace in medieval literature, as we can see from the words of the yeoman-devil in Chaucer's *Friar's Tale* to his human colleague, the summoner, who has just asked where his companion's dwelling might be:

> "Brother," quod he, "fer in the north contree
> Where-as I hope som tyme I shall thee see." (III.1410-11)

The northeast is the outer zone of hell, on the map roughly the land of Gog and Magog, where the unclean semi-human monsters roamed. On the stage, it is the locus of Covetyse, the sin of cupidity, which, though part of the domain of hell, is singled out as a place of especially heinous liminal transgression. The ditch around the stage can be equated with the *circumfluent*, and the castellated Tower of Perseverance in the middle of the *platea*, the locus of the regenerated *Humanum Genus* and of the seven virtues, occupies the dead center occupied on the map by the earthly Jerusalem. The *imago mundi* is unmistakably a link between the world and the theater.

The spectator who was familiar with the *mappa mundi* design would have to assume that the stage was in fact a replica of the world and that the action, which traversed the area from the center, the castle, to the circumference, the region of the uninhabited and the excluded, imitated the exploration of the marginal, such as we find in travel and pilgrimage accounts. Most important, however, is the moral nature of this stage journey—its orientation, as the word implies, to the east, but its transgressions associated with the perimeter, where the invasive forces of the World, the Flesh, and the Devil,

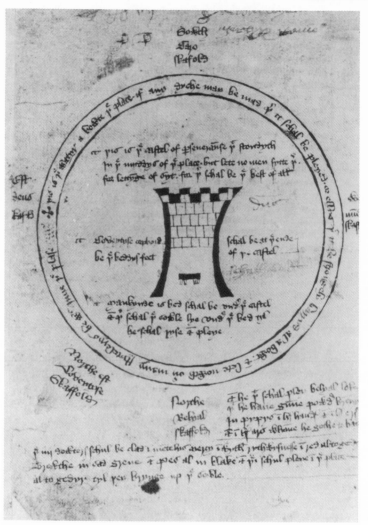

Figure 7. Stage Plan for Castle of Perseverance (Macro MS, early fifteenth century)

the three figures of the temptation, with their helpmates, the Seven Deadly Sins, attack and cajole man from the margins. The association of geographical zones with moral transgression is made especially graphic as a stage picture when the Hereford map is superimposed on the action.

•   •   •

When we turn our attention to actual medieval cities as sites of theatrical festivals, we note that the configuration of the *mappa mundi* exists there as well. Most medieval cities were surrounded by high, crenellated, circular walls and by a moat for defensive purposes. Seen as a cultural inscription for theatrical performance, this design is indeed the same as that of the world map or, in miniature, the map of Jerusalem (see the center of the Hereford map in fig. 1). York, as the second largest city in England, serves as a prime example with its medieval walls that still stand. The York cycle transformed York into a *theatrum mundi* as its pageant wagons moved slowly through the city, past its city hall, its churches and hospitals, its monumental Minster, to the central marketplace. As a mystery cycle it encompasses all of sacramental history from the creation to doomsday, and while the play-text does not undertake to identify sites inside the city with geographical locations, it suggests in a metadramatic sense that the itinerary of the play replicates man's pilgrimage on earth. The great Micklegate, still one of two chief entry points into the city, was the site at which the dramatic journey began. The Pavement was the place of its denouement, the center point where the Passion and the Resurrection were played out in their final performances along the cycle's itinerary.[16] As in the famous painting of *The Passion of Christ* by Memlinc, which made a biblical stage out of the city of Bruges (see fig. 8), the spectator undoubtedly was acculturated to visualize the contemporary city as Jerusalem.[17] The urban festival drama of Corpus Christi, with its scope of dramatic action spanning all time, was performed in ritual space that had the power to replicate itself into a plan of the universe.

At appropriate moments the play-texts themselves call attention to the world as stage. In the very first speech from the heaven pageant, God the Father in all the cycles proclaims the dimensions of the theatrical space when, as in Towneley, he says:

> At the begynnyng of oure dede
> make we heuen & erth, on brede,
> and lyghtys fayre to se. . . .
> In medys the water, bi oure assent,
> be now maide the firmament,
> And parte ather from othere. (1.19-21; 31-33)[18]

The stage plan of the world, inscribed for the spectator by God himself, defines the *theatrum mundi* from the outset. And it is echoed by the villains as well. For example Herod, self-proclaimed "Kyng of Kyngys," virtually replicates the regions of the T-O map when he rants in alliterative fustian that all the following now obey him:

Figure 8. Hans Memlinc, *The Passion of Christ* **(showing city of Bruges)**

> Tuskane and Turky,
> All Inde and Italy,
> Cecyll and Surry
> Drede hym and dowtys.
> From Paradyse to Padwa
> To Mownt Flascon,
> From Egyp to Mantua
> Vnto Kemptowne,
> From Sarceny to Susa
> To Grece it abowne
> Both Normondy and Norwa
> Lowtys to his crowne. . . . (16/62-73)

The world from every perspective is shaped for the spectator as the ubiquitous stage.

The *theatrum mundi* consequently stands as a living, cultural imprint of the *mappa mundi*. The latter, with its composite view of the earth and its accumulated history and mythology, is the imagined site of the newly emerging vernacular stage in England and on the Continent. As ludic space, it is especially appropriate to the holiday of

Corpus Christi. Like Corpus Christi, the *mappa mundi* signifies the body of Christ, wherein Christ's head and shoulders appear at the top marking the east, his feet at the bottom or the west, and his two hands at the North and South Poles so that the globe and the body are indeed one (see fig. 2). While Corpus Christi only gradually became the occasion for the midsummer holiday performance of religious cycles in England, it is clear that both the feast and the play are celebrations of the body of Christ.[19] Indeed, the body in all its significations lies at the heart and soul of the Christian drama. It is, after all, the drama of the Incarnation, and it is also the drama of a social body, which bonds the community.[20]

In this spiritual setting, the actual shape of the space matters little. We have seen that the idea of the *mappa mundi* can be inscribed onto a dedicated theatrical space, such as the stage of *The Castle of Perseverance*, or it can serve as a superimposition to convert an entire city into a stage as happened at York and at Chester. It can also function as the stage plan for a more restricted site such as the urban marketplace. A good example of the latter is the Weinmarkt (formerly the Fischmarkt) at Lucerne. Fortunately, we retain two elaborate drawings by the city clerk and the director of the play, Renward Cysat, for day one and day two of the 1583 production of the *Luzerner Osterspiel* (figs. 9 and 10). In coverage, the play was as extensive as the English Corpus Christi plays, except that it did not include the Ascension, Assumption, or Last Judgment. The Weinmarkt, which still stands almost unchanged from its sixteenth-century appearance, is the most prominent square in Lucerne. It was (and largely still is) surrounded by six- to seven-story private houses and guild halls that were separated by four large and four small exits from the square. Serving as the site for the Easter play (actually performed every five years early in the sixteenth century and later once in ten or more years, on Thursday and Friday following Easter) and for several other types of performances including saints, Last Judgment, and carnival plays, it was fitted out for the various civic and festival productions as a theater in its eastern half. The space around its perimeter was taken up with stations for the actors (also used at times for the performance proper) and specially built stands for spectators. In its eastern location was the *Haus zur Sonne*. It served as the heaven scaffold, in front of which Paradise was erected for the first day and converted into the Garden of Gethsemane on the second day. Hell was situated near the butcher shop on the northern side of the stage. The ornate Gothic fountain stood opposite the *Haus zur Sonne* at the western periphery of the *platea*. The square itself extended for half again its length to the west, and here the most prominent spectators sat in stands to

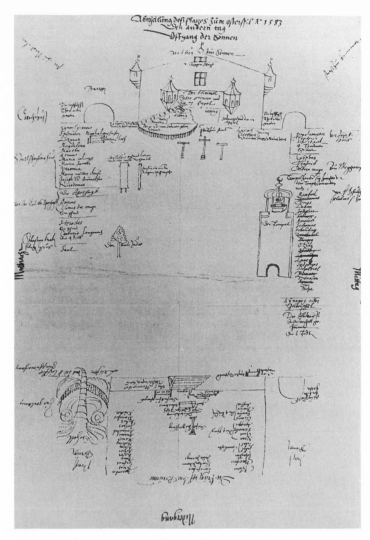

Figure 9. Renward Cysat, Drawing for *Luzerner Osterspiel* (1583)

watch the performance. The fountain served many functions, but during the first day its most prominent role was to conceal the figure of Adam, until the Creation scene, when God came down from heaven, traversed the square, and made Adam, who miraculously materialized out of a handful of dirt on which God had blown the breath of life.[21] Later it served as the tomb of Christ. The most prominent scaffold on the southern side of the square was the Temple, the setting for all of the tyrants.

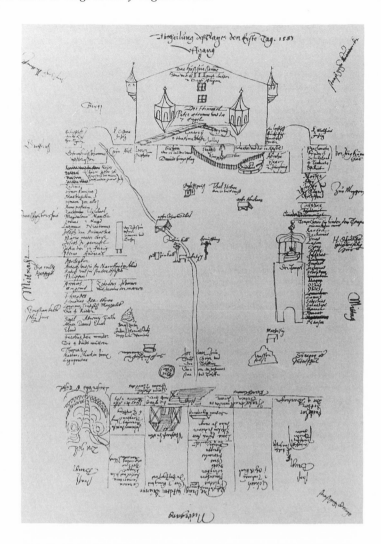

Figure 10. Renward Cysat, Drawing for *Luzerner Osterspiel* (1583)

In all important respects the Lucerne marketplace stage replicates that of *The Castle of Perseverance*. While the chart does not present us with compass points to mark the location of its major stations, the "House of the Sun" stands in the east, and it is to the heaven platform and the throne in its center that *Pater aeternus* and his company of angels ascend during the grand procession (of 300 actors) at the opening of the play. Since the official beginning of the play took place at 6:00 A.M., one must visualize the sun rising in the background and, at least on a good day, providing the natural light suggestive of the Creation. The heaven scaffold was populated with a large company of performers, who proceeded into the Weinmarkt at the very end of the grand entrance procession. They included, besides God the Father and twenty angels, the four archangels, two heralds on either side, and on the right side of heaven the prophets Isaiah and Jeremiah and the four fathers of the church, each with an acolyte carrying a book. On the left side (i.e., to the right of God), Jesus and the twelve disciples (including Judas) assembled. All of the remaining actors stood in their places in a ring around the *platea* until the Proclamator gave his opening speech, whereupon all sat down in their appointed seats ("So erst man in platz kompt, gat Pater aeternus vnd die Engel in Himmel. Die uebrigen personen all dess Spils stellend sich an einem Ring herumb, bis der Proclamator . . . geredt" [thus, when first (the company) comes into the place, "Pater Eternus" and the angels go into heaven. All the remaining characters of the play place themselves in a circle around (him), until the "Proclamator" . . . begins to speak]).[22] No opening curtain could have produced a more impressive and powerfully dramatic stage picture than this. The periphery of the performance place, while not precisely circular, laid out a pattern that put hell into the northern quarter, and the Temple as site for the rulers of the world in the southern and southwestern zone. The Garden of Eden was a permanent station for the first day, with a fence around it, immediately below the elaborate heaven scaffold, reminiscent of its placement on the Hereford *mappa mundi*. The Lucerne play, consequently, provides one of the most graphic pictures of the cosmic stage that survives from the late Middle Ages.[23]

•   •   •

The foregoing illustrative sketch of the medieval *theatrum mundi* can help us to understand the underlying design of the popular stage in the early Renaissance. I do not mean to suggest here that the construction of the large outdoor playhouses consciously carried forward the design of the medieval stage any more than I assumed a conscious connection between the emerging *theatrum mundi*, the design of the cathedral, and the *mappa mundi* in the Middle Ages. What does seem likely is that the Renaissance inherited a scheme, or an abstraction of a design, that governed its theatrical outlook and its dramaturgy.

First and foremost, the Renaissance drama, and especially that of Shakespeare, conceived of the stage as a "world." This construct, while certainly no longer visibly that of the Hereford or Ebstorf map, and while no longer associating the stage with the four compass points, did assume that the performance space was cosmic and therefore infinitely adaptable to the spatial needs of the playwright's imagination. The very name of Shakespeare's great outdoor amphitheater, the Globe (the "wooden O"), reflects the indebtedness of the Elizabethan theater to the idea of the *theatrum mundi*. This Globe theater could be conceived as the world of the spectator, and its size was astonishing for it could accommodate an inordinately large audience, often estimated at 3,000 or more. Its circular roof, which protected the best paying customers from the rain, was in fact referred to as the heavens (suggestive of the starry skies in the great movie palaces of the 1930s and 1940s in America). Even more important, however, the very name of the theater carried forward the tradition that the stage is potentially that of the world or any of its parts. Conversely, the discourse of the plays themselves reinforced for the audience that the world as imagined by the playwright is indeed a stage. Here is the image in the words of Antonio to Gratiano at the very beginning of *The Merchant of Venice:*

> I hold the world but as the world, Gratiano,
> A stage where every man must play a part,
> And mine a sad one. (1.1.77-79)[24]

The Shakespearean equation of world with stage is surely best known from the exchange on melancholy between Duke Senior and Jacques in *As You Like It:*

DUKE SENIOR
> Thou seest we are not all alone unhappy.
> This wide and universal theatre
> Presents more woeful pageants than the scene
> Wherein we play in.

JACQUES
> All the world's a stage,
> And all the men and women merely players.
> They have their exits and their entrances;
> And one man in his time plays many parts
> His acts being seven ages. . . . (2.7.136-44)

Quite apart from the fact that "the wide and universal theatre" with its "woeful pageants" may well be an allusion to the processional Corpus Christi play, the conception of the *theatrum mundi* underlies

Shakespeare's discursive world. The association of stage with world, and vice versa, is reinforced by the angry Northumberland, who at the beginning of *2 Henry IV* calls for *real* action rather than the more comfortable imitation of an action on a stage:

> Let heaven kiss earth! Now let not Nature's hand
> Keep the wild flood confin'd! Let order die!
> And let this world no longer be a stage
> To feed contention in a ling'ring act;
> But let one spirit of the first-born Cain
> Reign in all bosoms, that, each heart being set
> On bloody courses, the rude scene may end,
> And darkness be the burier of the dead! (1.1.153-60)

These allusions are indicative of a tradition being brought into critical, metatheatrical play. Now, for the sake of rhetoric, the stage is playfully and artfully deconstructed so that it can be transformed into the very world that gave it shape in the first place. The stage-world that Shakespeare inherited from the popular medieval play may no longer be the image of a map, but it has fully appropriated the cosmic analogy so that stage and world have become poetically interchangeable subjects.

Perhaps the greatest contribution that the *theatrum mundi* of the Middle Ages made to the native dramatic tradition is the introduction of universal time, space, and action.[25] These concepts are, of course, directly antithetic to the classical unities. They introduced a dramatic design that was to influence the English stage, in its construction and its dramaturgy, throughout its history. It is only when a stage of fully open representation comes into being that the playwright has the freedom to allow the signification of place and time as he pleases. In the Shakespearean history plays, which span nearly a century, we do, indeed, have what O. B. Hardison, Jr., called "the secular equivalent to the sacred cycle of the Middle Ages."[26] What subsumes this development, however, is not the secularization of the doctrinal content and ritual form (as Hardison argued), but rather the idea of cosmic time that the Corpus Christi cycle provided and the image of cosmic space that was appropriated from the *mappae mundi*. It is this model that allows the Muse of Fire in *Henry V* to transform an "unworthy scaffold" (Prologue, 10) into a "kingdom for a stage" (Prologue, 3). It is also this model that allows the spectator to

> Suppose within the girdle of these walls
> Are now confined two mighty monarchies,

Whose high upreared and abutting fronts
The perilous narrow ocean parts asunder. (Prologue, 19-22)

In fact, I think it could safely be said that in the role of the Chorus for *Henry V*, Shakespeare is the first to theorize the meaning, the potential, and the artistic intention of the open stage as it developed in the native dramatic tradition.

Notes

1. O. B. Hardison, Jr., in his groundbreaking study of *Christian Rite and Christian Drama in the Middle Ages* (Baltimore: The Johns Hopkins Press, 1965), was the first modern historical critic to give serious consideration to the subject of the continuity between medieval and Renaissance drama. Unfortunately, his own model of a ritual sacred stage, which he traces to the Lenten Agon of the Christian liturgical year, raises more questions than it answers. Hardison begins with an incisive critical examination of E. K. Chambers's premises in *The Mediaeval Stage* (London: Oxford University Press, 1903), showing that Chambers relied on Social Darwinism and a strong anti-Catholic bias to argue implicitly against the continuity of medieval and Renaissance drama. For Chambers, the development of the native stage experienced a "mutation" in the sixteenth century. While Hardison rejects this notion, and in fact finds a common pattern in the cycle plays and the history plays, he finally terms this pattern "of minor significance in itself" (290). Indeed, Hardison's overview does little to correct the notion that a mutation occurred, and he, too, seems to believe that the medieval drama was replaced by something new in the Elizabethan period. He did, however, call for a study of the continuity of the ritual pattern inherited from the mass as an important link between the medieval Christian stage and that of the Renaissance (291).

2. It would appear likely that Shakespeare knew the medieval cycles from their performance at Coventry, where the mystery plays continued to be played until 1580. Coventry was the most famous site for performance of the Corpus Christi cycle—the place favored by royalty for seeing the play. An eyewitness account tells us that "the confluence of people from farr and neare to see that Shew was extraordinary great, and yielded noe small advantage to this Citye" (Reginald W. Ingram, ed., *Coventry*, REED [Toronto: University of Toronto Press, 1981], xviii). Since Stratford is a mere fifteen miles away from Coventry, it seems entirely possible, perhaps even inevitable, that Shakespeare saw one or more productions of the Coventry play. Emphasis on the separation of the medieval and Renaissance drama often causes us to forget that what we insist on calling "medieval" plays were still popular in Shakespeare's lifetime. He was twenty years old when the city of Coventry decided to perform a sequel to the Passion play by staging a lavish "Destruction of Jerusalem," and that event, we should remember, preceded the first performance of

Shakespeare's own first history play (*1 Henry VI* in 1589 or 1590) by only some five years. There are those who would argue that if Shakespeare saw popular street performances he surely would have referred to them in the body of his plays. They claim that there is not a single reliable trace of that drama in Shakespeare's text. Yet, even if we disregard the very probable dramatic origin of Hamlet's "out-herods Herod" and the point of reference for the meckanicals in *A Midsummer Night's Dream*, the influence of the popular street drama was far more important for its conceptual contributions than for any direct or even conscious applications that it might have occasioned.

3. Glynne Wickham, *Early English Stages, 1300-1660*, vol. 1 (London: Routledge, 1963).

4. Brian Stock, "Historical Worlds, Literary History," *The Future of Literary Theory*, ed. Ralph Cohen (New York and London: Routledge, 1989), 45.

5. For a full discussion, see Harold Gardiner, *Mysteries' End: An Investigation of the Last Days of the Medieval Religious Stage* (New Haven: Yale University Press, 1946).

6. The theatrical metaphor of "the world as stage" has received a good deal of scholarly attention. Of special interest is Ernst Robert Curtius's treatment of the subject in *European Literature and the Latin Middle Ages*, trans. Willard R. Trask (New York: Pantheon, 1953), 138-44. While he traces the concept back to Plato, Curtius concentrates on the genesis of the world-stage metaphor especially as it emerges in the European North in the twelfth century. He attributes its wide influence to John of Salisbury, whose *Policraticus*, which contains two formative chapters on the world-as-stage metaphor, was widely and frequently translated in the Renaissance and may well have been one of the sources for the emergence of the new playhouse in the late sixteenth century. The other influential scholar who has written extensively on the "world as stage" is Frances A. Yates in *The Theater of the World* (London: Routledge, 1969). Her approach to the topos differs fundamentally from Curtius's in that she regards the classical revival as its source: "A theatre with a name such as the Globe . . . *must*, in my opinion, have beeen based on the classical theatre plan of the equilateral triangles within the circle of the zodiac" (134). What both of these illuminating and fundamental studies disregard is the treatment of the world as theater on the popular religious stage throughout Western Europe.

7. The theater, as Chaucer describes it, was built by the best craftsmen and artists that Theseus could find. The description emphasizes the compass points: in the east is the altar and oratory of Venus, the patron goddess of Palamon, the appellant, who always entered the lists from the east (see Edith Rickert, ed., *Chaucer's World* [New York: Columbia University Press, 1962], 152); in the west is Mars and his retinue; in the north is the temple of Dyane; see *The Canterbury Tales*, I.1901-8. There is much here that suggests the theater of the world, with Theseus "arrayed right as he were god in trone" (I.2529) and the action taking place in a *platea* with the compass points situated as *sedes* in the perimeter and taking on a moral

significance not so different from the stations as mapped in the diagram
of *The Castle of Perseverance* (see fig. 6).

8. All quotations of Chaucer are from *The Riverside Chaucer*, gen. ed. Larry
Benson (Boston: Houghton Mifflin, 1987).

9. Victor Turner, *The Anthropology of Performance* (New York: PAJ
Publications, 1987), 25.

10. See the discussion by Stuart Chase, *The Power of Words* (New York:
Harcourt, 1954), 146.

11. See A. L. Moir, *The World Map in Hereford Cathedral* (Hereford: n.p.,
1979), 8.

12. For a full description of these and other exotic and monstrous races, see
John B. Friedman, *The Monstrous Races in Medieval Art and Thought*
(Cambridge: Harvard University Press, 1981).

13. Marcia Kupfer, "The Lost *Mappamundi* at Chalivoy-Milon," *Speculum* 66
(1991): 569.

14. The comparison of the *mappa mundi* and *theatrum mundi* is not original
with me. To my knowledge it was first proposed by A. C. Cawley, "The
Staging of Medieval Drama," *The "Revels" History of Drama in English*, ed.
Lois Porter (London and New York: Methuen, 1983), 6-7. It was further
explored by Catherine Belsey, who sees an "emblematic geography" in
both the map and the stage of the world (*The Subject of Tragedy* [London
and New York: Methuen, 1985], 19-21). My discussion expands on those
of Cawley and Belsey as a design that is applicable not just to the fixed
stage of theater-in-the-round as we find in *The Castle of Perseverance* plan
but also to the religious stage of the urban Corpus Christi cycle, which
Belsey ignores completely (throughout her book) and which Cawley
does not mention directly in this connection. The application of the
mappa mundi would discourage the practical reading of the *Castle* plan
provided by Richard Southern, which interprets the ditch around the
playing area as a device to deny access to gate crashers (*The Medieval
Theater in the Round* [London: Faber, 1954]).

15. The *Castle of Perseverance* stage plan differs in its topographical alignment
of the compass points with most medieval maps. Usually, in the latter,
either north or east is at the top (see P. D. A. Harvey, *Medieval Maps*
[Toronto: University of Toronto Press, 1991], 19). The fact that south is
at the top and east at the left in the *Castle* plan may reflect the layout of
the stage in relation to the entrance of spectators into the playing area.
The east in any case is the focal point; as in church architecture, the
light of day first streams into the area from that direction. It may have
coincided with the opening of the play, as the sun rises upon the stage.

16. The "Pavement," which served as the central marketplace in medieval
York, was apparently named in the late Middle Ages. The name probably
had a practical origin—it was one of the few paved spaces in York—but
probably it also echoes the name of the site at which Pilate handed
Christ over to his executioners at high noon on Good Friday; see John
19:13. While it is not known whether folk practices and/or the Corpus
Christi play were the immediate source of the name, the location of the

Pavement is virtually at the dead center of the city. Invariably, this site was the last stop of the dramatic procession—I have argued that it may well have been the place where an in-the-round "final" stage was created for the itinerant performance (see Martin Stevens, "The York Cycle: From Procession to Play," *Leeds Studies in English*, n.s. 6 [1972], 37-62)— as well as the place where the crucifixion took place and where the gallows stood—the place in anthropological terms of the blood sacrifice. If the plays were responsible for the application of the name, we can conclude that they did indeed inscribe the city. I have discussed the York processional and dramatic route for plays and royal entries elsewhere; see Martin Stevens, *Four Middle English Mystery Cycles* (Princeton: Princeton University Press, 1987), chapter 1.

17. For a fuller discussion, see Martin Stevens, "Intertextuality of Late Medieval Drama and Art," *New Literary History* 22 (1991): 317-37.

18. Martin Stevens and A. C. Cawley, eds., *The Towneley Plays*, 2 vols. EETS s.s. 13-14 (London: Oxford University Press, 1994). All citations are to this edition.

19. See V. A. Kolve, *The Play Called Corpus Christi* (Stanford: Stanford University Press, 1966), chapter 3.

20. For a ranging discussion of this topic, see Peter W. Travis, "The Semiotics of Christ's Body in the English Cycles," *Approaches to Teaching Medieval English Drama*, ed. Richard Emmerson (New York: Modern Language Association, 1990), 67-78.

21. The stage direction reads as follows: "Mitt dissen Worten nimptt Gott vatter den Erdklotz in die hand, thutt, alls ob er inne formierte, vnd soll Adam daby verborgen ligen, demnach soll Gott vatter vff den Erdklotzen blasen, ergryfft damitt den verborgnen Adam by der hand, zücht in herfür. So sichtt Adam vmbsich alls einer, so vss einem schlaff erwacht . . . (With these words, God the Father takes the clump of dirt into his hand, acts as if he is forming it, takes the hidden Adam by the hand, leads him forward. Then Adam looks all around him, as if he had awakened from a sleep" [translation mine]) (Heinz Wyss, ed., *Das Luzerner Osterspiel* [Bern: Francke, 1967], 1:84).

22. Quoted in M. Blakemore Evans, *The Passion Play of Lucerne: An Historical and Critical Introduction* (New York: Modern Language Association, 1943), 217. Translation mine.

23. While the dramatic performance took place entirely within the confines of the Weinmarkt, Lucerne celebrated the source stories of several dramatic genres as decorations on all three of its famous wooden bridges, which gave access to the city from the south. Interestingly Renward Cysat, the director and dramaturge of the play, was also responsible for the inspiration and execution of the picture cycles represented on triangular panels that were installed on the inside of the peaked wooden roofs. There were three medieval bridges that led to the city over the River Speuer, of which now only one, the Speuerbruecke, still stands. (The *Kappellbrücke* was destroyed by fire in August 1993, but the City of Lucerne has decreed that it will be rebuilt and entirely restored.) The

first of these, the *Hofbrücke*, contained a cycle of 230 Old and New Testament scenes. The second, the *Kapellbrücke*, featured a historical cycle of Lucerne and the Confederation as well as the lives of two saints, SS. Leger and Maurice, the patrons of the town. The third bridge, the *Speuerbrücke*, contains a full cycle of Dance of Death paintings. These bridges undoubtedly created a variegated pictorial program that produced for its traversers a cultural panorama of the city as theatrical space. Interestingly these bridges collectively focused on the popular genres of the early drama: the historical play, the saints' play, the biblical play, and the morality. In a sense, therefore, the bridges advertised the drama of the marketplace, and both came together in creating a universal stage. For a discussion of these bridges, see Adolf Reinle, ed., *Die Luzerner Holzbrücken* (Lucerne: Räber, 1972).

24. All Shakespeare quotations are from David Bevington, ed., *Complete Works of Shakespeare*, 3rd ed. (Chicago: Scott, Foresman, 1980).

25. For a full discussion, see Martin Stevens, "The Theatre of the World: A Study in Medieval Dramatic Form," *ChR* 7 (1973): 234-49.

26. Hardison, *Christian Rite and Christian Drama in the Middle Ages*, 290.

Asleep Onstage

David Bevington

Characters asleep onstage are not especially common in ancient and modern drama. The few examples one can find do not suggest a thematic or dramaturgic pattern. Strepsiades, in Aristophanes' *The Clouds*, finds his horse-loving son Pheidippides asleep one morning, farting happily under the blankets, but the device serves only to characterize a lazy adolescent who must be routed out of bed and set to some kind of profitable schooling. The ghost of Clytemnestra berates the Eumenides for sleeping at the start of Aeschylus's play, though we do not see these chorus figures asleep once they enter. Professor Serebriakov dozes briefly in act 2 of Chekhov's *Uncle Vanya*, but chiefly as a way of suggesting the lateness of the night and the turmoil into which he has thrown the household by his waspishness. One can think of a few other instances.[1]

In medieval and in Renaissance English drama, on the other hand, sleeping onstage is a recurrent and widespread motif with thematic and theatrical significance. The characters who sleep in view of the audience make an impressive roster. First are those who appear in the Corpus Christi cycle plays, Saint Nicholas plays, and other church drama of the Middle Ages and on into the Renaissance: Adam and Eve, the shepherds who witness Christ's birth, the Magi, Joseph, Pilate's Wife, Mary Magdalene, the disciples in the Garden of Gethsemane, the soldiers guarding the tomb at the Resurrection, the five foolish virgins, and the wayfarers who are vindicated by Saint Nicholas. Then, in Renaissance English drama, the list is a steady one in the late fifteenth and sixteenth centuries: the title figure in *Mankind* (ca. 1465-1470), Wit in John Redford's *Wit and Science* (ca. 1530-1548), Hans the drunken Fleming in *Like Will to Like* (1562-1568), the mad Bomelio in the anonymous *The Rare Triumphs of Love and Fortune* (1582), Sappho in John Lyly's *Sappho and Phao* (1584), the title character and Sir Tophas in Lyly's *Endymion* (1588), the young travelers who serve as listeners in the framing device of George Peele's *The Old Wife's Tale* (ca. 1588-1594) and several characters in the play proper, Friar Bacon and his poor scholar Miles in Robert Greene's *Friar Bacon and Friar Bungay* (ca. 1589-1590), Revenge in Thomas Kyd's *The Spanish Tragedy* (ca. 1587), Mercury in the opening scene of Christopher Marlowe and Thomas Nashe's *Dido Queen of Carthage* (1587-1593), the title characters in Marlowe's *Doctor Faustus* (1588-1589) and *Edward II* (1591-1593), Sloth in the A- and B-texts of *Doctor Faustus*, Benvolio in the B-text version of *Doctor Faustus* (1602-1603), Friar Barnardine in Marlowe's *The Jew of Malta* (1589-1590), Christopher Sly in Shakespeare's *The Taming of the Shrew* (1590-1593), Titania and Bottom and the four lovers in *A Midsummer Night's Dream* (1595), the title character, the Duke of Clarence, and the Earl of Richmond in *Richard III* (1592-1594), Falstaff in *1 Henry IV* (1596-1597), King Henry in *2 Henry IV* (1597-1598), Juliet in *Romeo and Juliet* (1594-1596), Lucius and two guards (Varro and Claudius) in *Julius Caesar* (1599), the Player King in *Hamlet* (1599-1601), Desdemona in *Othello* (1603-1604), Kent and the title character in *King Lear* (1605-1606), the title character in *Pericles* (1606-1608), Imogen and Posthumus Leonatus in *Cymbeline* (1608-1610), Miranda and some members of Gonzalo's court party in *The Tempest* (1611), Queen Katharine in *Henry VIII* (1613), and still others, not to mention Shakespeare's early poem on *The Rape of Lucrece*.

The device remains quite common in Jacobean and Caroline drama, although, as we shall see, with a shift of tone and thematic emphasis. It is rarely found in a few major dramatists of this period, including George Chapman and John Webster, but is employed by a number of others, such as Thomas Heywood, Henry Chettle, Anthony Munday, Thomas Dekker, Ben Jonson, John Fletcher, Francis Beaumont, Thomas Middleton, Philip Massinger, John Ford, William Davenant, Richard Brome, James Shirley, John Suckling, and Henry Killigrew, along with a group of lesser-known dramatists such as Thomas Goffe, Robert Davenport, Anthony Brewer, Arthur Wilson, Gervase Markham, W. Rider, Jasper Mayne, Thomas Nabbes, Thomas Berkeley, William Cavendish Duke of Newcastle, and some who remain anonymous.

Here then is a theatrical motif that seems to connect Tudor and Stuart English drama with medieval drama. Sleep is often compared to death, as in the Raising of Lazarus, the Resurrection, the death of Humanum Genus in *The Castle of Perseverance* (1405-1425), and the death of the title character in *Everyman* (1495-1500). Both characters and audience have difficulties at times distinguishing sleep from death, as in Helena's exclamation on seeing Lysander stretched out on the ground, "Dead, or asleep?," and in Thisbe's "Asleep, my love? / What, dead, my dove?" (*A Midsummer Night's Dream*, 2.2.107, 5.1.321-22).[2] In *2 Henry IV*, in a last poignant token of misunderstanding between father and son, Prince Hal concludes that his drowsing father has died before the end actually occurs (4.4-5). Sleep can connote spiritual laziness and unpreparedness. Because sleep is the time for dreams, the sleeping state is also associated with prophecy and divine intervention in human affairs.

At the same time, theatrical exploitation of sleeping onstage undergoes considerable change over time. Sleep becomes a more ambiguous state in Renaissance drama than in its earlier manifestations; it grows more difficult to "read" as a theatrical signifier, and more consciously connected by Renaissance dramatists with the very business of writing and acting plays. As sleep becomes more metatheatrical, it serves as an apt vehicle for explorations of carnival inversion, indeterminacy of meaning, uncertainty as to the will of Providence, and the ironies of human lack of self-awareness. The medieval legacy of this stage metaphor is pervasive in Elizabethan drama, but it is also transformed.

Is there a continuity in stage tradition, a conscious reworking of the configuration of sleeping onstage that gains in richness through theatrical experimentation? I should like to argue that such a continuity is demonstrable, and that the continuity helps us understand why the motif flourished to a remarkable degree in a particular kind of theater—the kind that Francis Fergusson speaks about in his book, *The Idea of a Theater*.[3] In the theatrical world that extends from the earliest medieval plays through *Hamlet*, heaven and hell are visible, felt presences. Human action takes place on earth, in the center, with the heavens above and hell beneath. Heaven and hell are often represented in medieval cycle drama by scaffolds, contrastively decorated and present throughout a lengthy dramatic action; on the English Renaissance stage, the "heavens" are the symbolically decorated roof over the actors' heads, while hell is understood to be beneath the trapdoor in the stage. Effects from the underworld are sometimes auditory rather than visual. Thus the physical representations of the cosmos change materially in medieval and Renaissance drama. What remains constant is an awareness of the physically surrounding presence of that cosmos. In such a cosmic environment, human sleep takes on dimensions that it must lack in more "realistic" theatrical evocations of street scenes in perspective or interior rooms.

Sleeping onstage first becomes a recognizable theatrical entity not in the cycle drama of the later Middle Ages but in liturgical drama around the twelfth century. The "theater" is the church or, rather, various churches of varying proportions employing widely varying liturgical practices. All the terms we use to describe dramatic activity—play, theater, stage, actors, stage directions, entries and exits, sight lines, audience, representation, mimesis, willing suspension of disbelief—need to be redefined or replaced in this environment or series of environments. Sleeping "onstage" means in this case lying down on the floor of the church building, be it monastery church or cathedral. The "audience" can include the members of a monastic community celebrating a religious festival among themselves, or lay persons connected with a monastic establishment, or the students of a cathedral school, or the members of a royal court, or townsfolk, or any combination of these. Theatrical practices must owe a great deal to local conditions of "performance"—i.e., of religious celebration.

The Service for Representing Herod (*Ordo ad Repraesentandum Herodem*) from the Fleury Playbook, perhaps late twelfth century, offers what may be an early instance of sleeping onstage. The Fleury Playbook seems to have been copied at Fleury, a Benedictine monastery on the Loire, though whether the plays were actually performed there is hard to determine. In any event, this dramatic representation of the birth of Christ and the visit of the Magi appears to have been written for inclusion in the order of worship for January 6, the Feast of the Epiphany, celebrating the first manifestation of Christ to the Gentiles. The text concludes with a singing of the *Te Deum laudamus* at the end of matins. The *Ordo* begins with the angelic announcement of Christ's birth to the shepherds, who thereupon visit the manger and are asked "Whom do you seek?" (*Quem quaeritis*) in a sung passage directly related to the *Quem quaeritis* of the visit of the three Marys to Christ's tomb on Easter morning. Soon the Magi enter, following the star, consult with Herod about the stories they have heard of a newborn king and, leaving him in a paranoid rage, proceed to the manger, where they prostrate themselves before the babe and make their offerings. At this point the rubrics of the Fleury manuscript, in the guise of a stage direction, specify as follows:

> *These things done, let the Magi go to sleep there in front of the manger, until an angel, appearing from above, warns them in their sleep to return to their country by another way.*[4]

As the angel sings, the Magi, "*awakening*," arise ("Let us rise, therefore") and do as they are bidden. This dramatic insertion into the order of worship ends as they enter the choir, singing, "Rejoice, brethren, / Christ is born unto us, / God is made man." The cantor then begins the *Te Deum laudamus.*

How was this dramatic action staged in a monastic church on the Feast of Epiphany? The rubrics plentifully indicate that the entire church building was pressed into service. Angels appear *"on high"* (*in excelsis*), in a multitude, to the shepherds below. Whatever upper part of the church building is used, the effect is presumably awesome to spectators and shepherds alike; the angels are above, in glory, their voices evoking the beauty of heavenly song. This is an epiphany, indeed. The shepherds, for their part, are homely and earthbound; they fall prostrate to worship the child (*"procidentes adorent infantem"*), and then, rising up, *"invite the people standing around to worship the child."* The spectators are not monastics but lay worshipers (*populum*), standing in the nave near the rude crèche, located also in the nave. *"Meantime"* (*"Interim"*), say the rubrics, the Magi appear *"each from his own corner as if from his own land"* and *"come together before the altar or rising-place of the star."* Traversing the church in processional majesty from different directions signifying the four corners of the globe itself, they assemble in the east of the church, in the choir. They follow the star as it goes forward (*"Procedente autem stella"*), presumably on a guy-wire or carried aloft. As they reach the entrance to the choir, they ask directions of the "Citizens of Jerusalem," i.e., those *"standing by"* (*"astantes"*), including, it would seem, members of the congregation. They thus come to the attention of Herod and his men-at-arms, located evidently on a high and sumptuous scaffold near the crossings of the transepts. After an elaborate interview with Herod they proceed to the humble manger, where they follow the example of the shepherds in prostrating themselves before the Christ child.

What this encompassing stage suggests is that the sleep of the Magi takes place in a full and complex arena. Spectators are evidently all around the Magi as they lie down on the floor of the nave. Perhaps the "sight lines" are unorthodox from our point of view, but the action more than compensates by placing the sleep of the Magi right among the spectators as a gesture of spiritual significance. Just as the shepherds earlier had invited *"the people standing around"* to join in worshiping the child, the Magi worship on behalf of those who are present. The appearance of an angel *"from above"* to warn the Magi of Herod's hostile intent recapitulates the epiphany of the earlier appearance to the shepherds. Sleep thus takes on a double significance, as a demonstration of human frailty and of divine presence watching over those who are in need of guidance. Like the spectators around them, the Magi are well intentioned but easily deceived by villains; they are seekers who need direction; they are sleepers who, when awakened by angelic warning, will praise God and arise to a new life. The episode is based ultimately on Matthew 2:12, "And being warned of God in a dream that they should not return to Herod, they departed into their own country another way." The liturgical stage, like other medieval visual art forms, is able to give a graphic particularity to the process of dreaming, and to literalize in the theater the idea that dreams come from God. Small wonder that this sleep of the Magi became an iconographical favorite in the Middle Ages, as in the stone carving from Autun Cathedral in the mid twelfth century. Staging indications in the Benedicktbeuern Christmas Play, more or less contemporaneous with the Fleury play, call for a stage picture of the sleeping Magi that is essentially similar (line 516).

Other liturgical plays of the twelfth century confirm the iconographical import of sleeping onstage, and show how early a canon of interrelated episodes took form based on the motif of sleeping. Adam and Eve are created by God in *The Service for Representing Adam* (*Ordo Repraesentationis Adae*), written in Anglo-Norman French in the twelfth century; although the rubrics do not specify how the creation takes place, some symbolic action seems necessary, as in later cycle drama, to signify the archetypal moment when God has formed them "Of loam of the earth" (*"De limo terre"*). The creation occurs in Paradise, located evidently outside the church building in the midst of a multilevel set designed to encompass heaven, hell, and middle earth.

In the twelfth-century *Passion Play* (*Ludus de Passione*) from Benediktbeuern in the Bavarian Alps, Mary Magdalene is directed to *"go to sleep"* (*"Postea vadat dormitum"*) in her arbor. An angel appears to her in her sleep, calling her to an awareness of her sins and her need for Christ's salvation. She is distracted by her lover's approach and by her young women friends with whom she buys rouge from a merchant, but she soon falls asleep once again (*"Et iterum postea obdormiat"*), hears once more the angelic voice, and resolves at last to put aside her "worldly attire" in favor of a black mantle. Sleeping onstage here is essential to a portrayal of Mary's psychomachia; she is ambivalently responsive in sleep to carnal desires and to the voice of angelic exhortation. Her arbor, located evidently in the nave of the church, serves as a focus for her soul-struggle (like the Castle of Mankind's soul in the later outdoor production of *The Castle of Perseverance*) in the midst of other acting stations representing worldly tyrants such as Herod and the chief priests or, on the other hand, the beleaguered Christians at the Last Supper or at Golgotha.

In this same passion play, Christ ascends to the Mount of Olives twice and returns to the disciples only to *"find them sleeping,"* despite his strictures that they are to "Watch here and pray, that you enter not into temptation." As in the instance of the sleeping Magi, this image literalizes in the theater a Gospel narrative for which the scriptural text itself and patristic tradition provide a rich commentary: sleep is symbolic of human irresolution and proneness to temptation, demonstrating that "the spirit indeed is willing, but the flesh is weak" (Matthew 26:40-45). As Christ chides his disciples, "You could not watch one hour with me, you who used to protest you would die for my sake. Do you not see Judas, how he does not sleep, but hastens to betray me to the Jews?" (line 157).

Another important iconographic moment of sleeping in early liturgical drama portrays the sleep of the five foolish virgins in the eleventh- or twelfth-century *Sponsus* play from Saint Martial at Limoges. The stage action in this play gives us a straightforward visualization of Christ's parable of the foolish virgins who took no oil for their lamp when they went forth to greet a bridegroom and "all slumbered and slept" while the bridegroom tarried. The door shut upon them because of their unpreparedness is plainly indicative, in Christ's teaching, that one must "watch therefore, for ye know neither the day nor the hour wherein the Son of man cometh" (Matthew 25:1-13). In this instance, an entire dramatic representation serves to visualize a metaphor rather than a presumed historical incident; the dramatization of sleep gives rise to allegory rather than biblical drama in a strict sense, suggesting how broadly thematic is the idea of sleep as a state of unpreparedness or susceptibility of the human soul.

The Holy Resurrection (*La Seinte Resureccion*), an incomplete play in Anglo-Norman French, is missing the crucial scene of the Resurrection itself, but must have dramatized the dazed sleep of the soldiers guarding the tomb; before the manuscript breaks off, Caiaphas warns them to "Guard it absolutely. / If you sleep and he is taken, / Never again will you be good friends of mine" (lines 338-40). Sleeping is here a manifestation of Christ's compassionate observation about the self-unawareness of those who have persecuted him: "Father, forgive them, for they know not what they do" (Luke 23:34).

A Saint Nicholas play from the twelfth-century Fleury manuscript, *The Three Scholars* (*Tres Clerici*), shows the three victims in bed as they are about to be robbed and killed. The scholars, traveling among foreign peoples on their way to the university, seek lodging in the house of an impoverished elderly couple who then rob and murder their guests. Saint Nicholas, dressed as a traveler, restores them to life and brings the old couple to penitence. Despite the fact that this brief miracle play seems to have been intended for liturgical performance at matins in honor of Saint Nicholas, the rustic and folksy stage setting called for is strikingly different from that of Christmas and Easter drama: we are shown traveling students, old people, their house, a table, and a bed. Accordingly, the thematic import of sleep is new: it suggests victimization, the dangers of travel, and the need for divine protection in a bad world of sensational crime. At the same time the miraculous ending does invest sleep with the idea of death and resurrection, and is specifically associated here with the spiritual regeneration of penance and prayer.

Still other sequences from liturgical drama show how the dramatization of sleep onstage was often related to the ideas of death and resuscitation or spiritual rebirth. In Hilarius's twelfth-century play *The Raising of Lazarus* (*Suscitatio Lazari*), Christ observes to his disciples that "Lazarus sleeps," puzzling them as to whether he is referring to the restorative qualities of ordinary sleep. The Benedictbeuren *Passion Play* indicates too that this biblical conversation (John 11:11-13) is at the heart of dramatic interest in this event. Onstage, the configuration is like that of other sleeping scenes, with a recumbent figure who is induced to rise. The Fleury representation of *The Slaughter of the Innocents* centers on "the children lying slain" who rise finally "*at the voice of the angel*" who sings from above, "Suffer the little ones to come unto me." In the Fleury *Conversion of Saint Paul*, the central moment is visually similar: "*let Saul fall to the ground.*" Sightlines for performance in church must have presented difficulties and opportunities not unlike those of the sleep of the Magi before the manger: perhaps not all the congregation could see at once, but those close at hand were immediate witnesses to the fall and rise of characters who in various ways anticipate or imitate Christ in typologically meaningful stage action.

Later medieval vernacular drama elaborates the iconographical representations of sleep we find in liturgical drama, demonstrating stability in the canon of favorite stories and in the way they are visually interpreted. Adam and Eve arise out of the earth in the English cycle plays; in the Towneley *Creation* play, for example, God touches Adam ("*Et tanget eum*"), bids him "Rise up, and stand by me" (line 170), and proceeds to make Eve from one of Adam's ribs before they are led into Paradise by an angel. The sleeping disciples at the Garden of Gesthemane personify, in the N-Town cycle as in earlier liturgical drama, a failure in watchfulness that is all too typically human. In the Towneley *Lazarus* and in the Digby *Mary Magdalene*, Christ's miracle of rescuing Lazarus "from grevos slepe" is a demonstration to the disciples that human sleep alone "may stand him in no stede" (line 29). Also in the Digby *Mary Magdalene* the title figure is directed to "*lie doun and slepe in the erbyre*" (line 571 S.D.), located somewhere in the "place," where her conscience is awakened by the Good Angel as in the Benediktbeuern *Passion Play* some three centuries earlier. The Digby *Conversion of Saint Paul* uses scaffold-and-place staging to reenact the moment when Saul "*faulith down of[f] his horse*" (line 182 S.D.) in visual terms not unlike those of the twelfth-century Fleury play, even if the scaffolded *sedes* of that earlier production in a church interior did not encourage the same degree of simulated realism about the horses.

Because the staging of sleeping sequences in later vernacular drama is no longer confined to the church and its immediate environs, and because the plays are intended to reach a larger and more popular audience through guild performance, staging and thematic interpretation are at times more expansive. The famous *Second Shepherds' Play* from the Towneley cycle makes much of onstage sleeping in its imaginative additions to the familiar account. Mak lies down with his fellow shepherds, gets up while they are sleeping (*"surgit, pastoribus dormientibus"*), casts a spell to keep them oblivious, and mocks at them for their snoring. A good many lines of conversational exchange are devoted to the business of getting up and down (e.g., lines 253-68); directors of the play soon discover that they are faced with a stage littered with prone bodies. Associations of sleep with vulnerability, weariness, and cold (as in lines 255-57, for example) reinforce the play's insistent interest in the poverty and discouragement of spirit that Christ's birth is meant to address. Sleep is also a time of magic, of danger and deception. The first shepherd's exclamations as he awakes, "*Resurrex a mortruus!*" and "*Judas carnas dominus!*" (lines 350-51), remind us, in their imperfect Latin, of the deeply thematic connection between sleep and resurrection, between Christ's birth and his passion. Throughout the play the emphasis on sleeping anticipates the dual ending in which the shepherds first find a stolen sheep wrapped in swaddling clothes to whom Mak's wife sings lullabies (lines 433-48); then, after yet another lying down in the fields and rising to hear the angelic announcement (lines 633-39), they find the Christ child who "ligys full cold" (line 747). Sleeping onstage, then, offers a major visualization of the analogues between comic human frailty and divine incarnation for which this play is justly famous. The Wakefield Master's thematic use of sleep is strikingly imaginative, but it is also composed of traditional elements that had already been developed in medieval drama through centuries of use.

Other late medieval elaborations expand theatrical opportunities in similar ways. In the Towneley *Offering of the Magi*, the travel-weary kings find a fully spread bed ("a litter redy cled," line 590) thoughtfully provided for their comfort. This elaboration of the set is of a piece with the horses or simulated mounts that the kings repeatedly use (*"Here lightys the kingys of thare horses,"* line 504). A sleepy and bewildered Joseph, in the York *Flight into Egypt*, is comforted by the angel Gabriel, who bids him "Wakyn, and take entent"; God's assistance is at hand, and "Therefore I bidde the[e] slepe no mare" (lines 37-40). Joseph, worried about his vulnerability to cuckoldry in his old age, is an aptly comic figure with whom popular audiences might identify. The dream of Pilate's Wife becomes a central episode in the N-Town cycle, as Satan, alerted too late to the fact that his plot to kill Christ will undo the devil's work by means of Christ's great sacrifice, desperately attempts to persuade Pilate's Wife to prevent her husband from signing Christ's death warrant. A sleeping figure onstage thus becomes the focus of a cosmic contest of guile between Christ and Satan in which the latter will surely lose.

The Towneley dramatization of the Resurrection enhances the roles of the soldiers who attempt to guard the tomb only to fall into a stupor when Christ rises. This actualization in the theater of a favorite icon reminds us that it is based only partly on Gospel authority: Matthew is alone among the four Gospels in reporting that the chief priests and Pharisees set a watch over the tomb because, as they tell Pilate, "that deceiver said, while he was yet alive, After three days I will rise again" (Matthew 27:63), and even here we find only a hint of the thematic use of sleep as expressive of human incapacity to comprehend spiritual truth. The very act of visualization, in the theater as in other visual arts, invites the kind of interpretive reading that patristic scholarship of the Middle Ages is so ready to provide. Participants in the great moments of medieval iconography become dramatic characters whose actions and motives the spectators need to understand so that they may relate these events to their own lives.

•   •   •

Sleeping onstage becomes a staple dramaturgic device in sixteenth-century English drama, and yet so strikingly changed are the visual effects and themes as to challenge any previous idea of continuity and tradition. The cast of sleepers is no longer canonical, as it was in medieval drama, and correspondingly we find no body of lore incorporating a "received" tradition of interpretation in most cases. *Endymion* uses a mythological tale about sleeping, but even here Lyly radically invents the contents and potential significance of Cynthia's dream. Individual situations call forth varied configurations. The sleeper, as before, remains the focus of an epiphany, a meeting between mortals and immortals, but that meeting is more apt to be suggestive of ideas about the magic of theater than about providential concern with human destiny. At its most effective, the epiphany can combine these ideas into a single, unstable vision, one in which a continuity with medieval tradition is perceivable along with the transformation.

The sleep of the title figure in the anonymous *Mankind* (ca. 1465-1470) suggests how readily the morality drama could adapt to its own uses the themes that had become popular in medieval religious drama. The protagonist's giving in to slumber is the direct result of his impatience with his rural life and his inclination instead for gluttony and sloth (lines 581-606). Titivillus gains direct access to Mankind's vulnerable psyche through the suggestive medium of dreaming. In an apparent university play from the Winchester College MS 33 called *Occupation and Idleness,* from the mid-fifteenth century in the lower east midlands, Idleness steals upon the vulnerably sleeping Occupation in the play's opening scene with an intent to swindle him; later Idleness drunkenly resolves to "go wynke" for a while, though in fact he appears to remain awake (fol. 65ᵛ, lines 45ff. and fol. 67ᵛ, line 253).

The sleep of Wit in John Redford's *Wit and Science* (ca. 1530-1548) shows the transition at work in humanist drama of the early Tudor period. Wit's sleep is symptomatic of his spiritual laziness and self-indulgence, as in the case of Mary Magdalene. Redford is thoroughly familiar with a stage tradition in which sleep is associated with spiritual struggle, with costuming suggestive of the protagonist's fallen condition (here, the fool's cap and coat of Ignorance in which the sleeping Wit is dressed by Ignorance's mother, Idleness), and with the protagonist's confused sense of self. Wit's awakening in the company of the lady he hopes to marry, Science, and his chagrin at discovering that he literally looks like a fool, are clever recapitulations of the religious and moral drama that was still commonly performed in England. Yet the focus of Wit's spiritual crisis and eventual self-discovery is humanist learning. Although that learning is not at odds with religious faith, the dramatic impact is quite different from that of *Mary Magdalene.* The spiritual figures that Wit encounters in his sleep are moral abstractions, not angelic messengers from God; Ignorance and Idleness are personifications of Wit's inattentiveness to his studies, and are so plausibly human onstage that they might just as well be given names as Wit's idle and ignorant companions. Sleep has become a metaphor for a common obstacle to self-knowledge and educational reform.

In *Like Will to Like* (1562-1568), sleep takes on an even more mundane aspect as the consequence of drunkenness. The Flemish Hans, along with Philip Fleming, figures in a scene of antiforeign sentiment:

Hans enters pot in hand, sings stammeringly, and "sittith in the chair" as he drinks repeatedly and finally "snorteth as though he were fast asleep" (lines 490-560). In this instance sleep becomes little more than a sign of bestial oblivion. To be sure, it also betokens the kind of spiritual sluggishness that one sees in earlier religious drama, insofar as this play embodies morality play antitheses between good and evil, but the satirical and xenophobic focus here is really on deplorable social behavior.

The sleep of Endymion in Lyly's best-known play (1588) is a metaphor for a divided self, as in much medieval drama, but in terms that are romantic and political more than religious. Endymion is caught between the claims of Tellus and Cynthia. It is at Tellus's behest that the sorceress Dipsas casts a spell upon Endymion, putting him into a sleep that lasts forty or fifty years. Tellus, a Circean figure whose name bespeaks the fleshly desires of this world, employs cunning to immobilize Endymion, hoping that his absence will breed mistrust in her rival Cynthia. Tellus and Dipsas know that although they can "breed slackness in love," they cannot rule Endymion's heart (1.4.24-32).[5] When Cynthia awakens him with a kiss (5.1.24), he is restored to a secure and loving position as her favorite courtier. Even so, the long sleep is not simply a deliverance of one who has suffered for his loyalty; surely the paralysis afflicting him is at least partly the result of his venal longing for what he cannot have and of Cynthia's wish to discipline his affections. The conflict is internal. His sleep thus becomes, in effect, the main plot of this extraordinary play, beginning when Endymion is estranged from the queen he adores and ending with the resolution of his conflict.

Endymion rests on a lunary bank specially devised for his long theatrical sleep, and appears to remain there, visible at times to the audience and curtained from view at other times, from the end of act 2 until the kiss in act 5. Much action occurs onstage meanwhile; the stage is evidently designed to encourage visual juxtapositions between adjacent areas of focus, as in medieval drama. Dramatic ironies swirl about the present-absent Endymion, as Cynthia bids Eumenides search for his friend (3.1), and as Sir Tophas too sleeps onstage for a time in a comically exaggerated parody of enervation in lovesickness (3.3). These juxtapositions must have appealed to Shakespeare when he came to write *A Midsummer Night's Dream*. In both plays, the device of sleepers onstage unrecognized for a time by waking figures makes thematic connections between the multiple plots that are running concurrently. The device also encourages metatheatrical awareness, as we watch characters onstage being manipulated by techniques of illusion. We see what the fairies see, and share their immortal consciousness. In both plays, sleep is an unstable metaphor of the experience of drama itself. And in both plays the metaphor of theatrical illusion is enriched for an Elizabethan audience by a perception that the dramatic experience is partly about Queen Elizabeth's volatile relationships with her leading courtiers and with her nation.[6]

Sleep is thus capable of expressing a complex range of ambivalent feelings toward the rule of a strong, virginal queen: adulation, irritability, deference, suspicion, gratitude, resentment. It proves no less evocative as a means of exploring and even criticizing the inner feelings of such a regal person, for in *Sappho and Phao* (1584) it is Sappho, princess of Syracuse, who sleeps onstage. She enters "*in bed*" (3.3), evidently thrust forth onto the stage in a bed or alcove provided with bedcurtains so that she can be curtained from view. As with Endymion, her sleeping is associated with being in love. This state of emotion shows Sappho at her worst: she snaps at her women, is restless and petulant, is willful and yet cannot make up her mind. Still, the inward struggle is ultimately ennobling, for she masters herself and finally accepts the hard truth that a queen cannot compromise her position by giving her love to one of her subjects. Both praise for Queen Elizabeth and misogynistic resentment of her control over male destiny are transparent in Lyly's dramatic portrait.[7] As in *Endymion*, the sleeper's prolonged presence onstage, visible at times and curtained from view at others as she is intermittently awake and asleep, allows for ironic juxtapositions between her situation and that of her rival Venus. Similarly, her plight is visually juxtaposed with that of Phao, the beautiful oarsman whom she loves but cannot allow herself to marry. In Lyly's hands, sleep becomes a wonderfully delicate theatrical instrument for the exploration of tensions and ambiguities between men and women, rulers and subjects.

The metatheatrical potential of sleeping onstage, evident in the plays looked at thus far, is highlighted in the phenomenon of the sleeping figure in an induction or chorus. "Revenge, awake!" exclaims the distraught ghost of Don Andrea at the end of the long third act of *The Spanish Tragedy* (ca. 1587), when injustice seems out of control and Andrea's craving for bloody satisfaction is wholly unappeased. "Awake, Revenge, for thou art ill-advised / To sleep away what thou art warned to watch!" Revenge urges his fellow chorus figure to be patient: "though I sleep, / Yet is my mood soliciting their souls." If "Revenge hath slept," Andrea is bidden nonetheless to imagine "What 'tis to be subject to destiny" and to bide his time. One function of the play's choruses is to pace the expectation of the audience, as the play moves from exposition to complication to catastrophe and resolution.

Don Andrea is an onstage audience being watched by us: he is dispassionate at first, then engaged, then frustrated and furious, as witnesses to a tragedy of revenge should be. His companion, Revenge, is the puppeteer who controls the action, the surrogate for the dramatist. His sleep is literal and metaphoric: as he slumbers in his chair, the action seems to turn further and further from the purposes that Andrea (and we) had hoped to see accomplished. Yet we also sense that Revenge is biding his time, as is the dramatist. The stage metaphor of sleep thus controls the shape of the plot as it arches toward expectation and closure. The audience is invited to see itself in a dream, as in Shakespeare's *A Midsummer Night's Dream*, except that here the dream is a nightmare. The pleasurable terror of apparent loss of control in revenge tragedy, as perhaps also in a nightmare, arises from our perception that fiction can give shape to what seems threateningly inchoate. Revenge's awakening from his sleep offers promise to Andrea, and to us, that all will be brought to a conclusion, however terrible: "Nor dies Revenge, although he sleep awhile."[8]

Other sleepers in choruses make the point that the play itself is their dream. The students who lose their way at night and call upon an old woman for sustenance and a story in *The Old Wife's Tale* (ca. 1588-1594) help the spectators to experience Peele's play as at once quaintly folksy and psychically familiar, suitable for a bedtime story. The well-educated chorus figures provide us a sophisticated stance with which to condescend to a story deserving no more elegant a title than that of an "old wife's tale," and in which the ingredients are indeed so romantically heterogeneous and implausible that we laugh at the apparent simplicity; yet the ordering of these events as linked together by common folk motifs suggests a relevance to our deepest feelings about magic, love, and death. Sleeping onstage is associated repeatedly with magic: Eumenides, the wandering knight, awakens on his journey to find the Princess Delia just in time to pay for the funeral of the impoverished Jack, whose ghost will repay the knight by serving as copartner in his quest (lines 473-500); the braggart Huanebango is quelled by the sorcerer Sacrapant and is inertly carried off by Furies until he is roused by thunder and lightning, now deaf and hence a fit mate for the shrewish Zantippa (lines 582-675); and Eumenides, when he finally locates Delia with Jack's help, discovers her asleep behind a curtain until he wakens her with his lover's greeting thrice repeated (lines 880-84). When the storyteller herself is found asleep at the end of the play the audience is invited to think of the tale as her dream.

Similarly, in a play from the late 1580s that survives only in a "plot" or summary list of stage directions, *The Second Part of The Seven*

Deadly Sins, the slumbering figure of Henry VI remains onstage throughout as the chorus figure to whom, as in a dream allegory, the poet John Lydgate presents a series of episodes illustrating sloth, envy, and lechery.[9]

Christopher Sly's slumbering as he sits "*over the stage*" in the induction of *The Taming of the Shrew* (Induction 2:139) serves much the same purpose, whether or not he and his companions disappear halfway through the drama (as in Shakespeare's version) or remain to the end (as in the anonymous *The Taming of a Shrew*). To see the play itself as Sly's dream is to perceive connections between the Lord's hoodwinking of Sly and Petruchio's taming of Kate, along with other illusory happenings in the play such as servants pretending to be masters and an old Pedant assuming the role of Vincentio. Dramatic fiction is a kind of dream in which the audience can begin to grasp the uncertain relationship between life and art. Playacting is deceptive, illusory, unreal, and yet enjoys a paradoxical reality that gives lasting value to mimetic art. We are a long way from the providential assurances offered to sleeping characters in medieval drama.

Christopher Marlowe's approach to sleeping figures onstage is, as one would expect of him, sardonic and subversive. He deals in paradoxes and ironies of illusion, as do Lyly, Peele, and Shakespeare, but in such a way as to undermine the cheerful idealism with which those dramatists offset the potentially destabilizing experience of sleep and dreaming. Marlowe's iconoclasm is closer to that of Thomas Kyd. In *Doctor Faustus*, for example, Faustus sleeps "*in his chair*" in what appears at first to be a serious attempt to calm his despair at being "but a man condemned to die," but becomes instead a means of tricking the Horse-courser to whom Faustus has sold a magical horse. The Horse-courser, distraught at having ridden this horse into a pond and seen it transformed into a bundle of hay, finds the Doctor "fast asleep" and proceeds to "*Pull him by the leg, and pull it away*" (A-text, 4.1.139-74). Sleep is ambivalently both spiritually serious and a matter of cheap buffoonery; the tragic moment is undercut, as elsewhere in the play, by disillusioning practical joking. In a passage from the B-text version by one of Marlowe's revisers, probably Birde or Rowley, intermittently asleep, watches from a window as Faustus entertains the Emperor of Germany. The emperor is amused at the "sport" of seeing Benvolio awaken from his drunken sleep to find horns on his head. Faustus uses sleep to demonstrate his occult powers against those who have offended him, and to call the audience's attention to the theater as a place of magical shows (B-text, 4.1.124-32).

In *The Jew of Malta*, Barabas and Ithamore strangle the sleeping Friar Barnardine with his own belt and then prop him up as though still alive as a ruse to incriminate Friar Jacomo (4.2.131-206). The tricksters laugh gleefully at their grisly work ("Excellent! He stands as if he were begging of bacon. . . . Look how his brains drop out on's nose") and do everything possible to subvert serious issues of murder and deception. Christianity, it appears, is asleep on the island of Malta, and revenge bides its time, as in *The Spanish Tragedy*. In a similar way, Edward II dozes momentarily with his head in the Abbot's lap as he longs for release from the destiny that pursues him (*Edward II*, 4.5.39-45). Later, the imprisoned king sleeps on a bed provided for him by Lightborn as the latter sits close by; in his exhausted state, Edward desperately needs some rest, and yet he is tormented by grief and by fear for his life (5.5.70-110). His touching dependence on the comfort and companionship that Lightborn seems to offer him echoes the homosexuality that has created such difficulties in his kingship, and anticipates his gruesome death by means of a red-hot spit. Despite the continued preoccupation of Marlowe's plays with human destiny and its relation to the gods, the stage image of sleep is made violently physical and trivial as if in bitter laughter at the human condition.

Robert Greene's *Friar Bacon and Friar Bungay* (ca. 1589-1590) seems to echo and parody the serious subversions of Marlowe. If, as seems likely, Marlowe's *Doctor Faustus* is the earlier play,[10] Bacon's falling asleep as he is about to learn from his brazen head how to "girt fair England with a wall of brass" (11.20) recalls the proud ambitions of Faustus. The sleep appears to be a punishment for Bacon's blasphemous dealings with "th' enchanting forces of the devil" (line 18). Bacon's last speech before he falls asleep lays heavy stress on the need for watchfulness (lines 28-38), thus recalling medieval dramatic presentations of the five foolish virgins, the drowsy guards at the Resurrection, and the sleeping disciples at the Garden of Gethsemane. Miles's overtly comic slumbering underscores the parodic element in this dramatization of the futility of human striving to "be watchful" for selfish ends.

In several late Elizabethan plays, sleep is presented not as slothful or inattentive, as in so many medieval dramatizations, but as the innocent rest of those who are about to be victimized. Providential interpretation in the earlier drama gives way to a more sensational and historically particular kind of cruelty that is seen as an undeniable fact of human existence. Edward II's sleep before his murder is of this sort. Peele's *The Battle of Alcazar* (1588-1589) opens with a scene in which two young brothers of Muly Mahamet are shown to bed by their villainous older brother and "*betake them to their rest*," whereupon they are smothered to death in their bed by Muly and his brother

Abdelmunen. The episode no doubt reminded Elizabethan audiences of the murder of the two princes in the Tower of London at the command of their uncle, Richard of Gloucester—a scene that Shakespeare chose not to stage directly in his *Richard III* but which is narrated for us by Tyrrel in all its frightening particularity (4.3).

Similarly in *Thomas of Woodstock*, sometimes known as *1 Richard II* (1591-1595), the title figure is discovered asleep in his curtained bed by Lapoole and two murderers (5.1), in a scene of confrontation about the morality of killing that strikingly resembles the scene of Clarence's last moments in *Richard III* (1592-1594) and Edward II's demise in Marlowe's play. The order of dating of these three plays is uncertain; what seems clear is that the motif of the murder of sleeping victims had become something of a stage phenomenon during the early 1590s. It occurs also in Shakespeare's *2 Henry VI* (ca. 1591-1592); although we do not see Humphrey Duke of Gloucester asleep and then murdered onstage in the Folio version, we can look to the Quarto version (*The First Part of the Contention betwixt the Two Famous Houses of York and Lancaster*) for a more direct account in which "*the curtains being drawn, Duke Humphrey is discovered in his bed, and two men lying on his breast and smothering him in his bed*" (Malone Society Reprint edition, lines 1188-90). In the Folio version (3.2), we see "*two or three running over the stage, from the murder of Duke Humphrey*," and are shown his dead body in the bed later in the same scene (line 146 S.D.). In *The Trial of Chivalry*, perhaps by Heywood or Chettle (1599-1603), Navarre's daughter Bellamira is found "*sitting in a chair asleep*" by her villainous wooer, Bourbon, who, when she repulses his unwelcome suit, proceeds to poison her face in such a way that she resembles a hideous leper (2.3, sig. D). Soldiers are sometimes caught off guard asleep and drunk, as in the anonymous *King Leir* (lines 2436-2508) and *1 Henry VI* (2.1), though the actual sleeping is apt to be offstage.

Even when the innocent sleeper is saved from death or disfigurement (as, later, in *The Tempest*), the sleep can still betoken a dangerous vulnerability. When the virtuous Panthea, in *The Wars of Cyrus* (1587-1594), awakens in her bed to find that a Persian lord, Araspas, has employed a magician to place a love charm under her pillow, she escapes a fate worse than death like the Lady in *Comus* by the unassailable force of her chaste purity (3.2; sig. D2-D3). Robin Hood, in Henry Chettle and Anthony Munday's *Downfall of Robert Earl of Huntington* (1598), is found sleeping on a green bank by Marian's (or Matilda's) father, Lord Lacy (or Lord Fitzwater), shortly before his armed enemies arrive, but is warned in time by Friar Tuck (scene 11, lines 1490ff.). In *The True Chronicle History of King Leir* (1588-1594), the aged king and his courtier Perillus, awaiting Cordella, are set upon by a messenger sent by Conorill and Ragan to massacre them on the spot; only through the messenger's relenting are the intended victims spared (scene 19, lines 1438-1755).

• • •

To Shakespeare most of all belongs the achievement of bringing together the spiritual view of sleep as expressed in medieval theater and a Renaissance reinterpretation of sleep as an ambiguous state uncertain in its meaning. Relatively early in his career, *The Taming of the Shrew* and *A Midsummer Night's Dream* establish sleeping onstage (as in Lyly, Peele, and Kyd) as a metaphor for the fluid boundaries between reality and illusion, life and art, theater and dream. Falstaff operates along these theatrical boundaries. Many productions of *1 Henry IV* introduce him to the play asleep, since his first question in act 1, scene 2, "Now, Hal, what time of day is it, lad?" suggests a moment of awakening and of renewed encounter with a world where, as Hal says, "hours" might as well be "cups of sack, and minutes capons, and clocks the tongues of bawds, and dials the signs of leaping houses." Hal's first description of Falstaff is of one who is so "fat-witted with drinking of old sack, and unbuttoning . . . after supper, and sleeping upon benches after noon" that he has forgotten what time should be for.

Falstaff preens himself on being one of "Diana's foresters, gentlemen of the shade, minions of the moon" (1.2.1-26); he works best by night. Small wonder, then, that he should respond to the Sheriff's interruption of their late-night tavern revels by retiring into a hiding place where he is shortly discovered by Peto: "Fast asleep behind the arras, and snorting like a horse" (2.4.523-24). Falstaff is one whose presence fills a room, or a theater, even when he is asleep; his snoring, and the contents of his pockets, serve as the topic with which this scene is brought to a close. Falstaff's entrances and exits here are manifestly theatrical: Peto's "discovery" of him evidently unveils his bulky presence by means of pulling aside a curtain. We are treated to yet another little play-within-the play, serving as an encore to the play-acting that has just concluded about Hal and his father. The miniature scene concludes with the curtaining off of Falstaff once more behind the arras, allowing the actor to get offstage by means of an exit from the "discovery space," it would seem.

In a sense his presence is still felt, for he has never "exited" in the normal manner. Instead he is unveiled and veiled again, like King Herod on a medieval scaffold, and is invisibly "behind the scenes" even when not onstage in his triumphant flesh. The whole sequence at the end of act 2, scene 4, with its ambiguous connecting of sleep and theatrical magic, anticipates the moment in act 5 when Falstaff lies on the ground, seemingly dead to us and to Prince Hal, only to rise and rewrite history when Hal has exited from what he expected to be the finale of his own dramatic performance at Shrewsbury field (5.4.110-63). Falstaff exists in an eternal fictional world of his own devising,[11] and cannot be tied down to history. He embodies, in the proverbial sense, that which is "larger than life," by exploring the uncertain boundaries of sleep, death, fictionality, and theatrical illusion.

Sleeping onstage in Shakespeare often occurs at moments of otherworldly visitation, as in medieval drama, or evokes at least a powerfully ominous world of magic. The effect is at once reminiscent of medieval drama and disturbing in a new kind of uncertainty. The Duke of Clarence in *Richard III* dreams of death by drowning only a few moments before he is stuffed into a barrel of malmsey wine (1.4); Richard III and the Earl of Richmond sleep onstage in a symmetrically paired configuration, while the ghosts of Richard's many victims appear onstage to terrorize the conscience of the murderer and to comfort his opposite number with assurances of success in battle (5.3). These assurances seem divinely harmonious, but they are also contrasted ironically with the play's multiform historical ironies.

Juliet's deathlike trance in *Romeo and Juliet* points to the managerial role of Friar Laurence as resembling that of the dramatist; as in other plays, and in Prospero's boast of his ability to waken "sleepers" from their graves in order to bring them forth onstage (*The Tempest*, 5.1.48-49), the metaphor of sleep embodied in Juliet's trance is expressive of art's ambiguous potential for doing harm as well as good. The boy Lucius slumbers in *Julius Caesar* at the very moment when the spirit of Caesar makes his unnerving appearance to Brutus (4.3.277-307), and the failure of Lucius and the guards to have seen Caesar's ghost underscores the ambiguity of what it is that Brutus thinks he has witnessed. The connection of the sleeping boy to the ghost of a murdered man is evident in Brutus's term for sleep, "murderous slumber" (line 269)—that is, producing the likeness of death, but here with a special resonance that may arise from Brutus's consciousness of himself as one who has slain a friend.

Sleep in *Hamlet* occurs onstage not coincidentally in the play-within-the-play. The dumb show, presented in anticipation of the dialogue, dramatizes the ambiguous resemblance of sleep and death. The Player King "*lies him down upon a bank of flowers,*" whereupon the Player Queen, "*seeing him asleep, leaves him.*" After the murderer removes the King's crown and "*pours poison in the sleeper's ears,*" the Queen returns and "*finds the King dead*" (3.2.133 S.D.). In sleep and in death, an actor lies down and remains motionless to mimic death, though of course he may react to the poison in his ears before he dies. Our ability as audience to differentiate identical postures of proneness depends upon our acceptance of theatrical conventions. In this instance we are particularly aware of theatrical language, since we are watching an audience onstage attend to a play that is about to begin. In the dialogue version of "The Mousetrap" that follows the dumb show, sleep continues to show its thematic power of suggesting separation, aging, misplaced trust, and the illusory lack of clear distinction between sleep and death. Sleep is a liminal time of great danger; it is also suffused with a sense of divine warning and observation, for we can see that, in the theater, the murderer and the adulterous queen are observed (by two audiences) in ways they do not comprehend.

Act 5 of *Othello* similarly plays with theatrical convention. The fact that we as audience can scarcely distinguish between Desdemona sleeping and Desdemona dead, other than by what occurs and is said in between, reinforces Othello's reflection that he can "relume" his flaming torch but cannot restore to Desdemona the "Promethean heat" he takes from her (5.2.1-13). Stage picture thus adds theatrical immediacy to a thematic use of sleep that recurs repeatedly in the language of the play, as in Iago's observation that "Not poppy nor mandragora / Nor all the drowsy syrups of the world" can restore to Othello the "sweet sleep" he enjoyed only yesterday (3.3.346-49) and in Iago's dream of lying by Cassio (lines 429-41). The metatheatrical self-awareness of Desdemona's death scene reminds us too that the actions of Othello and Iago are not unobserved. As Emilia puts it, "'Twill out, 'twill out!" (5.2.226). The scene calls attention to its contrivance even while it also invokes, as in medieval drama, the human need to believe in divine intelligences that will demand a reckoning for what is done. Yet that divine agency is vested in the play's characters, not in deities onstage. "O, the more angel she, / And you the blacker devil!" exclaims Emilia of her mistress and of Othello. "She was heavenly true" (lines 134-35, 140). Othello looks downward to Iago's feet to see if they are cloven, like the devil's, but can only conclude, "but that's a fable" (line 294).

Kent's sleeping onstage in *King Lear* is an extraordinarily metatheatrical moment. He appears to remain in full view of the audience, in the stocks, as he waits for morning, from the end of act 2, scene 2 until he is found there by Lear in act 2, scene 4. The intervening scene (2.3) is devoted to a soliloquy by the banished Edgar, and apparently takes place somewhere else in Gloucestershire rather than in the courtyard of Gloucester's house where Kent has been stocked. Kent's sleep allows him to be inactive and "not there" as the previous scene ends. He dozes in his disgraced condition while Edgar, hunted by his father's household and fearing for his life, ponders how to disguise himself as a mad beggar. We as audience make the juxtaposition, aware that a flexible theatrical convention allows us to "place" Kent in the stocks and Edgar at some unspecified distance. Their nearness is thematic: two hunted and banished men face their trials with resourcefulness and stoic calm.

Lear's sleep in an outbuilding on Gloucester's estate is a fitting condition for a ruined old man who has just exhausted himself by arraigning a footstool as his daughter Goneril (3.6.51-101). Later, sleep is a restorative preparing the way for Lear's brief reunion with Cordelia (4.7.13-43); the motifs of "restoration" and "medicine" link Cordelia to sleep, and remind us too in an ironic way of Macbeth's despairing observations on "the raveled sleeve of care" (*Macbeth*, 2.2.41) that are occasioned in part by the sleepwalking of his wife. Henceforward in *King Lear*, and especially in the final scene, we will not often be sure whether Lear is sleeping or near death, mad or sane.[12]

In the late romances, Shakespeare finds onstage sleep an especially apt vehicle for exploring the ambiguous boundaries of sleep and theatrical illusion. The consciously old-fashioned character of the narratives he chooses to dramatize encourages a synthesis of an essentially medieval use of the sleep metaphor with Jacobean self-awareness of dramaturgic artistry.[13] When, for example, Marina is reunited with her grieving father onboard ship near Mitylene and tells him a tale of her being born at sea of a king's daughter who died in childbirth, Pericles stresses the dreamlike implausibility that we also recognize in such a story. "This is the rarest dream that e'er dull sleep / Did mock sad fools withal," he muses. "This cannot be / My daughter—buried!" (5.1.166-68). Death and sleep are superimposed in his vision of a history he believes to be irredeemably and tragically past. In the wonder of his reunion with his lost daughter, Pericles himself falls asleep onstage, in the pavilion where he has sequestered himself from all human comfort, and dreams that the goddess Diana appears to him with instructions that he proceed to her temple at Ephesus. Perhaps she descends from the theatrical "heavens" and reascends, for her entrance and exit are otherwise unmarked. Is she a "real" goddess or a figment of his dream? Her accurate knowledge of what will happen at Ephesus validates her role as deity, and yet the ambiguous character of sleep gives an uncertain resolution to the question. In any event, Diana's apparent descent from the "heavens" calls attention to this play's metatheatrical delight in a recently acquired device of staging in the public theaters, and strongly connects Pericles with two other late romances in which classical deities similarly manifest themselves: *The Tempest* and *Cymbeline.*

The Tempest combines this motif of the gods' descent with that of several sleeping figures onstage (Miranda and some members of Gonzalo's court party), whose subjection to the will of Prospero demonstrates the authority of that artist figure over his world, his island. The classical gods in *The Tempest* are illusory, since they are enacted by Ariel and his fellow spirits; we cannot be sure that the gods "exist" other than as devices created by the dramatist-magician whose power, though he is mortal, is supernatural. Prospero does readily acknowledge the authority of "Providence divine," to be sure, in the world outside his island (1.2.160), but on the island itself Prospero transforms a medieval Christian idea of benign divinity into his own humanistic mastery over plot, character, and destiny. Through Ariel's agency he devises tests, charming Alonso and his followers asleep so that Antonio and Sebastian, assuming incorrectly that they are unobserved, are given the seeming opportunity to murder for political gain. The potential hubris of Prospero's own self-assertion jars him, and so he draws back in pious renunciation, vowing to drown his books and free Ariel as he prepares for retirement and death. Prospero's unwillingness to step beyond certain bounds into the unnerving terrain of Doctor Faustus manages to preserve the fragile and self-contradictory harmonies with which the play closes. Still, the Promethean and magical vision suggests a greatly altered role for the sleeper onstage and that sleeper's place in the cosmos.

Cymbeline uses sleeping figures onstage perhaps more than any other Shakespeare play. Imogen, disguised as Fidele, takes a potion given her by the wicked Queen under the false assurance that it will cure her sickness, but because the substance is not in fact the poison that the Queen had hoped but one of Doctor Cornelius's concoctions, Imogen falls into a sleep resembling that of Juliet and appears to be dead to her grieving cave-mates. Arviragus and Belarius lay her out as a corpse and place beside her the headless Cloten, slain by Guiderius, dressed in Posthumus's clothes. Death and sleep look remarkably alike, especially in the theater; as Lady Macbeth says, "The sleeping and the dead / Are but as pictures" (*Macbeth,* 2.2.56-57). The theatrical ambiguity of Imogen's state is manifest in the Folio's stage direction: "*Enter Arviragus, with Imogen, dead, bearing her in his arms*" (4.2.197 S.D.). For a time, the audience cannot be sure if she is alive or dead—that is, whether the boy actor is miming sleep or death.

Metatheatricality is further reinforced when Imogen, reviving, mistakes the headless corpse for that of her husband. An event of high seriousness is given comic distance by the bizarre effect of manipulating theatrical conventions. We find ironic amusement in Imogen's mistake, however much we sympathize, and listen to her grieving cries with the godlike perspective of those who know that things are better than she supposes. Next, we are entertained by the misapprehension of the entering Lucius and his soldiers that the "page" who is prostrate on the corpse must also be dead, sleep and death being so outwardly alike. "Or dead or sleeping on him? But dead rather; / For nature doth abhor to make his bed / With the defunct, or sleep upon the dead" (4.2.359-61). Our superior awareness reassures us that we are watching tragicomedy, not tragedy, and that the magical world of the theater, with its manifold contrivances and deliberate improbabilities, is in control.

Posthumus Leonatus's sleep in jail, as he awaits execution with hope of deliverance from human suffering, reenacts the Jacobean and metatheatrical dimensions of Imogen's sleep and of Pericles's vision. There is something consciously medieval in the picture of a suffering, frail, human receiving divine visitation. "*Solemn music*" ushers in those who, "*in an apparition*," represent the members of Posthumus's family. "*They circle Posthumus round, as he lies sleeping*," beseeching almighty Jupiter to show his spite no more toward the penitent hero. Jupiter's appearance takes every technical advantage in its *coup de théâtre*: he "*descends in thunder and lightning*" from the theater's "heavens," "*sitting upon an eagle*." The stage directions do not specify how Jupiter is to throw "*a thunderbolt*," but the effect must be terrific. The ascent "to my palace crystalline" is no less striking. "He came in thunder; his celestial breath / Was sulfurous to smell," Sicilius marvels. "The holy eagle / Stooped, as to foot us. His ascension is / More sweet than our blest fields." The stunning effect continues to the very moment of his disappearance into the "heavens." "The marble pavement closes; he is entered / His radiant roof" (5.4.29-121).

The business of divine visitation can succeed brilliantly in twentieth-century productions of *Cymbeline*.[14] The more contrived are the effects, the more they work in a double way to impress us with the splendor of theatrical magic and at the same time to distance us by elegant artifice. We see that the story and stage picture are contrived, and that Jupiter is above all an image of artistic control. Of course all will turn out well for Posthumus and Imogen. Jupiter is a providential figure, for the play is full of providential metaphors: "Fortune brings in some boats that are not steered" (4.3.46). Still, Jupiter's role as Providence is an ambiguous one. Is he Fortune, or the Christian deity in classical disguise? More certainly, he is the guiding spirit of tragicomic form as artfully designed

by the omnipresent dramatist. The play's highly implausible denouement, with its multitudinous coming together of so many disparate
plots and characters, is a tour de force of the sort of comic Providence
Shakespeare perfects in his final plays. Nowhere do we see more clearly
his mastery of medieval conventions about sleepers onstage and his
transformation of that stage metaphor into his own exploration of the
potentialities of his art.

Dream visions are not uncommon in late Elizabethan and
Jacobean tragicomedy; as in *Cymbeline*, they are well suited to express
ideas of providential concern in a highly self-conscious theatrical
medium of otherworldly visitations, descents, and the like.
Shakespeare makes use of the device in *Henry VIII* (1613), when the
dying Queen Katharine is comforted by an elaborate vision of six
white-robed dancers (4.2.82ff.). Princess Elizabeth experiences an
otherworldly vision in Thomas Heywood's *If You Know Not Me You
Know Nobody*, Part I, or *The Troubles of Queen Elizabeth* (1603-1605), as
do Ascanio in *The Maid's Metamorphosis* (1599-1600), King John in
Chettle and Munday's *The Death of Robert, Earl of Huntington* (1598),
Bajazet in Thomas Goffe's *Raging Turk*, or *Bajazet II* (ca. 1613-1618),
the title figures in Gervase Markham's *Herod and Antipater* (1619-
1622), Anthynus in Richard Brome's *The Queen's Exchange* (1629-
1632), and a sleeping soldier in Brome and Heywood's *The Late
Lancashire Witches* (1634).[15] The sleeping figure onstage becomes a
significant means of exploring supernatural visitation in a theater
that is increasingly aware of its own potential for artifice and illusion.

Space does not permit the detailed exploration of sleeping onstage
in the Jacobean and Caroline period as a whole. Many thematic uses
we have already encountered are carried forward into this drama, as
when the Duke's daughter Infelice, in *The Honest Whore*, Part I, by
Dekker and Middleton (1604), wakens from the effects of a magical
drug that induces the appearance of death (1.3); the scene is a virtual
replay of *Romeo and Juliet*. Further study will suggest that those themes
and motifs are increasingly subjected to the ironic scrutiny of a theater
increasingly conscious of its effects, so that dreaming, the presence of
the gods, witchcraft, prognostication, and the like become the materials of a playful stage making sophisticated entertainment out of its
spiritual heritage. A tabulation of these effects in the appendix that
follows this essay will at least suggest the extensiveness of the device in
the Jacobean and Caroline theater right to the very eve of its demise in
1642. The particular instances of sleeping onstage also suggest how
the thematic emphasis has shifted to such areas as sensationalism and
sexual deceit (as in *The Revenger's Tragedy*) and murder in revenge of
adultery (*The Maid's Tragedy*). Clearly, the cultural rationale of the

stage's original fascination with sleeping and dreaming was already markedly deflected into self-conscious artifice in the theater of the Stuart years. The motif of sleeping onstage was not to find a major recurrence when the theaters reopened in the Restoration period.

Notes

1. At the end of Chekhov's *The Cherry Orchard*, the old manservant Firs (aged 87) decides to "lie down a bit" as the others leave for good; the audience is perhaps undecided as to whether he is going to sleep or is dying. Earlier, at the end of act 1, Anya dozes off in the nursery late at night, having been unable to get to sleep in her offstage bedroom, and is helped back to bed. The cook Christine falls asleep on a chair by the stove in the second scene of August Strindberg's *Miss Julie*. Hamm seems to be asleep at the start of Samuel Beckett's *Endgame*; later, Clove finds Hamm's father Nagg asleep inside his trash tin. Jennet Jourdemayne faints in act 2 of Christopher Frye's *The Lady's Not for Burning*, but fainting is not at all the same as sleeping onstage. Charlotte Corday is sleepy and slumped down as she awaits her moment to kill Marat in Peter Weiss's *The Persecution and Assassination of Jean-Paul Marat*. And there are others.

   I wish to thank Alan Dessen for his help on this essay; he has provided me with several examples of sleeping onstage from his impressive computer file of stage devices in Renaissance drama. Another important source of information has been Richard Hosley, "The Staging of Desdemona's Bed," *ShQ* 14 (1963): 57-65. Others who have helped me locate instances of sleeping onstage include Eric Rasmussen and Gerard NeCastro.

2. Textual references for Shakespeare throughout are to *The Complete Works of Shakespeare*, ed. David Bevington, 4th ed. (New York: HarperCollins, 1992).

3. Francis Fergusson, *The Idea of a Theater* (Princeton: Princeton University Press, 1949).

4. "*Istis factis, Magi incipiant dormire ibi ante praesepe, donec angelus desuper ap[p]arens moneat in somnis ut redeant in regionen suam per aliam viam*" (line 98 S.D.). Textual references to medieval plays are to *Medieval Drama*, ed. David Bevington (Boston: Houghton Mifflin, 1975), for the following plays: the Fleury *Service for Representing Herod* and *The Slaughter of the Innocents*, the Benedictbeuren Christmas and Passion Plays, the Anglo-Norman *Adam* and *Holy Resurrection*, the Beauvais *Play of Daniel*, Hilarius's *Raising of Lazarus*, the Fleury *Service for Representing the Conversion of the Blessed Apostle Paul*, the Towneley *Creation*, *Raising of Lazarus*, *Second Shepherds' Play*, *Offering of the Magi*, and *Resurrection of the Lord*, the N-Town Passion sequence, the York *Flight into Egypt*, the Digby *Conversion of Saint Paul* and *Mary Magdalene*, *Mankind*, and John Redford's *Wit and Science*. Other plays, including the *Sponsus* play from Saint Martial at Limoges of the wise and foolish virgins and the Saint Nicholas play, *Tres*

Clerici, can be found in Karl Young, ed., *The Drama of the Medieval Church,* 2 vols. (Oxford: Clarendon Press, 1933). *Tres Clerici* appears also in Joseph Q. Adams, ed., *Chief Pre-Shakespearean Dramas* (Boston: Houghton Mifflin, 1924). *Occupation and Idleness* can be found in Norman Davis, ed., *Non-Cycle Plays and the Winchester Dialogues,* Leeds Texts and Monographs (Leeds: Leeds University Press, 1979).

5. Textual references to Tudor Renaissance plays are to the Revels editions of Kyd's *The Spanish Tragedy,* Peele's *The Old Wife's Tale,* Lyly's *Sappho and Phao,* Marlowe's *The Jew of Malta* and *Doctor Faustus* in the A- and B-texts, ed. David Bevington and Eric Rasmussen (1993); references to Lyly's *Endymion* are to a forthcoming edition by David Bevington for Revels. The following editions are cited in the Malone Society Reprints series (Oxford University Press): *Like Will to Like,* in *Two Moral Interludes*; *The Rare Triumphs of Love and Fortune*; *King Leir*; *The Downfall of Robert Earl of Huntington*; *The Death of Robert Earl of Huntington*; and *If You Know Not Me You Know Nobody. The Trial of Chivalry* is cited in the Tudor Facsimile Texts edition. Other editions cited include: Marlowe, *Edward II,* ed. H. B. Charlton and R. D. Waller (London: Methuen, 1933); Greene, *Friar Bacon and Friar Bungay,* ed. Daniel Seltzer, Regents Renaissance Drama Series (Lincoln: University of Nebraska Press, 1963); and *The Wars of Cyrus,* ed. James Paul Brauner, University of Illinois Studies in Language and Literature, 28 (1942).

6. Louis Adrian Montrose, "'Shaping Fantasies': Figurations of Gender and Power in Elizabethan Culture," *Representations* 1.2 (1983): 61-94; Mary Beth Rose, *The Expense of Spirit: Love and Sexuality in English Renaissance Drama* (Ithaca: Cornell University Press, 1988), 12-42; Philippa Berry, *Of Chastity and Power: Elizabethan Literature and the Unmarried Queen* (London: Routledge, 1989), 111-33; Marie Axton, "The Tudor Mask and Elizabethan Court Drama," *English Drama: Forms and Development,* ed. Marie Axton and Raymond Williams (Cambridge: Cambridge University Press, 1977), 24-47; and Susan Frye, *Elizabeth I: The Competition for Representation* (Oxford: Oxford University Press, 1993), 17.

7. Theodora A. Jankowski, "The Subversion of Flattery: The Queen's Body in John Lyly's Sapho and Phao," *MRDE* 5 (1991): 69-86.

8. *The Spanish Tragedy,* 3.15.23. On reflexivity and language in *The Spanish Tragedy,* see Peter Sacks, "Where Words Prevail Not: Grief, Revenge, and Language in Kyd and Shakespeare," *ELH* 49 (1982): 576-601, and Frank Ardolino, "'Veritas Filia Temporalis': Time, Perspective, and Judgment in *The Spanish Tragedy,*" *Studies in Iconography* 3 (1978): 57-69.

9. See W. W. Greg, ed., *Dramatic Documents from the Elizabethan Playhouses,* vol. 2, *Reproductions and Transcripts* (Oxford: Clarendon, 1931), and David Bradley, *From Text to Performance in the Elizabethan Theatre: Preparing the Play for the Stage* (Cambridge: Cambridge University Press, 1992), 98-100.

10. On the likely dating of *Doctor Faustus* in 1588-89, see David Bevington and Eric Rasmussen, eds., *Doctor Faustus, A- and B-Texts* (1604, 1616), Revels Plays (Manchester: Manchester University Press, 1993), introduction, 1-3.

11. James L. Calderwood, *Metadrama in Shakespeare's Henriad: "Richard II" to "Henry V"* (Berkeley: University of California Press, 1979).

12. Sleep is a restorative in the earlier *The Rare Triumphs of Love and Fortune*, 1582; when the exiled Bomelia goes mad as a result of losing his magic books, Mercury puts him into a charmed sleep until he can have his health and memory restored by a sprinkling of blood on his face (Malone Society Reprints, 1930, act 5, lines 1620ff.). As in *King Lear*, the remedy is accompanied by music.

13. Arthur C. Kirsch, *Jacobean Dramatic Perspectives* (Charlottesville: University Press of Virginia, 1972).

14. I think especially of the Chicago Shakespeare Repertory Theater production in 1991, directed by Barbara Gaines, with brilliant flashing lights, rich costumes, thundering music, and other sound effects, all in a theater space that was otherwise devoid of realistic scenic effects.

15. Princess Elizabeth's sleeping vision in Part I of *If You Know Not Me You Know Nobody* (1603-1605) takes the form of a dumb show in which her Catholic enemies (during the reign of Mary, 1553-1558) assemble to murder her, led by a Friar; they are driven back by two angels, who then put the English Bible into the Princess's hands (MSR edition, 1934, sc. 14, lines 1049-53). In act 2 of *The Maid's Metamorphosis* (1599-1600), the Duke's son Ascanio, in search of his banished beloved Eurymine, falls asleep on a "grassy bed" in the forest and experiences a dream vision of the gods: Juno, angry at Venus for practicing her "wanton pranks" on Ascanio and Eurymine, dispatches Iris to the cave of Somnus with a request that a vision reveal to Ascanio the way to Eurymine. The drowsy god obliges by sending his eldest son, Morpheus, in the shape of Eurymine. In Chettle and Munday's *The Death of Robert Earl of Huntington* (1598), John receives three visitations, one from Ambition in the form of a temptation to seize Austria, one from Insurrection in a prophecy of young Arthur's death, and one from his Queen Isabel and from Matilda betokening John's indifference toward his own wife and sons (MSR edition, 1965, lines 924-93). The ghosts of Mahometes, Zemes, Trizham, Mahomet, Achmetes, Caiubus, and Asmehemides, led in by Nemesis, "*encompass Bajazet in his bed*" in *The Raging Turk* (1613-1618), (MSR edition, 1968, 5.9, lines 3380-85).

At 5.2.95 of Markham's *Herod and Antipater*, Antipater, the bastard son of Herod, "*sits down and slumbers.*" On another part of the stage representing the palace, Herod congregates with the Emperor Augustus and others. As Antipater slumbers, Herod guiltily beholds in a vision his sons, whom he has slain, and his queen Marriam. When Herod in turn slumbers, Antipater sees the ghosts of his victims. The double appearance is not unlike that in act 5 of *Richard III*. Afterward, Antipater, misled into thinking that Herod has committed suicide and that Antipater's way is now clear to being king of Judah, is taken to the palace only to experience a just execution that is simultaneous with the death of his father Herod. In Brome's *The Queen's Exchange* (1629-1632), Anthynus, son of the banished Segebert, sees as in a trance a vision of six Saxon ghostly kings, the last of whom picks him up and leaves him standing upright, though he collapses once again and is carried off "asleep" (3.1). In *The Late Lancashire Witches* (1634), by Brome and Heywood, a soldier is ordered to stand guard over a property that is rumored to be haunted by witches and that turns out to be so indeed. Witches and spirits come about him "*with a dreadful noise*" and engage with him in a pitched battle (act 5); the effect is hilarious, and lends itself to a thorough spoofing of otherworldly phenomena.

Appendix

What follows is a tabulation of occurrences of sleeping onstage in Jacobean and Caroline plays not discussed in the present essay. They are presented more or less in chronological order. The dates given at the head of each item indicate what is known about dating, often only approximate. I would be glad to know of other instances.

1605-1606 *Volpone*, by Ben Jonson. In act 1 Volpone pretends sleep as part of his ruse to deceive the acquisitive Voltore, Corbaccio, and Corvino; Mosca bids his master "Betake you to your silence and your sleep" (1.4.1), and moments later Mosca and Corbaccio find Volpone "Upon his couch . . . newly fall'n asleep" (line 8). Corvino is encouraged by Mosca to shout insults at the seemingly insensate Volpone as he lies abed, and to let Mosca "stifle him rarely with a pillow" (1.5.68) or "pull the pillow from his head" (2.6.87). Corvino agrees to put his wife Celia to bed with the supposed valetudinarian.

1606-1607 *The Revenger's Tragedy*, perhaps by Cyril Tourneur or Thomas Middleton. In 2.3 the disguised Vindice leads Lussurioso, the Duke's son and heir, to the Duke's bedchamber under the supposition that they will find the Duchess sleeping with Lurrurioso's illegitimate brother Spurio; instead, they find the Duke with the Duchess in bed. The Duke plausibly assumes that Lussurioso is out to kill him, and has him seized.

1607 *The Devil's Charter . . . containing . . . the life and death of Pope Alexander VI*, by Barnabe Barnes. In 4.5 the villainous Alexander dispatches the sleeping Prince Astor and his brother Philippo with two asps in boxes, making it appear that they died from being overheated at tennis. Before they die, the two young men speak in their sleep of angels and golden light, as though anticipating their own deaths.

1608-1611 *The Maid's Tragedy*, by Beaumont and Fletcher. In 5.1 Evadne, the unfaithful wife of Amintor, does penance for her unchastity by going to her royal lover at night, tying the arms of the sleeping king to his bed, and stabbing him to death after he has awakened and begged for mercy.

1604-ca. 1617 *The Woman's Prize, or The Tamer Tamed*, by Fletcher. In 5.1 of this comic inversion of *The Taming of the Shrew*, Livia, the sister of Petruchio's second wife Maria, is "*discovered abed, and Moroso by her*," feigning illness and representing herself as penitent for having abused her aged wooer so. This is all part of her ruse to abuse Moroso and escape from him, as her cousin Bianca indicates in appreciative asides. Livia also uses her apparently immanent death as a ploy to subdue her favored suitor Rowland into signing papers that are favorable to her.

1610-1615 *The Valiant Welshman*, by "R. A." In 5.1 Gald (the brother of the King of Britain) and the magician Bluso hide in the chamber of Gald's wife, Voada, daughter of Cadallan the prince of March, to observe Marcus Gallicus (son of the Roman Lieutenant Ostorius) approach Voada's bed, candle in hand and sword drawn, like Tarquin. Gald and Bluso burst forth from their hiding, "*tumble Marcus over the bed*," and convey Voada away to safety. Marcus Gallicus penitently interprets the interruption as a heaven-sent deliverance of sacred chastity.

1613-ca. 1621 *The Faithful Friends*, authorship uncertain. In 4.1 the weary Armanus is found asleep in a forest by his "faithful friend," the general Marcus Tullius, husband of Philadelpha—who, however, is convinced at present that his wife is unfaithful and Armanus false. Tullius draws his sword but cannot complete the stroke. The awaking Armanus persuades the disguised Tullius of his and Philadelpha's fidelity, and the two friends are reconciled. In scene 4 Tullius hides in his wife's bedchamber ("*a rich bed is thrust out*") and is convinced of her goodness when she spurns the advances of King Titus Martius.

1610-ca. 1616 *Monsieur Thomas*, by Fletcher. In 5.1 "*a bed discovered, with a black moor in it*" is a comic trap for Monsieur Thomas, who is deceived into believing the sleeping figure in the bed to be Mary, whom he is pursuing. Mary is one of those present who are enjoying the discomfiture. He's so vexed he'd rather marry the devil. The black maid Kate is rewarded with various gifts for the pommeling she receives and the bed is drawn in offstage.

1616 *Love's Pilgrimage*, by Fletcher. In 1.2 Theodosia and Philippo "*enter on several beds*" that are evidently "thrust out" at the start of the scene. Theodosia is occupying a room in an inn, disguised as a man, in order to look for her absent lover. When a shortage of beds leads to her sharing the room with a stranger, Philippo, she confesses her female identity and name to her roommate only to learn that he is her dear brother, whom she fears she has dishonored by her unseemly disguise.

1607-1617(?) *The Lovesick King*, by Anthony Brewer. In 3.2 (line 1201) Cartesmunda, the fair nun of Winchester, finds her beloved Canutus, King of Denmark, asleep as music plays. She smoothes away his fearful dreams with a kiss; he bids her sleep, too, and he will guard her. Lord

Harrold, who believes that a conquering king must be a soldier and eschew love, is distressed to find the king so lovesick.

1607-1621 *Thierry and Theodoret*, by Fletcher, Massinger, and perhaps Beaumont. In 5.1 Thierry, the dying King of France, enters "*on a bed*" attended by doctors. In his distempered speech he bids one of his attendants lie down and sleep that he may behold what blessed rest his own eyes are deprived of. His queen, Ordella, dies with him.

1619 *Sir John van Olden Barnavelt*, by Fletcher and Massinger. In 3.6 Leidenberch, oppressed by his own failure to save Holland and encouraged by Barnavelt to take his own life, sends his son to bed off-stage while he prepares for "the iron sleep of death." The boy has premonitions of a heavy doom, and cries out in his sleep as the moment of suicide approaches.

1621 *The Wild Goose Chase*, by Fletcher. In 4.3 Oriana enters "*on a bed,*" pretending to be mad and dying for love. She appears dead, indeed, and nearly succeeds in tricking her marriage-shy lover, Mirabel. Alerted to suspicion by his friend Belleur, however, Mirabel suspects a ruse and elicits a confession that she is shamming. The "wild-goose" eludes capture on this occasion, however, only to succumb to yet another device in act 5.

1622 *The Spanish Curate*, by Fletcher and Massinger. In 4.5 Diego, sexton to Lopez, the Spanish curate, enters "*in a bed*" as part of Lopez's Volpone-like trick to fool Bartolus, the covetous lawyer, into thinking that Diego is dying a rich man and hence a fit victim for a lawyer. Bartolus, promised the role of executor, cringes as the list of donations on Diego's will and testament gets longer and longer. The wife's lawyer is in on the joke. At last Bartolus confesses "the lawyer is an ass."

1619-1623 *The Two Noble Ladies and the Converted Conjurer*, anonymous. In 5.2 Justina, princess of Antioch, "*is discovered in a chair asleep, in her hands a prayer book, devils around her.*" This is the work of the conjurer Cyprian, who has been obliged to use magic on her since she has paid no heed to his wooing speeches. When even the spirit Cantharides is unable to do anything with her on Cyprian's behalf, the conjurer calls up "lust-provokers from black hell" to "present her fancy with lascivious visions." All is of no avail; she looks "heavenly sweet" in the midst of hell's enchantments. She stirs, sleeps again, starts awake when he attempts to kiss her, and forces the spirits to fly from her by her holiness. He is converted to penitence by her example.

1623 *The Wandering Lovers, or The Lovers' Progress*, by Fletcher and perhaps Massinger. In 3.1 Lysander is escorted by night to the bedchamber of Calista, the virtuous wife of Cleander. Lysander finds Calista "*sitting behind a curtain*" and "*asleep.*" She wakens; he woos her; she urges him to behave honorably, but is drawn to him and allows a number of kisses. When her husband arrives, taper in hand, she conceals Lysander behind the hangings. Her husband has had a nightmare of a dragon coming to her chamber. When Cleander has departed, Calista persuades Lysander to leave.

1624 *The City Nightcap*, by Robert Davenport. In 2.1 "*a bed thrust out*," with "*Lodovico sleeping in his clothes*," and Dorothea, his wanton wife, "*in bed.*" Lodovico's habit of coming in tired and drunk, and sleeping so soundly in his clothes that nothing can wake him, makes him the perfect target of a cuckolding jest, one that requires the servant Francisco to be brought into the bedroom and to approach Dorothea while the husband sleeps on.

1627 *The Cruel Brother*, by William Davenant. In act 5, the Duke of Sienna "*on his bed is drawn forth*" onstage. Count Lucio and his dependent, Foreste, awaken and confront the Duke with hard questions as to whether he has sought to corrupt their wives with gifts, but are at last reluctant to slay their anointed sovereign.

1626-1629. *Albovine, King of the Lombards*, by William Davenant. In act 5 "*A canopy is drawn, the King is discovered sleeping over papers*," and hence an easy prey for Paradine, a captive soldier and the King's onetime favorite, who is on a mission of vengeance for having been cuckolded by the King. But Paradine relents upon seeing that the King has been reading some papers about Paradine with indulgent care. Paradine confesses to having whored the Queen first. They fight; Paradine delivers the King a fatal blow and falls on his own sword, but survives.

1628 *The Lover's Melancholy*, by John Ford. In 2.2 Cleophila "*draws the arras*" and discovers her much-wronged father Meleander "*in a chair, sleeping.*" He is so distracted by "the cunning / Of tyrants" that he is slow to recognize his daughter and their servant Trollio.

1629-1630 *The Inconstant Lady, or Better Late Than Never*, by Arthur Wilson. In 5.3 the Duke of Burgundy is escorted by Millecert to the bedside of Emilia, where she lies asleep, veiled to conceal her identity. The Duke is under the apprehension that he is about to enjoy Cloris, Emilia's sister. Millecert, hoping to keep the Duke from "the adulterate sheets / Of foul Emilia," now reports (falsely, but in accord with what Emilia believes) that Cloris has been poisoned by her inhuman sister, who hopes to take Cloris's place in the Duke's desires and become duchess. The Duke unscarves Emilia, who confesses her guilt. Eventually Cloris is revealed to be alive; all are reconciled and forgiven.

1633-1634 *Tottenham Court*, by Thomas Nabbes. In 4.7 the tailor Stitchwell is found "*in a chair, asleep,*" or seeming so, for he is thus able to listen in on Changelove's wooing of Stitchwell's wife and to the wife's complaining of her husband's drinking, his paying no attention to her advice, etc. When Stitchwell remarks in an aside about horns, the wife assures her suitor that her husband talks in his sleep; and when the supposed sleeper pulls Changelove by the ears, the wife chalks this up to a fit in his sleep.

1634 *Love's Mistress, or The Queen's Masque* (*Cupid and Psyche, or Cupid's Mistress*), by Thomas Heywood. In act 5 of this classical legend play, Psyche opens a box she has received at Pluto's fearful court in the underworld from Proserpina, containing "celestial beauty." Though forbidden to inspect it, she yields to temptation in her desire to be beautiful, and at once "*falls asleep.*" The Clown takes up the box for his mistress Amaryllis, but Cupid then "*charms him asleep*" and removes the box from him, leaving in its stead a counterfeit that proves to be full of ugly painting. Psyche, awaking, is told by Cupid to take the real box to Venus and be deified with her.

1634 *A Very Woman, or The Prince of Tarent,* by Massinger and perhaps Fletcher. In 4.2 "*A bed drawn forth, Martino upon it, a book in's hand.*" As his father, the Duke of Messina, explains to the witnesses, Don Martino Cardenes is laboring under a melancholy imagination of the wrongs he has committed against Don John Antonio, the prince of Tarent. A doctor uses various impersonations in an ultimately success- ful attempt to cure his patient.

1625-1655 *The Twins,* by W. Rider. In 5.2 (1655 edition, p. 43) "*A curtain drawn, and Carolo discovered asleep in a chair.*" He is found there by Julio, the banished duke, who is tempted to kill "Laberio" (i.e., Carolo) as a supposed murderer; indeed, Carolo "*talks in his sleep,*" confessing to having killed Alphonso, Julio's son. But Julio's eyes dazzle and he puts up his sword rather than indulge in a cowardly action. The supposed violent acts in this comedy, in any event, are all the result of mistaken purposes and identities.

1635 *The Platonic Lovers,* by William Davenant. In act 2 the young Duke Theander is led to his mistress Eurithea by her woman, and "*draws a canopy. Eurithea is found sleeping on a couch, a veil on, with her lute.*" He wakens her with welcome rhapsodies of love and bids her unveil her beauty to him. In the purity of their love, they part company, each wishing the other sweet dreams.

1635 *The Conspiracy* (*Pallantus and Eudora*), by Henry Killigrew. In act 2 the young prince Cleander, later to become king, "*is discovered sleeping*" by Achates and awakened by him into an unwelcome consciousness.

1635-1637 *The Princess, or, Love at First Sight,* by Thomas Killigrew. Tullius, a humorous companion of the lieutenant and others, enters sick "*on his bed*" in 3.3 and again "*sick in his bed*" in 4.4. He pleads, "Let me sleep then, quiet those drums" in the second of these scenes, though he appears to stay awake and indeed becomes quite drunk.

1637-1638 *The Lost Lady*, by Thomas Berkeley. In act 5 the Moor Acanthe is "*thrust out*" on her bed, groaning, convinced that she has been poisoned, longing for death. She is perhaps insensible when they "*draw in the bed.*"

1637-1638(?) *The City Match*, by Jasper Mayne. In 3.2 the merchant's son, Timothy, is discovered "*asleep like a strange fish*" when Captain Quartfield "*draws a curtain*" for the edification of the gentlefolk (including Timothy's mother) who have paid good money to see this well-advertised prodigy.

1638 *The Antipodes*, by Richard Brome. Peregrine, the son of an old country gentleman named Joyless, is subjected to a cure for his bookishness by a pretend "voyage" to the Antipodes that involves a drugged wine and a series of staged illusions. In 2.4 he is brought in "*in a chair*" by two sailors and is solemnly informed that his "sleeping fit" has lasted some eight months.

1639-1641 *Brennoralt, or The Discontented Colonel*, by John Suckling. In 3.4 the discontented Brennoralt finds the Governor's daughter, Francilia, in her bedchamber, asleep. "*He draws the curtains*," awakens her, and distresses her with accusations of injustice for having aroused his passion for her without reciprocating it.

ca. 1639-ca. 1640 *The Country Captain* (*Captain Underwit*), by William Cavendish (Duke of Newcastle) and James Shirley. In 3.1 Sir Richard (the country gentleman) and his wife are discovered "*in bed*" early in the day. He wishes to hunt for a brace of hares but bids her to take her ease in bed still. She is in fact expecting a lover, and nearly gives herself away when she hastily says, looking out of the bedcurtains, "For heaven's sake, my husband is not gone," only then realizing that her husband has returned, but she "*feigns sleeping*" as a cover for her confusion and concocts a dream of being attacked.

Acting Mary: The Emotional Realism of the Mature Virgin in the N-Town Plays

Alexandra F. Johnston

The founding almost thirty years ago of the *Poculi Ludique Societas*, the medieval and Renaissance play group of the University of Toronto, can be attributed directly to the enthusiasm of Arnold Williams for the production of early drama. At a meeting of the seminar which he founded in association with the Modern Language Association, John Leyerle caught his excitement and returned to Toronto to make the production of a medieval play (inevitably *Everyman*) part of his first graduate seminar. Two years later Professor Leyerle's Seminar (PLS) became independent of the course and the rather pretentious Latin words that fitted the initials were chosen for the group. The group has passed through many phases since then but it remains at the center of much of what we now know about early drama. I have been associated with the *PLS* since 1974. What follows is based on my experiences as an actor and director, bringing my scholarly knowledge and training to the realization of the mature figure of the Virgin Mary in the N-Town plays.[1]

Recent feminist scholarship has begun to uncover some unsuspected complexities that underlie the texts of early drama. In her essay on feminist approaches to the Corpus Christi cycles, Teresa Coletti centers much of her discussion on the figure of the Virgin Mary and examines "the many roles and meanings attributed to her during the Middle Ages."[2] Three other recent publications have focused our attention on the figure of the N-Town Virgin. Peter Meredith has abstracted the play on the childhood of the Virgin from the manuscript and published it as a separate play.[3] Martin Stevens emphasizes Mary's role in the Birth sequence but sees her importance, as well, in the episodes after the Resurrection. In N-Town, the risen Christ appears first to his mother and she then becomes, according to Stevens, "the presiding spirit of comic resolution" for the entire sequence.[4] Most particularly, however,

85

a consideration of Mary and her cult forms a large part of Gail McMurray Gibson's fine book on East Anglian lay spirituality and the drama. She writes:

> The incarnational preoccupation of the late Middle Ages tended to make the Virgin Mary—perhaps even more than Christ himself—the very emblem of Christian mystery. Mary of Nazareth had been chosen God's bride and God's mother; her body had enclosed divinity, had given Godhead a human form and likeness, had finally been transported to heaven, where Mary, ever Virgin, reigned not only as Queen of Heaven, but as Gabriel extols her in the N-Town "Salutation and Conception," even as "empres of helle." The Virgin Mary was for late medieval Christendom a mother goddess of powers conceivable and inconceivable, a saint raised uniquely among the whole company of saints to the highest pantheon of the sacred Trinity.[5]

Although my own approach has been influenced by these works, it has been through the experience of acting Mary and discussing the issues with my students that my ideas have been formed.[6]

Much of the concern in feminist approaches to the Virgin has been focused on her physical role as mother. Stimulated by the gynecological preoccupation of the plays on the Nativity themselves, attention has been given to the young Mary, the Mary of the Christmas story. Although this young figure seems in many ways to have dominated much of the thinking about Mary in the late Middle Ages, she remains removed from the everyday experience of ordinary women. There is an essential alterity about a virgin mother who bore her child without pain. This alterity sometimes expresses itself in the art of the period, as in the famous east window of the church in East Harling, Norfolk, where the figure of the Virgin remains young and blonde throughout the depiction of the sequence of events that covers more than fifty years. For many artists and theologians the figure of the Virgin remained the unattainable, beautiful child chosen by God to redeem the world, a child whose very physical purity was a constant rebuke to unbelievers.

Yet the dramatic character of this Mary, based on the legends of her childhood and the miraculous events that led to the birth of Christ, is of less interest to me than that of the mature Mary of the Passion story, the post-Resurrection appearances, and the plays treating her death and assumption. In the York and N-Town dramatizations of the return of Joseph, for example, her ecstatic reply to his demands to know the father of the child—"God's and yours"—is the reply of someone living in a private world where no one can follow her. The mature Virgin, on the other hand, is a woman whose experience and sufferings have been shared by many women. I believe it is from a deep understanding of the emotions of mature women that the older Marys of the N-Town plays are drawn.

Other dramatic versions of the Passion treat Mary differently than she is portrayed in N-Town. In the Bodleian *Death and Burial,* for example, Mary speaks 379 lines of formulaic lament which includes a *planctus Mariae,* spoken over Christ's body, that is 184 lines long. Together her lines make up 44 percent of the entire episode.[7] The laments in York and Towneley are equally stylized but form only a small percentage of the action of the plays on the death of Christ.[8] In York the Virgin speaks 42 out of the 416 lines of the episode of the Death of Christ (or 10 percent), and in Towneley she speaks 86 out of 666 lines (or 13 percent). Chester, with its greater emphasis on sign rather than word, gives Mary only 21 lines out of 479 (or 4 percent).[9] These versions are all in contrast to the extraordinary naturalism of the Mary in N-Town where the character progresses from self-pitying despair to joyful confidence.

The N-Town Passion Play, unlike the Passion sequences in the three other biblical collections, is conceived as a unit although apparently played over two years. This makes it quite different from the more episodic collections. The York cycle, for example, has sixteen Christs and two Marys in a Passion sequence that unfolds with the linearity of processional performance. N-Town has one Christ and one Mary whose characters grow within the constant world of staging in the round. Mary appears first at the end of Passion Play 1 as Mary Magdalene brings her news of Christ's arrest. Her speech is full of questioning and concern. She understands the theological significance of what is happening but she continues to demand "May man not ellys be savyd"?[10] The final line of this part of the play is addressed to her absent son "thynk on þi modyr þat hevy woman" (28, 192).

It is a woman heavy with grief who enters partway through Passion Play 2, supported by the three other Marys and John, to confront Christ as he hangs on the cross. Her first outburst of anger, shock, and shame is followed by a descent into self-pity:

> A, my good Lord, my sone so swete!
> What hast þu don? Why hangyst now þus here?
> Is þer non other deth to þe now mete
> But þe most shamful deth among þese thevys fere?
> A, out on my hert—whi brest þu nowth?
> And þu art maydyn and modyr and seyst þus þi childe spylle!

How mayst þu abyde þis sorwe and þis woful þowth?
A, deth, deth, deth! Why wylt þu not me kylle? (32, 93-100)

And, as the rubric tells us, here she swoons.

If you have never been called on to act this role, and if you are familiar with the other lamenting Marys in medieval drama, speeches such as this one can be passed over as painful, but formulaic. However, when you have to examine each word to understand fully what is being said and convey that to an audience, you discover that this is anything but formulaic. The tangle of emotions represented here and the implications of what she is saying for the characterization of this Mary are quite astonishing. All the complex stages of grief are here—the anger with the loved one who is dying, the sense of outrage that such a thing is happening to the mourner, the conviction that somehow this situation has been created simply to make her suffer. Mixed in, as well, is the sense that by dying between thieves, Christ is bringing shame to his respectable mother.

Christ, seemingly ignoring his mother, forgives the thieves. The gracious words "þis same day in paradyse / With me, þi god, þu xalt þer be" (32, 131-32) are barely uttered when Mary again bursts in with her self-centered grief:

> O my sone, my sone, my derlyng dere!
> What! haue I defendyd þe?
> þu hast spoke to alle þo þat ben here
> and not o word þu spekyst to me.

> To þe Jewys þu art ful kende:
> þu hast forgove al here mysdede.
> And þe thef þu hast in mende:
> For onys haskyng mercy, hefne is his mede.

> A my sovereyn Lord, why whylt þu not speke
> To me þat am þi modyr, in peyn for þi wrong?
> A, hert, hert, why whylt þu not breke,
> þat I were out of þis sorwe so stronge! (32, 133-44)

This is hardly the hieratic Mary of the iconographic tradition.

Christ's next speech is a direct rebuke of her selfish extravagance. After he has committed her to John's care with the words one "clene mayde xal kepe another" (32, 148), he reminds her through his pain of the purpose of the Incarnation and her part in it, "I was born of the, / To þe blys þat man had lost man aȝen to restore" (32, 155-56). But she does not listen. Here the rubric tells us that the Virgin "xal

ryse and renne and halse þe crosse." She falls at the foot of the cross
embracing it while Mary Magdalene and John try to take her away.
She cries out in her grief:

> I pray ȝow alle, lete me ben here,
> And hang me up here on þis tre
> Be my frend and sone þat me is so dere
> For þer he is, þer wold I be. (32, 161-64)

The force of the emotion that was evoked in all of us acting this scene
was such that every night we played it, I acquired new bruises on my
arms where John and Mary had tried to pull me away from the cross. I
never felt the pain. There is nothing controlled here, nothing cere-
bral. The character of Mary is completely given over to hysterical grief.
At this moment, Mary becomes so overcome that she must be looked
after by others.

The almost unbearable tension is broken as she is led aside and
the scene gives way to the high priests and Pilate as they come to affix
the "Iesus Nazarenus Rex Iudeorum" emblem to the cross. She
stands, supported by John and Mary Magdalene, in silence, as his enemies inflict the last physical abuse on Christ. When he dies she moves
forward this time to lament in measured eight-line stanzas. The grief
is there but the frenzy has passed and she is able, with John, to reiter-
ate the purpose of the sacrifice (32, 254-55) before she stoops with
great dignity to kiss the dead feet. She is again in control, in command, as she asks John to take her to the temple where she will pray.

Here the figure of Anima Christi appears, addresses the audience,
and crosses the platea to enter hell. Meanwhile, Nicodemus and
Joseph of Arimathea ask for the body and Mary returns to the foot of
the cross for the Deposition. Sadly, Joseph lays the body on Mary's
knees and in a living icon of the pietà she gently prepares it for burial:

> A, mercy! Mercy myn owyn son so dere,
> þi blody face now I must kysse.
> þi face is pale, withowtyn chere;
> Of meche joy now xal I mysse.
> þer was nevyr modyr þat sey this,
> So here sone dyspoyled with so grete wo.
> And my dere chylde nevyr dede amys.
> A, mercy, Fadyr of Hefne it xulde be so. (34, 126-33)

These stark, poignant lines are in sharp contrast to the wordy
lament in the Bodleian version. Yet the point is superbly made

through word, action, and stage image. This is a conscious return to the Mary of the Nativity caring for the helpless body of her son. Here the figure of Mary finds again the center of her being and finally accepts Christ's death. Her parting from Joseph and Nicodemus after the committal is that of a great lady dismissing her servants, regal, gracious, and controlled:

> Farewel ȝe jentyl princys kende.
> In joye evyr mote ȝe be
> þe blysse of hefne withowtyn ende
> I knowe veryly þat ȝe xal se. (34, 154-57)

The Mary of the N-Town Passion moves from self-centered hysteria to outward-looking dignity as she is carried along through the stages of mourning. Yet there is still another emotion that she must portray. Christ appears to her first after the Resurrection and so it is she who must express the first joy at the completion of God's plan. Her litany of praise beginning with "Welcom, my Lord! Welcom, my grace/ Welcome, my sone and my solace!" (35, 97-98) sets the tone for the first formal greeting, but as Christ takes his leave, the tone changes from ritual to lyric,

> Farewel, my sone! Farewel, my childe!
> Farewel, my Lorde, my God so mylde!
> Myn hert is wele þat fyrst was whylde.
> Farewel, myn owyn dere love! (35, 121-24)

This Mary must interact with her child, her God, and her beloved. In a complex way, the N-Town Mary is both a mourning mother and a bereaved lover. The playwrights conceived this character not as the awesome, ever-youthful Mother of God but as a woman who experienced all emotion from ecstasy to despair, a woman set apart by God yet at one with all women as the mother and mourner, caregiver and lover. She is not only "God's bride and God's mother" (Gibson, 1989, 137); she is God's widow.

The Assumption Play is an interpolation in the highly complex and controversial N-Town manuscript. As Stephen Spector, the most recent editor of the plays, has said, "It is not mentioned in the Proclamation, is written by a different hand on different paper from that found elsewhere in the codex and is prosodically, stylistically, and orthographically distinct from the other plays."[11] Indeed, this play has suffered in comparison with the Passion Play. Rosemary Woolf, for example, condemns the text as "wooden, stilted and lifelessly aureate in diction."[12] It is true that the verse lacks the flexibility of the Passion Play, yet the characterization of the Mary of the Assumption Play is remarkably similar to the Passion Play Mary. She is specifically made sixty years of age:

> At fourten yer sche conseyved Cryste in hire matere clere,
> And in the fiftene yer sche childyd, this avowe dar I;
> Here lyvyng wyth that swete sone thre and thretty yere,
> And after his deth, in erthe xij yer dede sche tary.
> Now acounte me thise yeris wysely,
> And I sey the age of this maide Marye
> When sche assumpte above the ierarchye
> Thre score yer as scripture dothe specyfye. (N-Town, 41, 5-12)

Like the playwrights of the Passion sequence, these playwrights did not conceive a Mary who was eternally and impossibly young for all of her life. This is a mature and weary woman longing to be taken from this life to the life that her son had promised her. Although the play closely follows its sources, the *Legenda Aurea* and the *Transitus Mariae*, the dramatic version bestows on Mary the same earthly authority that she assumed in the Passion Play after the burial of Christ. The play also manages, again through the arrangement of the lines and the subtle use of stage icons, to reinforce the multilayered relationship between Mary and Christ.

The only other dramatic version of the legend of the death, assumption, and coronation of the Virgin is in the York cycle. The series of three plays plus a later fragment that come just before the *Last Judgment* in that cycle have a complex history of their own. The funeral of the Virgin with the episode of the conversion of the unbelieving Jew (popularly called the "Fergus" play in York) has not been preserved. In 1431 the Masons petitioned the city to be able to give up the "Fergus" play because "in sacra non continetur scriptura & magis risus & clamorem causabat quam deuocionem."[13] Although there is some indication that the Linenweavers were responsible for the "Fergus" play in 1476 (Johnston and Rogerson, 1979, 110), it was not copied into the official civic "register." In its place was entered a play on another aspect of the legend—the appearance of the Virgin to Thomas as she is being assumed. Nevertheless, the other two plays in the York series—the *Death of the Virgin* and the *Coronation of the Virgin*, which have close affinity to the N-Town *Assumption*—allow us to make fruitful comparisons.

Mary first appears in the N-Town *Assumption* on her knees begging Christ to take her to him. This follows the source closely expressing in Middle English the urgency of the Latin verbs:

Me longith to youre presence, now conj[u]nct to the Vnyte,
Wyth all myn herte and my sowle, be natures excitacyon,
To youre dominacyon. (41, 100-3)

It is Mary who precipitates the action both in N-Town and in the
Legenda Aurea. By contrast, the York *Death of the Virgin* (play 44) opens
with the speech of Gabriel in the second annunciation. The York
Mary is a passive figure while the N-Town Mary is an active one. In N-
Town Christ responds to his mother's prayer by sending Gabriel to
her. The N-Town Mary initiates the request that the disciples be with
her at her death while in York the disciples simply appear. The N-
Town Mary makes her request that she not see the Devil during her
conversation with Gabriel while the York Mary makes the request
directly to Christ as she is dying.

The second major contrast between the two treatments of Mary is
in the interaction between Mary and Christ. In York Christ remains in
heaven sending his angels first to take the soul and then to take the
body. The relationship between them in the northern cycle is strictly
that of mother and son. This is made very clear in the dialogue
between them as she reaches him in heaven:

Maria
    Jesu my sone, loved motte þou be,
    I thanke þe hartely in my þought
    þat þis wise ordand is for me,
    And to þis blisse þou haste me broght.
Jesus
    Haile be þou Marie, maide bright,
    þou arte my modir and I thy sone,
    With grace and goodnesse arte þou dight,
    With me in blisse ay schall þou wonne. (York, 46, 85-91)[14]

Even the music from the Liturgy of the feast of the Assumption that is
such a feature of the Assumption play (play 45) in York is sung in
polyphony by the angelic chorus that summons Mary to Christ. The
relationship is formal, liturgical, and distant. It is Christ who initiates
and controls the action in York. There is none of the sense of a
domestic world ordered by Mary, a matriarchal relationship with the
disciples and a strong sexual undercurrent in her relationship with
Christ, that makes the N-Town *Assumption* such an effective piece of
theater.

Again, it was in performance that the realism of the N-Town Mary
became apparent to me. It had been eight years since I had played

the Passion Play Mary. Yet despite the significant differences in prosody as well as in codicological features between the Passion Play portion of the N-Town manuscript and this play, I felt that his characterization of Mary had much in common with her other mature East Anglian portrayal.

Until her death she is always in control. First, as we have seen, she initiates the action and then takes control of her own deathbed as she instructs the disciples and shares with them her last loving moments on earth:

Maria

Now I thanke God of his mercy. An hy merakle is this!

Now I wyl telle yow the cause of my sonys werkyng.

I desyrid his bodily presence to se.

Johannes

No wonder, lady, thow so dede ye.

Maria

Tho my sone Jesu of his hye pete

Sent to me an aungyl, and thus he sayd,

That the thredde nyth I schuld assende to my sone in deité.

Thanne to haue youre presence, brether, hertly I prayed,

And thus at my request God hath you sent me.

Petrus

Wys gracyous lady, we are ryth wel payed.

Maria

Blissid brethere, I beseke you than, tent me.

Now wyl I rest me in this bed that for me is rayed.

Wachith me besily wyth youre laumpys and lithtis.

Paulus

We schal, lady. Redy allthyng for you dith is.

Maria

Now sone schul ye se what Godis myth is.

My flech gynnyth feble be nature. (N-Town, 41, 287-302)

This Mary becomes weaker as death approaches but she does not complain of her sickness or the awkwardness of her handmaidens as the York Virgin does. Instead she faces her death with the calm assurance that she has set her affairs in order.

Peter then instructs each of the disciples to light a candle and in an allusion to the parable of the wise and foolish virgins (Matthew 25:1-13) urges them all to watch lest the lord should come and find them wanting (N-Town, 41, 303-9). Into the stage silence that follows, reverberating with the bridal images of the parable, Mary cries:

> A, swete sone Jesu, now mercy I cry.
> Ouyr alle synful thy mercy let sprede. (N-Town, 41, 310-11)

Her dying intercession calls to her bedside not just the heavenly host as in York, but Christ himself. For our production we had built a large winched hoisting device that brought Christ—masked, crowned, and dressed in gold from the highest of heaven where he and the angels had been observing the action—to Mary's bedside. Her greeting reflects again the emotional combination of lover, mother, and child of God:

> A, wolcom, gracyous Lord Jesu, sone and God of mercy!
> An aungyl wold a ssuffysed me, hye Kyng, at this nede.
> (N-Town, 41, 314-15)

The last line, so easy to pass over in reading, once again reminds us of the Passion Play Mary by revealing a depth of realism unexpected in such a play. Mary has been longing for this moment, has prayed and planned for this very encounter and yet, when Christ comes to her, she says, in essence, "I know you're busy, dear, you needn't have come yourself." Only in production can this kind of characterization be felt. The line places the relationship between Christ and the Virgin on a level of domestic intimacy that transforms the seemingly formal exchange that follows into a dialogue reverberant with multiple meanings. Christ and Mary, with the disciples joining them for one response, sing excerpts from the liturgy of the Assumption, the *Song of Songs,* and the Magnificat antiphonally. In production, the bed of the Virgin is center stage with Mary lying on it. Christ stands over the bed leaning toward her as the beautiful evocative words of Scripture float over the scene. The verses rise to this ecstatic exchange:

> Dominus
> > Veni de Libano, sponsa mea; veni, coronaberis.
> Maria
> > Ecce, venio quia in capite libri scriptum est de me,
> > Vt facerem voluntatem tuam, Deus meus,
> > Quia exultauit spiritus meus in Deo salutari meo.
> > (N-Town, 41, 326-29)

And she dies.

The erotic intimacy of this scene is startling. The density of image and association continues as Christ takes the soul of Mary. Following the iconographic tradition, we represented the soul as a doll dressed in white satin. The actor playing Christ took the doll and, holding it in his arms in a conscious reversal of the Nativity iconography, ascended to heaven on the hoist.

The rest of the play centers on the funeral of the Virgin and the conversion of the unbelieving Jew. The text allows the procession to leave the playing area while the antagonists briefly take center stage. This allowed us to effect a costume change so that at the end when Mary is raised bodily, she was dressed like the doll-soul in white satin, not in the blue habit worn at her death.

After the final unbeliever has been dragged to hell, Christ once again descends with the archangel Michael carrying the doll-soul. He greets the disciples who are watching the grave of the Virgin, and then, moving to the bier as he had moved to her bed, he returns the soul to the body with the words,

> Go thanne, blyssid soule, to that body ageyn.
> Arys now, my dowe, my nehebour, and my swete frende,
> Tabernacle of joye, vessel of lyf, hefnely temple, to reyn.
> Ye schal haue the blysse wyth me, moder, that hath non ende.
> For as ye were clene in erthe of alle synnys greyn,
> So schul ye reyne in hefne clennest in mend. (N-Town, 41, 509-14)

Mary's response as she rises and kneels before him, now dressed in the white garment of innocence, reinforces the mystery of the Incarnation while claiming her right to be with her son, her lover, and her God:

> A, endles worchepe be to you, Jesu, relesere of peyn.
> I and alle erthe may blisse ye, com of owre kend.
> Lo me, redy wyth yow for to wend. (N-Town, 41, 515-17)

As Christ and Mary step onto the hoist, Michael announces that "God throw Mary is mad mannys frend" (41, 541). The hoist ascends as the angelic host sings the great antiphon from the liturgy of the feast, "Assumpta es, Maria, in celum." When they reach heaven, Christ places the crown on her head and, in our production, the host also sang a coronation anthem.

Despite the apparent differences in style, the characterizations of Christ and Mary in the Passion and Assumption plays are strongly similar. The assumption of Mary into heaven brings this vision of the divine comedy to a close. The lovers who parted in sorrow and longing after the Resurrection have been reunited. This Mary is indeed "a saint raised . . . among the whole company of saints to the highest pantheon of the sacred Trinity" (Gibson, 1989, 137).

In *The Theater of Devotion,* exploring the possible patronage of East Anglian drama, Gail Gibson sees in the expressions of spirituality and affective piety among the laity a ready audience for the drama. Part of her discussion focuses on Margery Kempe, the crying mystic of Lynn. *The Book of Margery Kempe* is the record of a remarkable spiritual journey of a fifteenth-century matron who sought, with ecstatic longing, true union with Christ.[15] She led a "life of extremely literal and concrete achievement of those very spiritual exercises" that had been set out in the Franciscan *Meditationes vitae Christi* (Gibson, 1989, 49). So real were her visions that at one point she is present with the Virgin and Christ after the Resurrection (Meech and Allen, 1940, 196). At another, she envisions herself taking the Virgin home and caring for her after the burial of Christ: "Than þe creatur thowt, whan owr Lady was comyn hom & was leyd down on a bed, þan sche mad for owr Lady a good cawdel & browt it hir to comfortyn hir. . ." (Meech and Allen, 1940, 195). The meditations that led to these concrete descriptions of scenes and events from sacred history were part of the same impulse to affective piety that produced the plays. Indeed, Mary's anguish at the Crucifixion in the N-Town Passion Play is matched by that of Margery as she experiences the death of her Lord in her visions.

Much of Gibson's discussion, however, focuses on women for whom the excessive piety of Margery might appear unseemly. One such woman was Anne Harling of East Harling, a pious woman of substance three times widowed. Dame Anne stands for many late medieval women whose lives were punctuated by the deaths of children and of marriage partners. The portrayal of Mary the matron in the N-town plays would speak directly to the life experience of these women. Martin Stevens has quite rightly suggested that the N-Town Mary is both learned and cloistered. Anne Harling was a lay sister of five monasteries, including the royal convent of Syon. Gibson has described her as "indominable and sentimental, intensely religious and rigorously practical" (Gibson, 1989, 77). These are adjectives that describe the character of the Virgin in the Passion and the Assumption plays. I am not suggesting that Mary is modeled on Anne Harling, or rather on the Anne Harling whom Gibson has re-created from her will. Instead I am suggesting that the mature N-Town Mary, like Anne Harling, exhibits the characteristics of an East Anglian pious widow of the late fifteenth century.

The study of woman's spirituality in the late Middle Ages has too often been centered on Margery Kempe and Julian of Norwich. More recent work on the Brigitines of Syon and the study of women testators are broadening our picture of a large and important segment of late medieval society whose devotional needs were served in many ways. Many were literate and owned their own missals and service books. In a recent essay P. J. P. Gilbert has demonstrated that "Bequests of service books along the female line or alternatively to the parish are not uncommon."[16] He has also traced through bequests a deep interest in the images in the parish churches such as the small coral beads that Alice Carre of Saint Stephen's parish, Norwich, left to be "daily about the image of St Anne" (110). Gibson has also shown the importance of the cult of Saint Anne in East Anglia. She describes it as "an undisguised celebration of family ties and relationships of kinship" (Gibson, 1989, 83). The portrayal of the Virgin in the N-Town Passion and Assumption plays as a mature woman whose life experience paralleled that of many members of the audience is yet another way that women's spiritual needs found empathetic expression. Emotional, dramatic, yet rooted in faith, this Mary provided for the mature women of East Anglia a mediatrix standing beside the throne of God with whom they could uniquely identify.

Notes

1. In 1984 the *PLS* was invited to take a passion play to an Easter festival of plays, the *Pasqua del Theatro '84*, in Rome. We took an abridged version of the N-Town Passion Play that we had performed three years earlier. The late Stanley J. Kahrl had modernized the text and acted as dramaturge for the original production, which was directed by Kathy Pearl. Pearl also directed the touring version and invited me to play the role of the Virgin Mary in that production. After the untimely death of Professor Kahrl in December 1989, a special seminar on early drama in his memory was organized for the meetings of the Medieval Academy of America meeting at his university, Ohio State University in Columbus, in March 1992. The *PLS* was asked to bring a play to the conference. Professor Kahrl had long been a friend of the *PLS* and we wanted to take a production that would truly honor his memory. In 1974 he had published an article making suggestions for a possible way to stage the N-Town Assumption. That article became the starting point of our production. I codirected the play with K. Janet Ritch as well as once again playing the role of Mary. Andrea Budgey was the music director. All citations of the N-Town cycle are to Stephen Spector, ed., *The N-Town Play*, 2 vols., EETS s.s. 11 (Oxford: Oxford University Press, 1991); citations are by play and line number.
2. Teresa Coletti, "A Feminist Approach to the Corpus Christi Cycles," in *Approaches to Teaching Medieval English Drama*, ed. Richard Emmerson (New York: Modern Language Association, 1990), 85.

3. Peter Meredith, *The "Mary Play" from the N-Town Manuscript* (London: Longmans, 1987).
4. Martin Stevens, *Four Middle English Mystery Cycles* (Princeton: Princeton University Press, 1987), 253.
5. Gail McMurray Gibson, *The Theater of Devotion* (Chicago: University of Chicago Press, 1989), 137.
6. I wish to acknowledge, particularly, three students—Bretta Pirie, K. Janet Ritch, my codirector, and Kimberley Yates, whose discussions of these issues have enormously stimulated my own thinking.
7. These figures are based on *The Digby Plays*, ed. Frederick J. Furnival, EETS e.s. 70 (London: Oxford University Press, 1897).
8. For editions of these plays, see Richard Beadle, ed., *The York Plays* (London: Arnold, 1982), and George England and Alfred W. Pollard, eds., *The Towneley Plays*, EETS e.s. 71 (London: Oxford University Press, 1897).
9. See Alexandra F. Johnston, "Performance Practice Informed by Image: The Iconography of the Chester Pageants," *Spectacle et Image in Renaissance Europe / Dans L'Europe de la Renaissance*, ed. André Lascombes (Leiden: Brill, 1993), 245-62. The Chester figures are based on the edition by Robert Lumiansky and David Mills, *The Chester Mystery Cycle*, 2 vols., EETS s.s. 3, 9 (London: Oxford University Press, 1974, 1986).
10. Stephen Spector, ed., *The N-Town Play*, 2 vols. EETS s.s. 11 (London: Oxford University Press, 1991), 28, 186.
11. *N-Town Play*, 527.
12. Rosemary Woolf, *The English Mystery Plays* (London: Routledge, 1972), 287
13. Alexandra Johnston and Margaret Rogerson, eds., *York*, REED (Toronto: University of Toronto Press, 1979), 48.
14. Quotations from the York cycle are taken from Richard Beadle, ed., *The York Plays* (London: Arnold, 1982).
15. Quotations from *The Book of Margery Kempe* are from the edition by S. B. Meech and H. E. Allen, EETS 212 (London: Oxford University Press, 1940).
16. P. J. P. Gilbert, "Women in Fifteenth-Century Town Life," *Towns and Townspeople in the Fifteenth Century*, ed. J. A. F. Thomson (Gloucester: Alan Sutton, 1988), 110.

The Performance of Some Wakefield Master Plays on the University of Illinois Campus

John B. Friedman

As a student thirty years ago in Arnold Williams's graduate course in Middle English literature, I heard him discuss the performance aspects of cycle drama and moralities in a way that was quite unfamiliar to me and, I suspect, to the other members of the class. Although this class was engaging in many ways, with wonderful readings aloud of texts and many memorable digressions on such things as how to smoke a salmon and make Anglo-Saxon mead with angelica flavoring, the moments of the semester that have stayed in my mind over the years were those in which Williams emphasized three characteristics of the Middle English cycle plays: their improvisatory and puppet-show-like qualities, their incorporation of popular and secular elements, and the fact that the actors playing divine or sometimes diabolical roles were usually ordinary townspeople well-known to the audiences.

About ten years after this class, I offered for the first time my own graduate course in medieval English drama at the University of Illinois, where Williams himself had taught as a visitor some years earlier. I had a rather small enrollment, seven students as I recall, and I gave them the option of writing a final paper or of performing one of the plays. The students voted to put on a play. Recollecting the rather novel way that Williams had talked about the staging of these plays and how valuable for my "closet" reading of them it had been, I decided to put some of his ideas into practice.

With two exceptions, the students in this course were not medievalists, and although they brought a wide variety of skills to the class, experience in acting—as tryouts soon showed—was not one of these. Most important, like other graduate students then and now, they all lacked funds. After our first meeting to discuss which play to stage, and how to pay for costumes, properties, and the like, it was clear that

99

some students were ready to return to the idea of a final paper. Nonetheless, the majority wanted to proceed with the production, and we settled on the Wakefield Master's *Noah.*

After passing a hat among the members of the class, into which I myself put five dollars, I discovered that our group, provisionally and perhaps optimistically named the Wakefield Players, had an operating budget of thirteen dollars. To this meager amount, however, we added a sufficient sum of resourcefulness. We found that an Urbana bicycle store was willing to give away a large number of cardboard bicycle cartons, which we cut up to use for properties and stage sets. Also a local farmer was willing to lend us his decrepit hay wagon, which was towed into my driveway. The thirteen dollars was used for tempera to paint the cardboard, while donations of old leotards and pieces of muslin and felt from another campus drama group provided us materials to costume Noah, his wife, his sons and their wives, God, and a herald. The herald was added because we planned to perform on the University quadrangle for an audience faced with many distractions, including a noontime evangelist, and we felt that a herald could focus attention on our performance. His speech, to be preceded by a Gabrielli trumpet overture, was rather heretically borrowed from the *Ludus Coventriae* proclamation. Before appearing in front of a potentially critical audience of university students, we decided to try the play out at the local grammar school and perhaps to close it there if the children were not enthusiastic. During our rehearsals, many of Williams's ideas on the improvisatory nature of this drama were put into practice, and they worked out—so we thought—extremely well. The guilds "made do," he often said, for the leet books show them using or reusing what was on hand. With this in mind, our scripts were in a modernized Middle English adapted from Martial Rose's *Wakefield Mystery Plays* (New York: Doubleday, 1962), used chiefly because I had the book and because it could be copied conveniently. We found that our play needed to fit into the lunch hour, since we had contracted for exactly forty-five minutes of performance time with the Office of Campus Space.

To heighten the production's visual interest and to make the most of our allotted time, we developed a pantomime of the seven deadly sins, whose prevalence among mankind brought on the Flood, and a rain dance of reconciliation performed by Uxor Noah, the sons, and their wives at the end of the play (this would move the actors out on the grass where they could circulate, hats outstretched, among what we hoped would be a generous audience). Noah's sons doubled in character as Covetousness, Sloth, and Gluttony, and the daughters-in-law as Lechery, Pride, and Envy. The dance and mime routines were choreographed by the director of a small local dance company.

A simple but effective ark, made from bicycle box cardboard stapled to some scrap lumber, graced our hay wagon. Rain sticks in the form of a cardboard black cloud stapled to a broom handle, and another piece of the broom with streamers of clear plastic hanging from a rake-like crossbar on it, were to be carried by our herald, whose activities would signify the changing situations and development of the Noah plot. Also a cardboard raven and a dove with a green branch in its beak were carried round and round the wagon by our herald, who, being a classicist of sorts, made enthusiastic Greek "Croaax" sounds at the appearance of the raven and cooed to symbolize the sunnier days of the dove. The beasts "two by two" were represented by six large cardboard animals (made by projecting 35-mm color slides of some medieval bestiary illuminations onto the bicycle box cardboard, tracing the outlines of animals, and then painting them with tempera to imitate the colors and patterns of the originals). Such Punch-and-Judy devices proved useful in rehearsal as signposts and allowed a certain amount of dialogue to be cut in favor of more visual ways of conveying action, especially appropriate to an audience of schoolchildren.

As much as possible, we tried to rely on impromptu and ad hoc prop solutions; these generally seemed to fit the plays better when they developed in the course of rehearsals and production. Members of the cast brought bags of odds and ends, children's toys, blocks, things pushed to the very back of the garage, to see what ideas might develop out of them. Thus, the water in the front of the ark, complete with painted octopus, was a strip of heavy canvas left over from a canoe-recovering project. God's gold headdress was made of a number of knitting-machine thread cones glued to a mask and then gilded; the whole effect was particularly successful on a sunny day. Looked at with hindsight, our properties probably reflected the interest in "happenings" and found objects so ubiquitous in the high arts of the 1970s.

Later versions of *Noah* used several puppet-show-like devices, some more successful than others. By means of a small rocket engine obtained from a hobby shop, we tried propelling the dove and raven onto the stage with wires, but this burned the birds, so we returned to the less flashy system of having them carried around the stage by a herald who blew duck and goose calls. It also seemed that our cardboard bad weather, thunder, and lightning did not have the majesty needed for the play, so during one performance we employed as clouds a large number of black balloons, inflated with helium, tied together like a bunch of grapes and painted with tempera highlights. This ominous cloud mass hung low above the stage, ready to be released into the heavens and disappear at God's forgiveness and "good weather."

Initially the cast of nine stood in the ark established on a wagon. This proved too confined a playing area, but we did gain some interesting insights into the probable limitations of wagons as playing areas in the original performances. The actors found it much more dramatic to leap down from the static space in front of the ark to a playing space on the ground, though God sat in eminence atop a ladder for much of the play. From his ladder *sedes*, suggesting an omniscient viewpoint as well as an amused and ironically detached interest in the action of the play, God displayed his displeasure and from time to time made rooting gestures for the other actors. The high point of the play was a confrontation between Noah and his virago of a wife, followed by a chase away from the playing area and out into the midst of the audience, which culminated in a good deal of rolling about and somewhat bawdy bestriding of the wife by Noah.

We learned a lot about the mechanics of performance on a wagon as well as what a play presented to an essentially preliterate group of children could and could not expect from its audience. These lessons proved valuable for the two performances at noon and four o'clock on the first clear day of May on the University quadrangle in front of the English department building. Use of a live trumpeter and some tape-recorded music and thunder added to the interest of the performances. For each, a considerable audience of students, faculty, and campus dogs gathered around the wagon ark. Given our location, the audience was made up largely of graduate students in English, who were seeing their colleagues in a new guise. Recognizing acquaintances as actors produced a good deal of heckling and interaction between audience and cast, as it must have done in the fourteenth and fifteenth centuries. The passed hat collected about fifteen dollars, which bought dinner for the players.

Although I was not scheduled to teach medieval drama again until 1977, I found that a number of students in the class wished to continue performing independently of the course. Still calling ourselves the Wakefield Players, we gave two performances each year, in the fall and spring, for several years. After trying the play of *Noah* at various parks and churches in the community (Unitarians seemed to like it best and Episcopalians least), we finally settled on a spring campus performance at two successive noon hours. The Wakefield Players' productions became increasingly complex, and were soon partially funded by the English Department and other agencies of the

University, which realized that they were good advertising for the Humanities on campus. By 1977 we had an assured operating budget of about $100; we had amassed a collection of costumes and properties; and most important, we had developed a permanent cast, some of whom were not students but accomplished local amateur actors who looked forward to performing year after year. Moreover, like a bread starter, a bit of the sourdough from one class of English graduate students seemed to contribute to the next class its enthusiasm for the plays. In all, the Wakefield Players lasted for nine consecutive years, performing the Wakefield *Noah, Second Shepherds' Play, The Killing of Abel,* and the Chester *Massacre of the Innocents,* as well as plays about the Fall and Harrowing of Hell adapted from several versions of these stories.

As each new class of students came to realize, the experience of play production brought a degree of textual understanding and awareness of staging problems that no amount of classroom analysis of the text could equal. For example, in later productions of the *Second Shepherds' Play,* we found that one of the puzzling features of this work is the change in locale from the moors to Mak's house and then to the Nativity at the end of the play. Though the changes would not, perhaps, require a suspension of disbelief worth dwelling on at length in the classroom, they become of great significance in a performance. Building on what we had learned from the *Noah* play about staging, we approached the problem in a way that allowed us to see that the quick shifts of location, far from being a flaw in the play's development, are really part of its genius. When the three shepherds have fallen asleep and Mak has described his magic circle, we simply pulled a large tarpaulin painted with "moor" contours over the sleeping shepherds and shifted the audience's attention to Gyl and the cradle by means of two characters wearing ox and ass heads (typologically preparing for the coming Nativity sequence) and holding a sign saying "Mak's house."

Another insight into the conditions of medieval play production emerged from our early experiments with sets on the wagon and concerned the role of weather and wind. Our sets and properties were elaborately but fragilely made of tempera-decorated cardboard, and strong spring winds or sudden showers could send us quickly indoors. Though we were never, in fact, rained out, many of the props had to be repainted because of squalls, and one wonders how the medieval pageants guarded against the vagaries of spring weather. Possibly the many references to weather in the *Second Shepherds' Play* added an ironic dimension during its original stagings.

Producing the Chester *Massacre of the Innocents* proved instructive in a number of ways. As in our productions of the Wakefield *Noah*

and *Second Shepherds' Play* where we emphasized for comic and satirical purposes the unruly female figures (for example, Noah's wife and
Mak's Gyl), so in the *Massacre* we continued the tradition of outspo-
ken, role-subverting women in how we played the mothers robbed of
their infants by Herod's knights. (Audiences so liked the pairings of
the large, aggressive, and rouged wife and the small, grey, henpecked
husband, as with Noah and his wife or Mak and Gyl, that we incorporated more and more of them into the plays. Soon God was always a
woman, and in the Wakefield *Killing of Abel,* Garcio was played by a
shrewish woman in a tightly fitted bodysuit with serpent-like touches
of decoration.)

One interesting issue of verisimilitude was also raised by the
Massacre performances. Herod's knights, ranting bullies at first,
became craven before the large, distaff-wielding mothers.
Nonetheless, they needed to slay the children, and in the first production of the play we used actual children (some belonging to cast
members), who were pursued and hacked down by the knights. It was
soon clear that this sort of casting was unacceptable to the audience,
for whom the line between drama and reality had already been weakened and threatened by their familiarity with the actors. So we substituted dolls which could be bounced off the scimitars like tennis balls
or tugged at by resistant mothers and eager knights.

Over the years our productions became increasingly elaborate.
Once it became apparent that the performances were greatly
enhanced by live music, for example, the Wakefield Players acquired
a group of musicians and a musical director. Between four and six
costumed musicians then sat to the side of the stage and played intermittently during the entire performance. Songs, along with drum and
tambourine passages to indicate changes of episode, were added to
the trumpet solos, and string players (on violins, viols, and other early
instruments) played nonhistorical but effective dance pieces such as
"La Rotta," which served to conceal set changes or distract the audience from exits and entrances.

In time, a different stage replaced the hay wagon. Six flats—made
of four-foot by eight-foot sheets of half-inch plywood nailed to six-
inch wide boards to raise the playing area above the lawn—provided
the main stage. These flats could be recombined in various arrangements, transported in a pickup truck for performances off campus,
and stored easily when not in use. Wooden standards were bolted to
the flats, and brightly colored strips of cloth were strung on lengths of
electrical conduit fitted between the wooden standards to make a
backdrop. Characters, especially diabolical ones, could wait behind
this backdrop or could, for an imposing appearance, emerge onto

the forestage from between two of the strips. This system was perfected in the *Massacre of the Innocents* and was not changed for the life of the company.

To the already fairly large cast of the *Massacre*—a Prologue, Herod, a sycophantic Preco, two knights, an Angel, Joseph, Mary, two mothers, and a devil—we added a second devil. The two devils were used to carry the body of our rather substantial Herod off the stage on a fluorescent rescue stretcher borrowed from a local surgeon. We also substituted a personification of death, Mors, for the original Doctor. Robed in a diabolical black inquisitor's costume, Mors mocked and parodied Herod and finally delivered his death blow with a large arrow.

In a late performance of the *Second Shepherds' Play* we added a number of animals, both symbolic and actual. It seemed that a good way to indicate the change from moor to Nativity setting, as I noted earlier, was to fit two of the players with ox and ass heads on a monumental scale, and place them behind the cradle as guardian figures. These heads, made of papier-mâché and fiberglass, were very dramatic but limited the vision of those wearing them. Since they could not safely leave the playing area, the "animals" served as ever-present stage hands, and this role turned out to have many advantages: two animal-headed characters stood on stage both to indicate the *sedes* of the Nativity and to move properties (for example, to pull the tarpaulin over the shepherds).

Although for several performances of the shepherds' play we had used a child's toy lamb in Gyl's cradle to represent the stolen sheep, we decided later to try for something a bit more adventurous. We made an arrangement with the manager of the University sheep farm to borrow a live lamb for the performance. Using an animal brought many problems. We needed a lamb sitter at each outdoor rehearsal to keep the animal under control and to ward off the campus dogs, who were magnetically attracted to it. Moreover, the lamb had to be different for every rehearsal since the shock of being separated for an hour or more from its mother was too much for the same animal to endure more than once. Also, lambs grow rapidly. In the course of our rehearsals, the winsome animals of the early weeks became in the later ones stolid and blocky sheep. They also posed certain dangers to the actors, as the youngest shepherd, Daw, found out. At the climactic moment of the play, that is, when Gyl's baby is held aloft and revealed to be the stolen sheep, our Daw was drenched with a stream of lamb urine. This provided good theater but made it difficult to recruit future shepherds.

Perhaps the most challenging play for the Wakefield Players to stage was the *Killing of Abel*, which we performed for the first time in

1982. Besides changing the gender of Garcio and God to female, we added a team of animals to pull Cain's plow onstage—the ubiquitous ox and ass of the shepherds' play. We also added a devil in a fright mask. A multilevel stage placed against the curtain backdrop in a totemic position consisted of a three-tiered altar on which Cain and his brother offered their sacrifices to God, who sat high above the curtain. This altar could also be mounted by the actors, so that Cain and Abel could be elevated above the other characters at the moment of their sacrifice

Like Milton some centuries later, the Wakefield Master had seen that sin and vice were dramatically more interesting than virtue. Cain and Garcio proved to be the true stars of the play. This became evident in tryouts for the roles. For Cain we chose a person who had never acted but who had dense, blue-black whiskers, long, rock-star hair, and extremely hairy legs. Wearing a pair of combat boots and shorts, our Cain was bound to show that he took none of his part seriously, and for some reason his hamming and self-parody worked extremely well in the role. I made an ass's jawbone of fiberglass, ornamented with tempera paint to indicate white teeth set in pale pink gums, to serve as Cain's club and his symbolic property. His opposite was cast as slender, pale, unctuous—a former boy scout, a born victim, walking about ostentatiously holding a toy lamb—an Abel whose death, one felt, would make the world a better place. Cain arrived on stage as a Caliban-like man at work, guiding a plow drawn by two actors in animal heads. After God's rejection of Cain's sacrifice, Abel, blowing on the flames of his own sacrifice, managed to direct its smoke, a stink bomb obtained from the local magic shop, into Cain's face with predictable results. To add a certain tragic note to the comedy, Garcio tormented everyone on this post-Lapsarian stage. This play, in my opinion, while less elaborate and spectacular than the other jewels in the Wakefield Master's diadem, is one of great richness and offers many opportunities for interpretation and experiment.

•   •   •

In the twenty odd years since the Wakefield Players first staged their *Noah*, much has happened with the performances of cycle plays in North America and England, and considerably more scholarly attention has been given to the conditions of early productions. In 1985 some twenty-five different companies of actors from all over North America gathered in Toronto to stage various plays in the Towneley cycle, including the University of Toronto's own *Poculi*

Ludique Societas company. Much of this production activity is now available from the University of Toronto in the form of videocassettes of the various performances. In the United States there were noteworthy performances of *Wisdom* by Milla Riggio at Trinity College, Hartford, in 1985, and by Edgar Schell at the University of California at Irvine in 1985-87. In England William Bryden mounted a cycle of mysteries in three parts for the National Theatre; other productions at the University of Bristol and some of the *Cornish Ordinalia* done by Neville Denny have been captured on film by John R. Elliott. Some of Elliott's thoughts on these productions appear in his "Medieval Acting," *Contexts for Early English Drama*, ed. Marianne Briscoe and John Coldewey (Bloomington: University of Indiana Press, 1989), 238-51. These visual materials should be seen in conjunction with Sheila Lindenbaum, "York Cycle at Toronto: Staging and Performance Style," *Medieval English Drama: A Casebook*, ed. Peter Happe (London: Macmillan, 1984), 200-11, and Martin Stevens, "*Processus Torontoniensis*: A Performance of the Wakefield Cycle," *Research Opportunities in Renaissance Drama* 28 (1985): 189-200. A fascinating account of production experiences somewhat akin to those of the Wakefield Players is given by Martin W. Walsh in "The Harlotry Players: Teaching Medieval Drama through Performance," *Approaches to Teaching Medieval English Drama*, ed. Richard Emmerson (New York: Modern Language Association, 1990). I believe that Arnold Williams would have smiled happily at Walsh's statement of his group's aims:

> The Harlotry Players' orientation in the field of medieval drama is towards the low and popular traditions, rather than the ecclesiastic. It is primarily interested in what the Victorians might have termed the contaminations of medieval drama. This approach has generally made the medieval drama more accessible to the majority of students who have little or no relation to the traditions of medieval spirituality. (136)

These visual records and responses to contemporary play production have been matched by a wealth of scholarly material useful for the teaching and staging of the cycle plays. Among many fine studies, one might mention William Tydeman's *English Medieval Theatre, 1400-1500* (London: Routledge, 1986), which considers both cycle plays and moralities. *Aspects of Early English Drama*, edited by Paula Neuss (Cambridge: Brewer, 1983), is rich in information on all aspects of the production of medieval plays: an essay by Richard Rastell offers many insights on the music of the performances, another by Peter Meredith gives a very clear account of the various manuscripts of the cycles with facsimile pages, Meg Twycross offers a good discussion of costume based on records of costings (she makes the important point that the costumes were consciously different in period from those of the audiences, indicating that the audiences were perfectly well aware of a "past"), Tony Davenport examines costume for the later period of drama, and Darryll Grantley discusses the problems of staging, including contemporary applications.

For groups wishing to stage the cycle plays, there are now a number of performance texts not available to us in the 1970s, from John Russell Brown and Edward Burns among others. Up-to-date bibliographic studies have been done by Sidney Berger and Clifford Flanigan, and there is now a journal devoted to the medieval drama, *Medieval English Theatre* (1979-).

Finally, I should like to record my own debt to Laurence Ross's "Symbol and Structure in the *Secunda Pastorum*," a somewhat undervalued essay, in my opinion, despite the fact that it was reprinted in Jerome Taylor and Alan Nelson's useful collection, *Medieval English Drama: Essays Critical and Contextual* (Chicago: University of Chicago Press, 1972). I first heard the outlines of Ross's essay as one of his graduate students at Johns Hopkins University in 1962. His approach to the plays by way of the visual arts helped to shape my thinking about medieval literature and its relationship to medieval art generally. It is a pleasure to mention this magnificent essay once again.

The Problem with Mrs. Noah: The Search for Performance Credibility in the Chester Noah's Flood *Play*

William G. Marx

irectors who approach the Chester *Noah's Flood* play may find themselves intimidated by the character of Mrs. Noah.[1] She sits at the very center of the play, apparently an implacable, sharp-tongued shrew. She disputes the judgment of her husband and abandons the family's boat-building labors to carouse with her gossips. She rebuffs Noah's entreaties and those of her sons, and refuses to board the ark. She boxes Noah's ears as she is wrestled aboard the ark, and then as one last rebuke to her tormented husband spits out her final line in the play: "Have thou that for thy note!" (246).[2] Mrs. Noah may seem such a perfect caricature of shrewish wives that she becomes *the* archetypal shrewish wife. Directors who find typological significance in this play may see Mrs. Noah as a type of the unrepentant sinner and the peril to which her pride brings her as a type of last judgment. Mrs. Noah may thus appear so to dominate this play that she becomes both the focus of its conflict and its most interesting character. In all this, these directors would share judgment with many others—directors and scholars alike—who have considered the structure and meaning of this play. But Mrs. Noah and this play deserve, and can sustain, interpretations and performances that are far more meaningful and credible.

The Chester *Noah's Flood* play ought to appeal to directors because its overarching theme is not the destruction of the world, but the reconciliation of God and his creation—the very theme of the whole cycle itself. This theme depends on the successful resolution of several compelling and believably human conflicts, conflicts between Noah and God, between Noah and his family, and between Noah's family and the external threats of worldly sin and natural catastrophe. That these conflicts are successfully resolved and that God is reconciled with his creation are evident in Noah's completion of the ark, his rescue of his family and the world's creatures, his sacrifice of thanks, and his receipt of God's rainbow covenant. The problem with Mrs. Noah, then, is that her character cannot be interpreted simply and easily to be a stereotypical shrew or static theological type without destroying the play's dramatic structure and undermining its moral lessons. If this play is to effect reconciliation between its characters and God, if it is to communicate its moral lessons effectively to its audiences, then Mrs. Noah has to participate in—indeed, contribute to—all of the play's reconciliations. She must grow and change. To give Mrs. Noah a human character and to integrate her role into the dramatic progress of the *whole* play, directors need to help their actors preserve Mrs. Noah's feisty spirit and comic action while they bring that spirit and action to the service of higher—in fact, transforming and transcending—purposes. This essay, then, records one director's search for ways to achieve that end.

The search covers, first, what scholars have said about the English flood plays, Mrs. Noah, and medieval misogyny; second, what significance may be seen in the conflict and reconciliation of Noah and his wife; and, finally, what sort of credible character interpretations and actions the play itself will sustain.

Mrs. Noah may seem to dominate *Noah's Flood* because her apparently shrewish character and knockabout conflict with Noah dominate the scholarly discussion of at least four, if not five, versions of the flood play: the Chester, York, and Towneley cycles, the Newcastle fragment and, perhaps, the Cornish *Creation*.[3] The conflict between Noah and his wife is unique to the medieval drama of England. Among the extant cycles, only the flood play in *Ludus Coventriae* omits it.[4] In all of the rest, Mrs. Noah is a spirited antagonist, seemingly disagreeable by nature and combative by choice. A. P. Rossiter asks, rather plaintively, why medieval preachers " 'picked on' the harmless necessary wife of the biblically intemperate but certainly not henpecked Noah."[5] Rossiter's own answer to this question is that this "age-old staple of farce—marital difficulties—slipped in from minstrelsy" (1950, 69).

Scholars since have been generous in their supply of other answers to Rossiter's question. Arnold Williams suggests that the themes of aged and befuddled husbands and shrewish wives may be found "in Chaucer, in Langland, and in a dozen other authors, and they have been traced back to Horace and Juvenal and Propertius, who doubtless took them from Greek poets, and they in turn from Egyptians or Babylonians."[6] V. A. Kolve says that Mrs. Noah became a "comic character and a dramatic tradition . . . so familiar and loved in the English Middle Ages that she became a kind of paradigm of human character:

she was the root-form of the shrewish wife," and that at "the level of
this interpretation, Noah's wife might be a character out of the *fabliaux*, the usual genre for such character studies."[7] Rosemary Woolf
notes that *Ludus Coventriae* and the Newcastle fragment dramatize Mrs.
Noah's refusal to board the ark as a yielding to demonic temptation.[8]
Mrs. Noah in these plays becomes a kind of second Eve.[9] In other
flood plays, says Woolf, Mrs. Noah conforms to the "stock figure of the
shrewish wife common to all misogynistic literature, Latin satire, sermons, comic poems and fabliaux" (1972, 138). Woolf quotes Andreas
Capellanus's *Art of Courtly Love* on the *proprietates mulierum* as typical:

> Furthermore, not only is every woman by nature a miser, but she is also
> envious and a slanderer of other women, greedy, a slave to her belly,
> inconstant, fickle in her speech, disobedient and impatient of restraint,
> spotted with the sin of pride and desirous of vain glory, a liar, a drunk-
> ard, a babbler, no keeper of secrets, too much given to wantonness,
> prone to every evil, and never loving any man in her heart. (138)

Woolf could have added these lines by Capellanus as well, had she
had the Chester Mrs. Noah specifically in mind:

> Again, every woman is a drunkard, that is, she likes to drink wine.
> There is no woman who would blush to drink excellent Falernian *with a
> hundred gossips in one day*, nor will she be so refreshed by that many
> drinks of undiluted wine that she will refuse another if it is brought
> her.[10]

Other scholars have elaborated on the misogynistic characterization of Mrs. Noah. Barbara Palmer puts Mrs. Noah in a long tradition
of medieval lyrics that painted dark pictures of marriage: the *chanson
de mal marié* and the *chanson de mal mariée*.[11] In fact, the Chester Noah
does complain formally about his wife and women in general, but
only briefly and only after Mrs. Noah has objected to his disruption of
the family's life:[12]

> Lord, that weomen bine crabbed aye,
> and non are meeke, I dare well saye.
> That is well seene by mee todaye
> in witnesse of yow eychone. (105-8)

Mrs. Noah's complaint, if it is a complaint, against her husband is
stated only implicitly in her decision to stay behind with her gossips,
for they at least loved her "full well" (205). The Mrs. Noah in Chester

has no more than this to say against her husband. She opposes his decisions but does not demean his character. Complaints about spouses, especially those of husbands about wives, were commonplace in the Middle Ages. As Howard Bloch reports, they were constituent elements in the larger "topos of *molestiae nuptiarum*, the pains of marriage, which was read, Jean [de Meun] maintains, 'in school.'"[13] Bloch traces the history of this topos from the Yahwist version of the creation of Eve as Adam's derivative helpmate through patristic commentary on the earthbound and sensual nature of women to medieval tracts on the fickleness of wives (1991, 13-63). By the time that the Chester playwright sat down to compose his flood play, the dichotomy between man and woman, spirit and flesh, was firmly established. The relationship between Noah and his wife, it seems, is necessarily to be one in which "man is associated . . . with spirit or soul formed directly by God, partaking of his divinity, while woman is assumed to partake of the body, fleshly incarnation being by definition the sign of humanity's fallen condition" (27). Noah hears the voice of God; his wife does not. From this one fact came all of the misunderstanding and conflict among the characters in our production of the play.

Behind the characters of Eve and Mrs. Noah lurks the legendary character of Lilith, Adam's first wife and the mother of innumerable demons. Louis Ginzberg recounts that Lilith

> insisted upon enjoying full equality with her husband. She derived her rights from their identical origin. With the help of the Ineffable Name, which she pronounced, Lilith flew away from Adam, and vanished in the air. Adam complained before God that the wife He had given him had deserted him, and God sent forth three angels to capture her. They found her in the Red Sea, and they sought to make her go back with the threat that, unless she went, she would lose a hundred of her demon children daily by death. But Lilith preferred this punishment to living with Adam.[14]

In the Chester flood play, Noah sends his three sons to bring their mother to the ark. Like the angels sent to Lilith, Noah's sons fail in their mission, too. Robert Graves and Raphael Patai report a variant of Lilith's story. When the angels approach Lilith beside the Red Sea, "a region abounding in lascivious demons," they order her: "Return to Adam without delay . . . *or we will drown you.*"[15] The Chester and Newcastle playwrights seem to have adapted this story to their dramatic purposes, and put Mrs. Noah's contrary actions into a context of external, corrupting influence visited upon her by gossips or devils.

Mrs. Noah in Chester may not have to be taken as contrary by nature, but as being contrary according to *circumstances*.[16] As her circumstances and understanding change, so also does her character. Unlike Lilith, Mrs. Noah is chastened by the threat of water; she accepts God's will and becomes Noah's helpmate.

Interpretations of the flood plays have also concentrated on the typological or allegorical significance of the conflict between Noah and his wife, and have explored less fully its more human cause or character or basis of resolution. The essence of typological or allegorical interpretation involves seeing one thing in terms of something else—the ark as a type of church, or Mrs. Noah as a type of unrepentant Christian, or Noah as a type of Christ. Augustine helped to set the precedent. In *The City of God* he writes that the ark "is certainly a figure of the city of God sojourning in this world; that is to say, of the church, which is rescued by the wood on which hung the Mediator of God and men, the man Christ Jesus. For even its very dimensions, in length, breadth, and height, represent the human body in which He came, as it had been foretold."[17] Augustine cautions that all other interpretations need to treat this story as an emblem of the church sojourning "in this wicked world as in a deluge, at least if the expositor would not widely miss the meaning of the author" (1950, 516).

John R. Elliott reports that Neville Denny, the director of a 1969 production of the Cornish Cycle, managed to convey some of the typological meanings of the ark by adapting its stage structure later on in his production to represent the Jewish Temple and then the sepulchre of Christ, thereby signifying "the old church . . . literally giving way to the new."[18] V. A. Kolve, describing a drawing of the flood in the *Holkham Bible Picture Book*, notes that Noah's holding of the raven and the dove in his outstretched arms demonstrates his "ecclesiastical importance as a figure of Christ" (1966, 69-70).[19] Kolve sees other "figural possibilities" in the story of Noah "too rich to be confined to a single interpretation" (67). Among these possibilities are visions of the Apocalypse, Last Judgment, and the intercession of the church through its sacraments, baptism in particular (67-69). He writes that even "in the cycles that do not develop the correspondence [between the flood and the last judgment] so carefully, that relationship—which existed long before the drama was ever thought of—is one of the reasons they all play the Flood" (68-69).

Despite Noah's obvious thematic importance and stage prominence, scholars seemingly cannot resist coming back to Millicent Carey's early judgment that Mrs. Noah is the "most interesting person in the play"[20] or to the sense that the "*dramatic portion of the play* begins immediately upon the departure of God from the scene, when

Noah turns from the problem as seen in terms of divine will, to the problem of overcoming natural domestic resistance."[21] Rosemary Woolf proposes that Mrs. Noah "represents the recalcitrant sinner . . . who refuses to repent and enter the church" (1972, 139). More important for the dramatic construction of the play, Woolf argues that the shrewish characterization of Mrs. Noah helped the cycle dramatists "motivate a highly implausible action," namely her refusal to board the ark (139). Mrs. Noah's professed desire not to desert her gossips, Woolf says, must be taken as a parable, "as otherwise the attachment of Noah's wife to her friends might be taken as a sympathetic sign of human feeling, which the authors manifestly do not intend" (140). When Mrs. Noah does board the ark, though, she has a dramatic but "psychologically unmotivated change of heart" (139). All this, Woolf thinks, is implausible "on the realistic level" (140). Medieval audiences were to understand that Mrs. Noah *represented* the sinner outside the church, unresponsive to Christ's entreaties. She was to be taken as an exaggeration of the defining trait of a class of people, and not as a real character herself (144).

• • •

Such stereotyping of Mrs. Noah is not always helpful to directors who must give their actors more plausible and concrete bases for characterization and stage action. Disproportionate attention given to Mrs. Noah may also create an impression that all of the English flood plays, except *Ludus Coventriae*, look to her character for their meaning, which may then be expressed in typological abstractions, rather than in human motivation and action. But Mrs. Noah cannot and does not account for all that happens in these plays. Besides, the actor who plays Mrs. Noah cannot play "something else"; she must play the character of Mrs. Noah complete in herself, as woman, wife, mother, and friend. For the actor, typological interpretations, despite all of their sophisticated allusions, reduce the complex human character of Mrs. Noah—the combination of her dramatic objectives, temperament, and stage actions—to mere convention.

The argument for this conventional interpretation of Mrs. Noah is that she is then at one with other women in the cycle plays, who almost always appear unsympathetic, shrewish, and without any apparent motivation beyond the desire to torment. Eve deceives Adam, Sara in the Dublin *Abraham* berates her husband, Gill flays Mak in the *Second Shepherds' Play* and becomes his willing co-conspirator and partner in crime, and the Pharisee, Scribe, and Accuser in *Ludus Coventriae* heap the vilest of abuse on the woman taken in adultery. Only the

Marian plays are more sympathetic to women. Even there, as in the "Trial of Joseph and Mary" in *Ludus Coventriae*, the moral character and actions of Mary herself can be the object of indelicate speculation. Mrs. Noah, however, can be played as an individual and sympathetic woman, and the modern actor who plays her needs more than the circular logic of convention to create a believable character or to justify her actions on stage.

Moreover, if the squabble between Noah and his wife were really the "dramatic portion of the play," then the Chester *Noah's Flood* is effectively over at line 249, when Mrs. Noah has finally boarded the ark, roughly two-thirds of the way through the play.[22] What are the actors to do for the next 126 lines? Why? More to the point here, what is Mrs. Noah to do for the rest of the play? She has no more lines to speak, but she neither forsakes her duties as wife and mother nor, as Millicent Carey assumes, "subsides into silence for the rest of the play" (1930, 89). Literary scholars may presume that an absence of words on paper means an absence of meaningful action on the stage, but such a presumption would be far removed from the reality of performance. The business of performance is to discover what combination of sights, sounds, and physical actions best reveals the meanings inherent in the text. Might not Mrs. Noah have important actions to perform in the last third of the play that could be performed without comment? Could she not be the one who brings her sons and their wives to follow Noah's lead in singing the psalm on board the ark? In the Towneley cycle, she selects the raven for Noah to send out from the ark (England and Pollard, 1925, 479-82). Could she not do the same in this play? Could she not, perhaps, restitch the red cross banner from the bowsprit into a chasuble that Noah may wear to perform the sacrifice of thanksgiving? Who could be better to bring the lamb to Noah for the sacrifice? Scholars may not need to know the answers to these questions or what business must occupy all of the actors throughout the play, but the director cannot direct and the actors cannot act without addressing them.

As the director of the *whole* play of *Noah's Flood*, I cannot construct a unified performance by basing my interpretation on the play's antagonist, instead of on its protagonist. Nor can I say to my actors, as Alan Nelson proposes, that the play becomes dramatic only after God exits the stage (1964, 394). Does the Chester play stop being dramatic when God returns to the stage the second time (113), and then does it become dramatic again upon his departure (144), and then off again yet once more (269)? I cannot tell the actors that they are dramatic only some of the time, or that some of them are not dramatic at all, without risking mutiny. Nor can I create a sense of credibility for

my actors or for the production if I accept one-dimensional stereo-
types, even one that seems so wickedly entertaining as the misogynistic stereotype of Mrs. Noah. Stereotyping Mrs. Noah and her husband
would reduce them to mere puppets in a clichéd and slapstick melo-
drama of marital conflict. In fact, such a reduction as this appears to
have happened. John R. Elliott writes that in "1709 the *Tatler*
reported the performance of . . . a puppet show in Bath in which
Punch and his wife were introduced dancing in the Ark" (1989, 13).
If the drama of Noah's struggle to obey the will of God is to have
credibility and meaning for modern actors and audiences, it must
look to the human nature of the characters themselves and to the
believable desires and frustrations that inform their conflicts and
motivate their actions. It must give just cause for the audience to
apply the lessons of this work of the playwright's imagination to the
actual circumstances of their own lives.

Josie P. Campbell offers a thematic basis for the play that can unify
and sustain the actors' work, without relying on the negative casting
of Noah as a fool or his wife as a shrew. In identifying God's love for
his creation as the animating force in all that happens in *Noah's Flood*,
Campbell gives the director and the actors an overarching and posi-
tive motivation for the action in the play. Writing about God's love
for Noah in the Wakefield flood play, she says that "it is this idea that
Noah must come to terms with on the human level if the world is to
be created anew. He may not intellectualize this idea, but, more
importantly, he enacts it."[23] We found that God in the Chester flood
play also loves Noah, so much so that he tells him:

> Destroyed all they worlde shalbe—
> save thou, thy wife, thy sonnes three,
> and there wyves alsoe with thee—
> shall saved be *for thy sake.* (37-40)[24]

Japheth makes God's love to the family explicit in his entreaty to his
mother to board the ark. He pleads that his mother "come into the
shippe . . . / for his [i.e., Christ's] love that [you] bought" (239-40).
The Chester play ends with God speaking to Noah in the most intimate and affectionate of terms:

> My blessinge nowe I give thee here,
> to thee, Noe, my servante deare,
> for vengeance shall noe more appeare.
> And now farewell, my darlinge dere. (325-28)

Noah's Flood in the Chester cycle begins and ends with an affirmation of God's love for his creation and for his servant people.

In between the beginning and the end of the Chester play, though, lies the family squabble with Mrs. Noah. Where does love fit into this part of the drama? Writing about the similar squabble between Noah and his wife in the Wakefield cycle, Campbell says that the "key" to the play is "love" and the "resulting commitment to act upon that love" (1975, 79). She says that the battles between Noah and his wife turn on a "wrong-headed notion of 'mastre'" (81), arising out of Mrs. Noah's "obstinate assertion of self" (82). Their last confrontation, she argues, results in "the disappearance of this notion of 'mastre'; it simply drops out of the play as an irrelevancy as a new spirit of accord takes over" (82). Unfortunately, Campbell can account for this new spirit of accord only by "the absolute physical exhaustion of both that forces them to relinquish the battle for authority" (83).

Campbell's insight that the confluence of divine and human love is the animating force in the flood plays became the foundation on which I based my interpretation of our play. Her essay, however, does not account for *why* Mrs. Noah resists her husband in the first place or why they eventually reconcile. Why is Mrs. Noah so "obstinate"? Why does her obstinate behavior in the Chester play manifest itself only *after* Noah proclaims that the family will take up boat building? Is there not some plausible reason for Mrs. Noah's reconciliation with her husband that an actor might play more purposefully than that of "absolute physical exhaustion"? I believe that there are "playable" answers to these questions and that they all stem from the love that emanates from God to his creation and from each member of Noah's family to all of the others.

I assumed that the conflict associated with the episode of the flood was atypical of Mr. and Mrs. Noah's roughly 600 years of married life.[25] I also assumed that Noah and his wife loved each other, that they had always loved each other, and that they would continue to love each other long after the business of the flood was behind them. Just think of this episode in human terms for a moment. Noah's first words to his family after he speaks with God have to come as a surprise and as a disruption to the daily routine of their lives:

> Have donne, you men and weomen all.
> Hye you, leste this water fall,
> to worche this shippe, chamber and hall,
> as God hath bydden us doe. (49-52)

Since Noah is a farmer (cf. Gen. 9:20) and the inventer of the plow, scythe, hoe, and "other implements for cultivating the ground" (Ginzberg, 1909-38, 1:147), his call to begin building a ship must strike his family as strange. The weather is fair, the family lives far inland, the ground is no wetter than usual, there is daily work to be done, and no one (Noah included) knows how to build such a thing as an ark. Noah's family humors him at first, but when they next speak to Noah in the play (after 120 years of construction have finally come to an end!), Noah still seems resolute—even giddy—about leaving all behind and "leaping" into his ark (97-98).

At this point, Mrs. Noah balks. She has been patient, but enough is enough. The words of her refusal are important. She says,

> In fayth, Noe, I had as leeve thou slepte.
> For all thy Frenyshe fare,
> I will not doe after thy reade. (99-101)

And when Noah insists, she replies:

> By Christe, not or I see more neede,
> though thou stand all daye and stare. (103-4)

These are increasingly forceful, but not hysterical, refusals. They do not belittle Noah's character, nor do they ask for a fight. Her insistence here that Noah demonstrate a "neede" for change that she can understand and accept is, I propose, the attempt of a devoted but thoroughly frustrated wife to bring her apparently addled husband back to the reality that she and her family understand.[26] Mrs. Noah, I believe, acts deliberately and with just cause, and not "suddenly," as Carey says, "with no apparent reason" (1930, 88). From her first objection to her final reconciliation with her husband, Mrs. Noah's attempts to bring Noah back to *her* reality become increasingly desperate, until they culminate in the "slap" at line 246. Her major objective in the play is to save her family, a character objective that is entirely "normal," given the apparently bizarre change in her husband's behavior. She misconstrues Noah's actions as a threat to the family, and not as a means to salvation. The desire to save her family is an objective that can support all of Mrs. Noah's comic behavior in the first two-thirds of the play. This objective can also sustain her actions through to the reconciliation with Noah and thereafter as his willing helpmate to the end of the play.

Mrs. Noah's very human objectives and frustrations establish the emotional linkages among the characters inside the play and the emotional ties between them and the audience. As Mrs. Noah becomes a realistic and believable character, this play of divine revelation and cataclysmic event takes on a direct and convincing relevance to the lives of the lay folk who were and still are its audience. Her excuses for not boarding the ark are eminently human. Arnold Williams writes:

> Each author seems to have been inspired by the very stockness of the character to do his best by way of making her credible. So in each play she is endowed with different expressions of her shrewishness, and not infrequently we are led to sympathize with her just as much as with her husband. In Towneley she wants to know where Noah has been—wives sometimes have good reasons for curiosity about their husbands' whereabouts—accuses him of laziness, calls his attention to the exhausted state of the family larder. The Mrs. Noah of York justifies her attitude by saying that Noah has been secretive, he spends most of his time away from home and does not tell her what he is doing. In Chester she cannot bear being separated from her friends. All of these are reasonable attitudes. A stock character Mrs. Noah certainly is, but she is also true to life. (1961, 121)

Williams also writes about Mrs. Noah's abrupt, seemingly "implausible" change of heart upon boarding the ark:

> Another sort of excitement is provided by the sudden changes of tone and mood. All the deluge plays except Ludus illustrate this device. Noah and his wife are having a violent quarrel. She refuses to get on the ark. The pleas of her husband and her family are to no avail. She will not budge. Noah has to resort to violence, and presently a fist-fight is in progress. Then within a few lines they all board the ark and Mrs. Noah is assisting her husband with the navigation. In Chester they even sing a hymn. Critics who have called this crude dramatic construction have missed the point. If we suppose some terrifying natural interruption to the quarrel, a monstrous peal of thunder or roar of high wind, the scene is not only playable, it becomes a theatrical triumph. (1961, 115)

These observations come from theatrical knowledge and experience. They remind us that the play's text is but the starting point in a complex creative process through which abstract ideas about human experience and conflict must necessarily become concrete events. They remind us, too, that universal truths on the stage emerge out of the interplay of characters whose circumstances, desires, and frustrations are much like our own. Finally, they remind us that on the stage words always yield place to action.

What happens, then, if after a "monstrous peal of thunder" has confirmed Noah's predictions and has scared the bejabbers out of Mrs. Noah, she then boxes her husband's ears, just because he seems to stand in the way of her panic flight to the safety of the ark? What happens if Noah breaks down in tears at this point? Could not Mrs. Noah then have that flash of insight that reveals the truth of what Noah has been saying all along and also reveals the tenderness and charity of his nature? Could she not then realize—finally—that she and her husband have had the same objective from the very outset, though they have each until then understood different circumstances? Could not their reconciliation then and Mrs. Noah's obedient and helpful behavior thereafter take on a deeply human meaning and poignancy? All this can happen in the action that surrounds and fills just four lines of the text.

At the moment that Mrs. Noah strikes her husband the play turns from apparent comedy to profound emotion and cosmic importance. Noah, with his arms outstretched in gladness and misunderstanding, cries out, "Welcome, wyffe, into this boote" (245). He is standing in Mrs. Noah's way, however, and causes a collision that makes her spill the household goods. She is flustered, panicked, and enraged all at the same time and slaps him ("Have thou that for thy note!" [246]). Noah is shocked ("Aha, marye, this ys hotte" [247]). All he meant to do was express his gladness in seeing his wife on her way to the ark— at last. The slap hurts; he has both misunderstood and been misunderstood in the most important moment in his life. His pain and disappointment overwhelm him, and he breaks down. Mrs. Noah is stunned, too. The action of the play comes to a long and painful halt. Everybody has a moment to think about what has happened—including the audience.

That moment for Mrs. Noah becomes an epiphany; she realizes that she has hurt the best friend she has and the means to her family's true salvation. She, too, is overwhelmed by remorse and guilt. She also breaks down, kneels to Noah, takes his hands in hers, kisses them, and asks for forgiveness. Noah responds, "Peace be with you," and Mrs. Noah answers "And also with you," a liturgical exchange that I inserted into the script after line 247 to make the moment and action of their reconciliation explicit and also to signal that their reconciliation had within it the spark of divinity. At that moment our production became more liturgical, and Noah began to fulfill his function as a kind of "priest" ever more explicitly. Noah knelt beside his wife, lifted her head, brushed back her tears, kissed her, and then quieted the panic in her soul, saying "yt is good for to be still" (248). As he raised his wife to her feet, Noah repeated his line, "Welcome, wyffe, into this boote," but then the line carried much greater import and emotional content. The sinner had been saved through her contrition and a kind of sacrament of penance that was administered by a husband who understood *what* he was forgiving. In that moment, Noah's character as a type of Christ and the importance of his priest-like actions should have been obvious to all. More than this, the moment had within it typological reverberations that echoed the mystical marriage of God and his church. Mr. and Mrs. Noah's moment of marital reconciliation was thus both intensely personal and universally significant.

Our playing of this scene seemed to me to offer a far simpler, more effective, and motivationally true dramatic moment than those proposed by Woolf or Campbell. Mrs. Noah made the play human. All of us at times need the truth to come crashing down about our heads to get our attention. V. A. Kolve writes:

> It was possible for the drama to show human goodness in relation to human nature only by allowing the good people an imaginative life larger than doctrine and story strictly require. They are given a certain independent dignity, most highly developed at those moments in which man serves God, but serves Him critically, not opposing His will, but reserving the right to voice a human judgment upon it. At such moments the medieval drama became most strongly an act of piety to man as well as to God, a religious drama written from *within* the human condition. (1966, 253)

Mrs. Noah is not the only character with "independent dignity" in this play. Noah, too, "reserves a right" to comment on his duty to obey God. When God appears to Noah the second time, his purpose is ostensibly to tell Noah what sorts of creatures he is to load into the ark (113-36), but he has more than that to say to Noah. Near the end of his lines, God presses upon Noah the urgency of his task:

> Seaven dayes bynne yett cominge;
> you shall have space them in to bringe.
> After that, it is my likinge
> mankynde for to anoye. (137-40)

Why should God say this to his "servante free" (17)? The answer comes in Noah's response:

An hundreth winters and twentye
this shippe-makinge tarryed have I,
if throughe amendemente thy mercye
would fall to mankynde. (149-52)

Despite receiving his charge from God himself, Noah dawdles
through construction of the ark to see if "mankynde" might be saved,
a charitable initiative that incurs a rather thunderous "hurry up" and
final deadline from the Almighty. Noah is an obedient servant but far
from a slavish one. His wife's displeasure is not the only nor the greatest of his concerns.

In our production Mrs. Noah gave her husband a newborn lamb
for the sacrifice of thanksgiving, which Noah in turn lifted toward
heaven. While the family sang a *doxology*, one of the angels descended
from heaven, took up the lamb and carried it to God, who accepted it
and cradled it in his right arm.[27] The production concluded with the
rainbow covenant and the family's response. Following Noah, they
rose from their kneeling positions and sang the *Nunc Dimittis* as they
exited the stage in solemn procession.[28] Thanks to the "independent
dignity" of Noah *and* his wife, our production became not solely a
drama of one righteous man's obedience to God, but also a drama of
the intimate and intensely human relations among family members
and between them and God.

Our production was warmly received by the audience, so much so
that they cheered the actual rain showers that began and ended virtually on the play's cue lines. We were also gratified to discover that our
solution to the problem of Mrs. Noah made the play a meaningful—
even moving—entertainment for those who attended. All of us who
saw the character of Mrs. Noah emerge through the rehearsal period
gained new insights into and heightened appreciation for the talents
of the playwright who created her. That her character became believably human suggests that the medieval playwrights may have had
greater insights into the workings of the human psyche and the construction of dramatic action than we might at first want to credit them
with. Mrs. Noah is essential to the dramatic progress of this play. She
anchors it in the world in which we all live. The priest-like actions of
her husband, however, are dominant, and to their ends she eventually
becomes a willing collaborator. Their conflict and reconciliation constitute the play's turning point, but not its climax, which is the return
of the dove, nor its denouement, which is the rainbow covenant.

The first step to salvation for the medieval Christian was penance,
the confession of sin accompanied by heartfelt contrition and repentance. Human will must bend itself to the divine. Salvation, however,

lies ultimately within the community of believers as it receives the redemptive sacrifice of Christ. Mrs. Noah becomes the model for the lay Christian, then, for she comes to accept her salvation on faith, without having heard God directly, as her husband did. More important for the play and its Christian audience, Noah's obedience to God's call and his construction of the ark betoken the outreach of a loving church, welcoming—in fact, rescuing—the souls of the faithful. Mrs. Noah and everyone else in the play come to God and salvation through Noah's mediation, charity, good will, and sacred acts. *Noah's Flood* begins and ends and is unified throughout by Noah's obedience to the will of God—the lesson replayed in one form or another throughout the cycle plays.

Notes

1. This essay is based on a production of the Chester *Noah's Flood* play that I directed at Michigan State University in 1992. The production was sponsored by the Department of English and acted by students enrolled in the graduate course in early English drama. Professor Arnold Williams recommended the Chester cycle's version of *Noah's Flood* to me, and he followed the progress of our production devotedly from its conceptual beginnings to its concluding performance. It was to be the last performance of a medieval play that he ever attended.

2. Quotations and line citations from *Noah's Flood* are taken from Robert M. Lumiansky and David Mills, eds., *The Chester Mystery Cycle*, 2 vols., EETS s.s. 3 and 9 (London: Oxford University Press, 1974 and 1986). Mills's edition of *The Chester Mystery Cycle* in modernized spelling (East Lansing, Michigan: Colleagues Press, 1992) that now makes the plays "readily accessible to teachers and students" (viii)—and to actors, I may add—was then unavailable to us.

3. The editions used for this essay include: Lumiansky and Mills, eds., *The Chester Mystery Cycle*; Richard Beadle, ed., *The York Plays* (London: Arnold, 1982); George England and Alfred W. Pollard, eds., *The Towneley Plays*, EETS e.s. 71 (London: Oxford University Press, [1897] 1925); Norman Davis, ed., *Non-Cycle Plays and Fragments*, EETS s.s. 1 (London: Oxford University Press, 1970).

4. K. S. Block, ed., *Ludus Coventriae or The Plaie Called Corpus Christi*, EETS e.s. 120 (Oxford: Oxford University Press, [1922] 1974).

5. A. P. Rossiter, *English Drama from Early Times to the Elizabethans: Its Background, Origins and Developments* (London: Hutchinson's University Library, 1950), 55.

6. Arnold Williams, *The Drama of Medieval England* (East Lansing: Michigan State University Press, 1961), 121.

7. V. A. Kolve, *The Play Called Corpus Christi* (Stanford: Stanford University Press, 1966), 146.

8. Rosemary Woolf, *The English Mystery Plays* (Berkeley: University of California Press, 1972), 136-38.

9. Anna Jean Mill cites a Russian legend in which "Satan always addresses Noah's wife as *Eve*"—"Noah's Wife Again," *PMLA* 56 (1941): 624n50.

10. Andreas Capellanus, *The Art of Courtly Love*, trans. John Jay Parry (New York: Norton, 1941), 207, emphasis mine. Tradition has it that Noah and his family became the first grape farmers and vintners only after the flood (cf. Gerf. 9:20-21). For our production, though, I assigned those occupations to Noah's family before the flood, too. Mrs. Noah's drinking bouts with her gossips were unexplainable otherwise. Anna Jean Mill confirms that there were persistent legends about beer and brandy drinking among the antediluvian Noahs (1941, 616-17).

11. Barbara Palmer, "'To Speke of Wo That is in Mariage': The Marital Arts in Medieval Literature," *Human Sexuality in the Middle Ages and Renaissance*, ed. Douglas Radcliff-Umstead, *University of Pittsburgh Publications on the Middle Ages and the Renaissance* 4 (Pittsburgh: Center for Medieval and Renaissance Studies, University of Pittsburgh, 1978), 3-14.

12. The *Towneley* Noah, in contrast, knows that his wife will be contrary *before* he delivers the news of the flood and ark:

    My [wife] will I frast what she will say,
    And I am agast that we get som fray
    Betwixt vs both. (184-86)

13. Howard Bloch, *Medieval Misogyny and the Invention of Western Romantic Love* (Chicago: University of Chicago Press, 1991), 13.

14. Louis Ginzberg, *The Legends of the Jews*, 7 vols., trans. Paul Radin and Henrietta Szold (Philadelphia: Jewish Publication Society of America, 1909-38), 1:65.

15. Robert Graves and Raphael Patai, *Hebrew Legends: The Book of Genesis* (New York: Greenwich House, 1964), 65-66, emphasis mine.

16. Graves and Patai write that Noah waited to marry "until God found him Naamah, Enoch's daughter—the only woman since Istahar to have remained chaste in that corrupt generation" (1964, 111). Ginzberg also describes Naamah as "pious" (1909-38, 1:159).

17. Augustine, *The City of God*, trans. Marcus Dods (New York: Modern Library, 1950), 516.

18. John R. Elliott, *Playing God: Medieval Mysteries on the Modern Stage* (Toronto: University of Toronto Press, 1989), 120.

19. Though our production stood alone, we also took advantage of the structure of the ark and the actions of Noah and his family to convey the play's ecclesiastical significance. We costumed God as a bishop and his angels as acolytes. The ark stood at upstage center, so that it and its mast/cross could dominate the stage. The ark's bowsprit was also cross-shaped, and on it Noah hung a white banner with the red cross of Saint George. The characters boarded and disembarked from the ark in solemn procession. While they were on the ark, the family arrayed

themselves as a congregation to face Noah, who led them in prayer and song. In our production Noah led his congregation in singing Psalm 78 in the Vulgate ("O God, the heathen are come into thy inheritance; they have defiled thy holy temple"). As the ark came to prefigure the church, so Noah, as captain of the ship and head of the "old church," came to prefigure the priesthood and Christ. Our production also included two devils, which I borrowed from the Newcastle fragment, and two angels, which I added to the script to be the mediators between God and Noah. The devils disrupted the household routine of the Noahs, spurred on the gossips' distraction of Mrs. Noah, and eventually dragged the gossips off stage as the waters rose to flood height. The angels delivered God's plans for the ark to Noah, played instruments to accompany the singing, announced the coming of the flood with cymbal (thunder) and sword (judgment), "caused" the waters to rise and recede, carried the raven and dove out from the ark and brought the dove back, received Noah's sacrifice of the lamb, and extended the rainbow above the ark.

20. Millicent Carey, *The Wakefield Group in the Towneley Cycle* (Baltimore: Johns Hopkins University Press, 1930), 87.
21. Alan Nelson, "'Sacred' and 'Secular' Currents in *The Towneley Play of Noah*," *Drama Survey* 3 (1964): 394, emphasis mine.
22. Our performance script included the forty-seven line raven and dove scene from the Harley manuscript, found in Lumiansky and Mills, Appendix IA (464-65).
23. Josie P. Campbell, "The Idea of Order in the Wakefield *Noah*," *ChR* 10 (1975): 77.
24. Line 40 here substitutes the variant from the Harley manuscript, empahsis mine.
25. Ginzberg says that Noah did not marry until he was 498 years old (159). Scripture says that Noah lived to be 950, and that he lived for 350 years after the flood (cf. Gen. 9:28-9). If Noah worked on the ark for 120 years, and the flood lasted for as long as a year, then he began work at age 479, and the flood began when he was 599 and ended when he was 600. But that sequence makes Noah's marriage dates inconvenient, since he already has a wife and family when God calls him. I set Noah's age at marriage at 350, thus giving him 129 years to raise a family before he is called to build an ark.
26. Mills writes that Mrs. Noah may be imagined as a "prosperous burgess' wife with a circle of drinking-companions whom she does not want to abandon to sail in an absurdly designed vessel" (49).
27. "Praise God, from Whom All Blessings Flow," the doxology that we used in *Noah's Flood*, was rather ecumenical, I confess. It was written by the Anglican bishop Thomas Ken (1637-1710). Our version came from the Presbyterian hymnal *The Worshipbook: Services and Hymns* (Philadelphia: Westminster, 1972), 272: "Praise God, from whom all blessings flow; / Praise him, all creatures here below; / Praise him above, ye heavenly host: / Praise Father, Son, and Holy Ghost." Also appropriate for the

dramatic moment would be an *offertorium* from the Mass, for example: "Laudate dominum quia benignus est psallite nomini eius quoniam suauis est omnia quecumque uoluit fecit in celo et in terra" (from Vulgate Psalm 134: 3, 6); see J. Wickham Legg, ed., *The Sarum Missal* (London: Oxford University Press, [1916] 1969), 79.

28. The actors sang the *Nunc Dimittis*, a metrical paraphrase of the "Song of Simeon" (cf. Luke 2:29-32), in Latin. The words are: "Nvnc dimittis seruum tuum domine secundum uerbum tuum in pace. Quia uiderunt oculi mei salutare tuum. Quod parasti ante faciem omnium populorum. Lumen ad reuelacionem gencium et gloriam plebis tue israel" (250).

The Theaters of Everyman

David Mills

E*veryman* occupies a special place in the revival of medieval drama in England in the twentieth century. The success it has enjoyed since the time of Edward Poel's revival of the play at London's Charterhouse in 1901 has not only made it, in the words of Arnold Williams, "the morality play best known and most widely performed in modern times";[1] its repeated revivals have also shaped the popular idea of the morality play and set a standard by which other plays in that nebulous genre are judged. Students of medieval drama, however, accept that *Everyman* is, as Williams said, "decidedly atypical." Williams emphasized two of the unusual features of the text— "its high serious tone" which set it apart from most contemporary English works, and its use of the pilgrimage motif (1961, 160-61). But behind the text lay problems of immediate and ultimate sources that concerned Williams as well as other critics.

Williams felt a tension between the play's moral philosophy and its ultimate source. As A. C. Cawley puts it, "Its teaching is a product of Western Christendom, its fable a product of the Buddhist East."[2] Williams thought that the Buddhist fable contained elements not readily assimilated into Christian belief. However, as Alan J. Fletcher has noted in discussing a particularly dramatic sermon analogue, "imported though *Everyman* may be, to an English audience its narrative would probably not have come entirely as a surprise," while Thomas J. Jambeck has stressed the importance of Bernardine theology to an understanding of the play.[3] Supplementing the list of sources and analogues in Cawley (1961, xvi-xix), these and other studies suggest that the tensions felt by Williams were not those of the contemporary audience or readership of *Everyman*.

As for the immediate source of the play, Williams accepted Henry de Vocht's arguments that the Dutch play *Elckerlijc* was a translation

127

of *Everyman,* whereas scholars are now inclined to accept the view of
E. R. Tigg that *Everyman* is a translation from the Dutch, with some
modifications.[4] We know considerably more about *Elckerlijc* than
about *Everyman.*[5] It was written by a certain Peter van Diest about
1470 and was the prize-winning play in a *Rederijker* play-competition
held in Antwerp about 1485. The play thus originates in a cultural
and theatrical context different from that found in England, and
the act of translating, "carrying across," this text into the society and
theater of England had potentially significant implications for its
interpretation.

In relocating the play in the English dramatic tradition, the scholar
must admit the possibility that the impulse behind the translation was
literary and devotional and that the text was intended for private
reading, not for theatrical performance. Some support may be given
to this view by the description of it as a "treatyse . . . in maner of a
morall playe" (Cawley, *Everyman,* 1) in the heading to Skot's edition.
Since four editions of the text are extant from the early sixteenth century, it seems to have been in wide demand.[6] Coming from a part of
Europe where religious controversy was strong, the text can readily be
regarded as a contribution to the pamphleteering debates of the
English Reformation. Though Cawley felt that, despite its date,
Everyman seemed "untouched by either Renaissance or Reformation,"
Bevington is surely correct in describing it as "designed for a crisis."[7]
Its confident affirmation of the centrality of the Catholic church, its
priesthood and sacraments to the salvation of humankind seems to
predicate an active but unstated opposition to such claims. The play
addressed a central area of contemporary controversy and derived a
topicality that is lost in a modern revival. As C. J. Wortham says in
placing the plays in their contexts of religious controversy, while
"*Elckerlijc* is *ante*-Reformation, *Everyman* is *anti*-Reformation."[8]

It is, of course, possible that the play was brought to England in
the repertory of one of the groups of English players who are known
to have toured in the Low Countries, or that it was commissioned as a
translation for a company by an English patron who had witnessed
the play abroad. Even if this were not the case, the casting of the
"treatyse" in the form of a play invites the reader imaginatively to
recreate the text and respond to it in terms of contemporary English
staging conditions. It is my purpose in this essay to argue that
Everyman's appeal and power result in large measure from the accommodation of familiar elements of performance to its metaphoric strategy, redesignating its acting spaces and drawing upon a variety of
dramatic and allegorical modes.

Drama as Metaphor

In the form in which it appears in the Dutch original, *Everyman* is a framed play. The action of Everyman's journey begins and ends at the heavenly *locus—*

> He thynketh on the in the heuenly spere (95)
> O gracyous God in the hye sete celestyall (153)
> God seeth thy lyuynge in his trone aboue (637)
> Now shalte thou in to the heuenly spere (899)—

which not only provides a visual and symbolic point of reference but also lends concrete expression to metaphorical usages such as "the hye luge" (245), "the hyest lupyter of all" (407). The most economical situation for this *locus* is above the House of Salvation, giving point to Everyman's prayer from the House (581-96). The line "O eternall God / O heuenly *fygure*" (581, italics mine) may suggest a distinction between God and the actor representing him. That God is an observer of the action that he has instituted in human affairs and is thus author and spectator of a play of his own creation is a a recurrent device of medieval theater, though exploited in an unusual way in *Everyman.*

Everyman takes from *Elckerlijc* the moralistic commentary upon the action that is offered by Knowledge toward the end of the play. But Everyman's journey is completed only after that commentary, and the play ends with a spectacular conclusion in which angels welcome the redeemed soul into heaven with music ("Me thynketh that I here aungelles synge" [891]). The historical action ends, as it began, in the heavenly sphere, with Everyman's journey visibly complete. The English translator has, however, accommodated this structure within a second, contemporary frame, which establishes the play as artifact and moves the audience to a contemplative distance from it. This frame, consisting of prologue (1-21) and epilogue (902-21), has parallels elsewhere in early drama.[9] The headings used for the speakers— headed "Messenger" for the prologue and "Doctour" for the epilogue—probably define their different functions in the play rather than indicating different actors. It would be appropriate for those functions to be signaled by different costumes, with the Messenger in the livery of a nobleman and the Doctor as priest or friar.

This outer frame not only denies the drama its theatrical autonomy. The prologue identifies the work by title and locates it generically as "by fygure a morall playe" (3). The speeches suggest a defensive stance toward the play, as if fearing misinterpretation or attack. But they distance members of the audience from the action, inviting them to reflect empathetically upon what they experience, much as Everyman reflects within the play upon his own experiences and learns. Lines 7-9

> This mater is wonders precyous,
> But the entent of it is more gracyous
> And swete to bere awaye,

suggest a contrast between the subject matter at literal level (*this mater*) and the edifying purpose that the performance is designed to convey (*the entent*). The opposition of *precyous* and *more gracyous* is more obscure, particularly since *precious* can have a spiritual reference (*MED, precíouse,* 2[a]); but I take this to contrast the visual impact of the play (*MED, precíouse,* 1[b] "beautiful, fair; excellent") with the doctrine of grace that the action transmits. The warning against responding to the play as a literal, sensory experience perhaps predicates a different initial expectation from its audience.

Through this outer frame, the play becomes a metaphor for the warning that God gives to humankind. Not only does it enact a *memento mori*, the coming of Death to Everyman to remind him of his mortality, it is itself a *memento mori* to members of the audience, serving to remind them also of their common fate. The Messenger of the play is analogous to Death as God's messenger, the play the message that he brings. God's play of Everyman becomes the playwright's play of God and Everyman.

This metaphoric use of drama extends to movement and playing time. It is self-evident that the action of *Everyman* is structured upon a journey. The image is biblical in its resonances,[10] but is found widely in other literature as well. It is also the case that in allegorical drama the movement of an actor in the playing place and his proximity to or distance from a number of symbolic fixed points or characters have meaning beyond the literal. *Everyman* makes this link explicit by incorporating the journey within the text as a recurrent image and enacting the journey upon the stage. There are at least two fixed symbolic points on the stage. One, I have suggested, is the House of Salvation with God seated above. The other is the visible presence of Goods at the extreme of the playing area:

> I lye here in corners, trussed and pyled so hye,
> And in chestes I am locked so fast,
> Also sacked in bagges. Thou mayst se with thyn eye
> I can not styre; in packes, lowe I lye. (394-97)

In a play with so little staging information, this is a remarkably detailed account, and the appeal to visible evidence demonstrates that the presence of Goods in material form throughout is essential to the impact of the play. Moreover, Goods lies *in corners.* The phrase predicates an enclosed playing space and suggests that at this important point in the play Everyman has reached the end of his physical and symbolic progress in one direction and is metaphorically "cornered." The playing area is defined between the House of Salvation/God and Goods, the extremes of grace and damnation since the love of money is the root of all evil. These extremes, however, also embrace the audience. Effectively, this is a theater in the round.

From the moment that God introduces the image of journeying (*a pylgrymage* [68]), travel across the acting place becomes symbolic as well as literal. Death's initial greeting, "Eueryman, stande styll? Whyder arte thou goynge / Thus gayly?" (85-86), becomes a question about the direction and purpose of life. Everyman's movements are seemingly random, following the movements of his mind, as he accosts Fellowship, then Kindred and Cousin, and finally Goods. His movement from Goods must reverse his previous direction, since he cannot continue forward. It is when he thinks of his Good Deeds that he begins his movement that will lead initially to her, then to the guide of Knowledge. His movements now become purposive. He is led into the House of Salvation to perform penance and receive absolution, then returns to the wider playing space. This movement is repeated when Everyman returns to the House of Salvation to receive the Host and extreme unction and then returns to the wider playing area to go, with a sense of world-weariness and release, to the grave.

The grave constitutes a further symbolic and literal point in the play. Whereas in *Elckerlijc* Good Deeds lies upon a sick couch, her words in *Everyman*—"Here I lye, colde in the grounde" (486)—indicate that she is lying in a grave, symbolically dead and, like Goods, unable to move. Encountering this emblem, Everyman seems to recognize both his need and the true nature of the action in which he is involved. The grave becomes the central point in his physical journey and spiritual understanding and presumably occupies a midpoint in the playing area. The text gives no indication of the form that the grave might take, though it was presumably a monument of some kind, perhaps the kind of table-tomb usually shown in art representations of the Resurrection and adopted in the mystery cycles. The resurrection of Good Deeds is perhaps the strongest theatrical moment of the play, reminiscent of the powerful impact of the resurrections of Lazarus and of Christ in the mystery plays. As Everyman scourges his body, a ritual act observed by the audience, the voice of Good Deeds calls the audience's attention back to that now-moving figure:

> I thanke God, now I can walke and go,
> And am delyuered of my sykenesse and woe.
> Therfore with Eueryman I wyll go, and not spare. (619-21)

This is a further extension of the journey image, as the steps of the strengthening Good Deeds correlate with the blows of Everyman. He cannot see her approach, presumably kneeling with his back toward the wider playing space, and must take the assurance of Knowledge: "Now is your Good Dedes hole and sounde, / Goynge vpryght vpon the grounde" (625-26). Everyman is reunited with Good Deeds and on his return to the grave, the tomb becomes both the literal grave of Everyman and the point of symbolic union between the soul and good deeds.

The play derives its emotional power not from its affirmative theology, which has attracted much scholarly attention, but from its realization of isolation, loneliness, and betrayal, which are offered as the natural conditions of existence. God sits alone above the audience, soliloquizing on the ingratitude of humankind, which has abandoned its natural love for him and become *vnkynde* (23). His visible isolation reinforces his own sense of rejection; he has been forgotten:

> I hanged bytwene two theues, it can not be denyed;
> To gete them lyfe I suffred to be deed;
> I heled theyr fete / with thornes hurt was my heed.
> I coude do no more than I dyde, truely.
> And nowe I se the people do clene for-sake me. (31-35)

The pointed contrasts of *lyfe-deed, heled-hurt, fete-heed,* and the double sense of *suffred* (*MED, sufferen* 1[a] "to undergo physical, mental or spiritual distress or affliction"; 7. "to allow an action to occur") intensify the sense of indignation, while the sequence of balanced half-lines lends force to the flatly prosaic line 34 with its final pleading *truely,* confirming the hurt bewilderment of these lines. Humankind seeks "after his owne pleasure" (40), not "the pleasure that I to them ment" (56), preferring the life of the world (38) to the heavenly company of angels (39). The play thus begins with God's sense of rejection. Unable to win humankind's fellowship by love, he applies fear (62). Death is his instrument of fear, the means by which he can coerce humankind to turn to him.

The fear that Death instills in Everyman separates the individual from his context, stripping him of social and physical support and identity until he is reduced to his essentials of his soul and his good deeds. The isolation of the individual soul before God translates into images of social rejection and abandonment in the two sets of "friends." The action of the first part of the play, in which he accosts Fellowship, Kindred and Cousin, and Goods, is a series of rejections that underline his exclusion from that society, to his growing bewilderment and despair. The cheerful self-regard of Fellowship, Kindred and Cousin, and Goods counterpoints Everyman's growing despair and contrasts with the sympathetic response of Good Deeds. Their mindless pledges to Everyman—Cousin's "For, wete you well, we wyll lyue and dye togyder (324)—and their conventional farewells—Fellowship's "To God I be-take the" (298) or Cousin's "Now God kepe the, for now I go" (377)—are grimly ironic. The false currency of language equates here with the false currency of Goods. Their failure imaginatively to grasp Everyman's plight, combined with scorn for Everyman's naivety, wins him our sympathies. Later, as the spiritually cleansed Everyman leaves the House of Salvation, we see him gather to himself a new society, that of his faculties, which, because he has summoned it, he believes he can control. "Lacke I nought" (680), he claims, ill-advisedly. The aging process is translated into a process of social abandonment as each of the friends whom he summoned wilfully departs. Despair returns: "O Iesu, helpe! All hath forsaken me" (851).

Everyman turns to God because he has nowhere to go. Nothing in the selectively constructed world of the play affords human comfort or consolation, and it is with a sense of relief that Everyman turns from it: "Frendes, let vs not tourne agayne to this lande, / Not for all the worldes golde" (790-91). The acts of charity that Everyman has evidently performed and that speak for him before God are never played. No human being shows him sympathy, and he dies without human companionship. The Earth is as God describes it, a place of sin: "For now one wolde by enuy another vp ete; / Charyte they do all clene forgete" (50-51). Dramatically, this is a bleak world of loneliness and fear.

Everyman is of interlude length and is the only medieval play of which it is possible to claim that playing time represents real time. The period between Death's summons and Everyman's actual death seems very short. The play seems to concentrate upon what are regarded as the last moments of an individual life, and in that respect differs from the lifetime span of *The Castle of Perseverance.* Much of the tension in the play derives from the fact that Everyman has very little time to prepare for his journey. Lines such as

> . . . without ony lenger respyte (100)
> Dyfferre this mater tyll an other daye
> Eueryman, it may not be, by no waye (123-34)
> I gyue the no respyte. Come hens, and not tary (130)
> For thou mayst saye this is the daye
> That no man lyuyng may scape a-waye (182-83)
> The day passeth and is almoost ago (194)

give point to Everyman's frantic movements about the playing place. Although the play literalizes the time available to Everyman, it also uses the brevity of time as a metaphor, both of the life of humankind and of the life of the world.

The idea of a human life as a day evokes both the *contemptus mundi* topos and biblical writing.[11] Something of this metaphoric sense is perhaps conveyed in the Messenger's line "How transytory we be all daye" (6). As Dennis V. Moran says, "The time allowed Everyman projects the fullness of life's experience."[12] Since, as we shall see, Death's initial commission is to warn, not to destroy, his coming can be read as a subjective realization rather than a physical attack by some terminal disease. Following his repentance, Everyman seems reinvested with the attributes of youth—Beauty, Strength, Five Wits, and Discretion—and returns to the wider playing area, apparently the world. It has been pointed out that the withdrawal of these attributes is an enactment of the aging process as well as of the process of death. Dying is not necessarily here the act of a few minutes but the inevitable outcome of a process of steady and inevitable decline, and the play advocates constant preparedness, not the importance of deathbed repentance.

The life of the individual is, however, microcosmic of the life of the world. *Everyman* is also a play of Judgment. Its outer frame is that of the "Doomsday" plays, and also to some extent the "Flood" plays, in the mystery cycles. God's speech in lines 22-63,

> I perceyue, here in my maieste,
> How that all creatures be to me unkynde,
> Lyuynge without drede in worldly prosperyte.
> Of ghostly syght the people be so blynde;
> Drowned in synne, they know me not for theyr God.
> In worldely ryches is all theyr mynde. . . .

metaphorically redesignates the performing space and assigns a role to the audience in the manner of the cycle plays where, as here, the literal gaze of the actor-God reconstitutes the audience as the totality

of humankind and extrapolates the common condition of humanity
from contemporary society:

> I God, that all this world hath wrought,
> heaven and yearth, and all of nought,
> I see my people in deede and thought
> are sett fowle in sinne. (*Chester Mystery Cycle*, play 3, "The Flood," 1-4)

Drowned in sin, a phrase without counterpart in *Elckerlijc*, might suggest that the English translator recognized the affinity with the
"Flood" plays. Throughout the speech, the blurring of the functional
distinction between generalizing word and specifying name allows the
combination of the general judgment at the end of time and the particular judgment that follows upon the death of the individual.[13]
    God's concluding words,

> They be so combred with worldly ryches
> That nedes on them I must do iustyce,
> On euery man lyuynge without fere (60-62),

would in the cycles be followed by the summoning of the angels to
sound their trumpets and display the instruments of the Passion.
Instead of this general announcement Death is commissioned, and at
line 66 the pronoun *him* signals finally the play's focus on the individual, and not the generality of humankind. But the wider perspective
is seen to return at the time of Everyman's death; the reference to
"whan Deth bloweth his blast" (843) may suggest a trumpet of doom
sounded by Death from the *locus* of heaven, and the reception of the
redeemed soul into heaven amid heavenly music is reminiscent of the
reception of resurrected and redeemed souls in the Judgment plays.
As Douglas Cowling has pointed out, the song is probably "Veni
electa mea," since the first line of the Angel's speech echoes the
opening of that text.[14] The Angel also refers to "the daye of dome"
(901) while stressing the "synguler vertue" (896) that admits the soul
of Everyman on his death; and the English translator recognizes the
same perspective. The concluding words of the Doctor's epilogue
allude to the general judgment, embrace *vs all* (918), and speak of
the uniting of body and soul (919). While there are significant differences between the specific and the general judgment, the play points
to affinities between the two both in theme and in theater. The
metaphor of time is further extended.
    One difference between *Everyman* and the "Doomsday" plays is
God's redesignation of the acting space and audience. Whereas the

God of the cycles constructs the city in which the cycle is performed as the world, in *Everyman* specific allusions to *worldly prosperyte* (24) and *worldly ryches* (60) characterize a more restricted society, one that is wealthy and materialistic. Although the play is frequently performed today in ecclesiastical settings, the text seems rather to predicate the secular setting of the hall and to address the society within it. Pressure from this context lends added resonance to the "Doomsday" commonplace of the Judgment as a "reckoning," itself an image of biblical origin:[15] "It ys full youre syns I beheight to make a reckoninge of the right" (*Chester Mystery Cycle*, play 24, "The Judgement," 9-10). The reference retains the specific force of fiscal accountancy. What is evidently a nobleman's hall thus becomes a metaphor of the world, its ostensible security the illusory materialism that is the prime initial target of the play, while the ambivalence of the accountancy image draws attention to its confused values. That image is actualized in the books of account that Everyman discovers beneath the feet of Good Deeds (or of Everyman, since he picks them up [500-8]).

The books are a property of major significance. They are held by Good Deeds, who brings them to Everyman from the grave—"Good Dedes, haue we clere our rekeynge? / Ye, in dede, I haue it here" (652-53)—and presumably carries them with her back to the grave. Opportunity exists for the illegible page to be displayed to the audience, and for the "clear" account to be displayed similarly. Such display of pages occurs elsewhere in medieval drama. In Chester's play 11, "The Purification," Simeon's "correction" of the biblical text is emended first in red and then in gold letters by an angel and evidently shown to the audience in evidence. The blotted record of Mischief's court in *Mankind* seems likewise displayed, for comic ends. Books are also employed in the Doomsday plays of the cycles.[16] The claim that "one letter here I can not se" (507) can be glossed from Goods' claim that "Thy rekenynge I haue made blotted and blynde" (419); the page is so blotted that the account cannot be read. Since the account has to be presented to God, it is possible that Good Deeds, who says "Fere not; I wyll speke for the" (876), presents the books to the angel after line 887, prompting the line "Thy rekenynge is crystall-clere" (898).

The "business" image is an extension of the wider distinction between treasure in heaven and treasure upon earth. Language plays its part in Everyman's confusion. The modern plural Goods, preferred in many editions, has ousted and hence obscured the force of the singular collective Good which is employed in the play. The combination of reference to material goods and to abstract virtue in the word provides the basis for ironic word play and pun—

O false Good, cursed thou be,
Thou traytour to God, that hast deceyued me
And caught me in thy snare (451-53)—

where the staging polarities are caught in the verbal link of *Good* and *God*, and *false Good* picks up not only the duplicity of worldly wealth but also the idolatrous love of it as a false God that leads to damnation.

The Theater of the World

God's instruction to Death, "Go thou to Eueryman" (66), initially seems to lack a reference. Everyman is Anyman among the audience gathered in the space before God, and the actor Death might draw any one of them into the play, just as Death might strike anyone. Death's promise, "Lorde, I wyll in the worlde go renne ouer-all / And cruelly out-serche bothe grete and small" (72-73), suggests that, like the Virtues in the N-Town "Mary" play, he descends from the heavenly sphere to audience level, in this case, the floor of the hall;[17] there he threatens the spectators with his dart (76) as he searches through them for his prey. The actor playing Everyman is either not present or—more likely—hidden among the audience, not obviously distinguishable by his dress. This easy interchange of actor and spectator is found in other hall interludes such as Medwall's *Fulgens and Lucrece,* where

There is so much nice array
Among these gallants nowaday
That a man shall not lightly
Know a player from another man!
(Glynne Wickham, ed., *English Moral Interludes*
[London: Dent, 1976], 42, lines 53-56)

Death's description of Everyman as going *gayly* (86) seems to confirm the impression that he is the young gallant, the youthful retainer who wears the livery of a great lord and flaunts the excess of his wealth in extravagant dress. As Tony Davenport says, "Man glorifies his flesh by assuming the trumpery finery of the world or of the court, and flaunts his short gown and immodest codpiece, his wide sleeves, his striped hose, his lace trimmings, the elegant smooth tightness of his hose, his open shirt, his slashed doublet and sleeves."[18] Such familiar finery signals Everyman's social identity and constitutes an index of his material priorities, which he must subsequently shed in preparation for his scourging (605-6). It is never resumed, for, as Davenport also notes, Knowledge gives Everyman in its place a *garment of sorowe* (638-41), which sets him apart from the rest of the audience and marks the change in his spiritual status.

As the quotation from *Fulgens and Lucrece* suggests, the livery of the retainer is analogous to a costume, assigning a role and, equally important, an identity to the wearer and encouraging him to act out his stereotypical part in a self-contained social drama. Death calls Everyman into a different play, that devised by God. But the values of Everyman are those of his society. Fellowship, the first friend to whom he turns, is the collective of such gallants (*MED, felaushipe*, 6. "An organized society of persons united by office, occupation, or common rules of living"). He voices the normative standard of conduct for the group, from which, like the servant B in *Fulgens and Lucrece*, he emerges. Fellowship's values confirm God's assessment of humanity. Fellowship proposes revenge ("If ony haue you wronged, ye shall reuenged be" [218]), gluttony and lechery ("And yet, yf thou wylte ete, & drynke, & make good chere, / Or haunt to women the lusty company" [273-74]), the sport of murder ("But and thou will murder, or ony man kyll" [281]), and the love of finery ("and thou wolde gyue me a newe gowne" [292]). Fellowship thus serves to define Everyman for us. The subjective sense of his name, "the mutual relationship, or characteristic behavior, of boon companions" (*MED, felauship*, 3) points to compatibility and may well suggest that the two actors are costumed identically.

Such concerns suggest affinities with the *Youth* interludes and seem to herald a sociopolitical critique on contemporary *mores* and crime. The play's date coincides with the popularity of the *Youth* plays,[19] and its affinities with the genre might therefore have seemed the more significant. Although, as Ian Lancashire points out, *Everyman* is a very different kind of play from *Youth* and *Hickscorner*,[20] the potential for development in the direction of social comment is not only present but to some extent exploited in this section of the play. Everyman is imprisoned within the literalism of the world that he inhabits and must be led to recognize that those around him, including himself, are bound up in their own allegorical limitations and ambiguities.

Continuing to search the playing area for help, he encounters two further representatives, Kindred and Cousin, his blood relatives. To some extent this might seem to repeat the encounter with Fellowship since they too reflect society and its values. But they also offer Everyman an alternative identity to that provided by society, that of descent, birth, and inherited rank. The word *kinrede* encompasses not only our modern sense of "kinsfolk" but also "stock, family, lineage, race" (*MED, kinrede*, 1). The personification here seems to take the form of an older, established member of society. The comment

> It auayleth not vs to tyse.
> Ye shall haue my mayde with all my herte;
> She loueth to go to feestes, there to be nyse,
> And to daunce, and abrode to sterte (359-62)

has the jocular tone of an older generation looking indulgently upon the pleasures of the young. The picture of a society feasting, dancing, and wandering abroad, and the use of *nys* with its semantic range from "frivolous" to "lascivious" (*MED, nice*), briefly calls to mind the errors of the spoilt child in morals of education such as *Nice Wanton*. In a hall setting, the allusion to feasting would be strongly underlined by the context, while the performance of a moral play would establish this occasion as distinctively different from those described. If the actors here double as the sisters, Good Deeds and Knowledge, then it would seem probable that Kindred and Cousin are also played as women, and that the maid is a lady's maid.[21]

Cousin seems closer to the age group of Everyman. We are half a century from the first *OED* example (1561) of the verb *cozen*, "to cheat, defraud by deceit," but it is difficult not to suspect a pun on the word in the otherwise surprising "Trust not to me, for, so God me spede, / I wyll deceyue you in your moost nede" (357-58). While no less firm in refusal than Kindred, (s)he identifes more fully with the plight of his/her kinsman, learning from his situation, almost as an example to the audience of their response: "Also of myne owne an vnredy rekenynge / I haue to accounte; therfore I make taryenge" (375-76).

As we have seen, the final encounter of this socially focused section of the play takes Everyman to the physical and moral limit of his travel through the literal and metaphorical acting space. He has now reached the heart of his own and society's corruption. Goods stands as the material wealth that sustains their pleasure and maintains their illusions of self-sufficiency. This is a society in which money can override all claims of morality and justice:

> For, parauenture, thou mayst before God Almyghty
> My rekenynge helpe to clene and puryfye,
> For it is sayd euer amonge
> That "money maketh all ryght that is wronge." (410-13)

The section thus ends with a critical observation on the contemporary values that structure Everyman's philosophical framework. He has extrapolated from the activities of the world in which he lives the values by which the universe operates, in ironic reversal of God's true intention.

The limited vision which these empirically deduced values promote is shown in Everyman's encounter with Death. Everyman's initial failure to recognize Death may seem to deny the literal level of the action in order to make an ironic allegorical point about Everyman's spiritual blindness. Death's self-description suggests that he takes the traditional form of a dart-armed skeletal figure (76), and although he does not verbally identify himself until line 115, he does announce himself as a messenger of God at the start of their dialogue (90-91). The problem is for a producer to address, though it admits of a number of possible solutions. Death may be literalized by Everyman as a curiously costumed actor, whose serious purpose only gradually penetrates his understanding. Alternatively, Death may speak at some distance from Everyman, calling out to him ("Loo, yonder I se Eueryman walkynge" [80]) and moving round him until he confronts him at line 115. Or he may be in cloaked disguise, revealing his identity visibly only at 115. Whatever the solution preferred, Everyman responds as if dealing with a normal master-messenger relationship of a kind he is accustomed to handling. He has received an unwelcome invitation, which he is not at the moment minded to accept (101, 113), and seeks to bribe the messenger to go away until a more suitable moment (122). His attitude is that of the busy man of the world, interrupted with an unwelcome bill at an inopportune moment. His "What desyreth God of me?" (97) is not, I think, a statement of surprise but a brusque, impatient remark on being jolted out of his reveries of lust and treasure.

The Theater of the Memory

Thus far, Everyman has occupied a timeless present; he expects past joys to continue unchanged, and that illusion has been translated into allegorical figures that outlast the life span of the individual. Goods says,

> For whan thou arte dede, this is my gyse—
> Another to deceyue in this same wyse
> As I have done the, and all to his soules reprefe. (448-50)

Now Everyman's punning progression from Goods to Good Deeds, from material to spiritual, corresponds to his change of physical movement as he turns away from the corner toward God. In so doing, he redesignates the acting space, from worldly society to the inner world of the mind. Whereas those whom he has encountered so far manifest themselves in familiar material guises, the appearance of the sisters Good Deeds and Knowledge is not readily determinable. Though they could be dressed in religious habits, such identification would seem to link them confusingly with the familiar social world, and a more anonymous dress, such as the linen gown of Lady Holy Church in *Piers Plowman*, might be more appropriate. The transition to this theater of the memory is, however, less abrupt than might at first seem, for *Everyman* has been, from the outset, a play about memory.

God's initial complaint is that his sacrifice is forgotten: "My lawe, which I shewed, whan I for them dyed, / They forget clean / and she-dynge of my blode rede" (29-30). Death comes to Everyman not to dispatch him but to remind him of what he already knows but has since forgotten:

> Full lyttell he thynketh on my comynge;
> His mynde is on flesshely lustes and his treasure. . . .
> Thoughe thou haue forgete him here,
> He thynketh on the in the heuenly spere. (81-82, 94-95)

Everyman does not think that he is immortal, and he knows from the start what is required of him and his unpreparedness: "Full vnredy I am suche rekenynge to gyue" (113). Death is not simply the destroyer of life; he is the messenger of God, sent to warn humanity, and as such is also a part of Everyman's consciousness. What he brings is a reminder of mortality into the mind of Everyman.

Even the theater of society has been in part a mental construct. Everyman has first to explore the concerns that were at the forefront of his mind when the realization of his impending death came before him. His physical and spatial progress is a mental progress, leading to the center of his own priorities and beliefs, and each dialogue is followed by a soliloquy in which Everyman reflects upon the process so far, clarifies his own false preconceptions, and moves on to the next possibility. As William Munsen says, "The rhythm of act and learning leading into new act shapes a local texture of continuous trial and correction."[22] The significance of Fellowship, Kindred and Cousin, and Goods is a projection of Everyman's own understanding. They are not as he constructs them. Goods, the inanimate object, states this point finally and clearly:

> Mary, thou brought thy selfe in care,
> Wherof I am gladde.
> I must nedes laugh, I can not be sadde. (454-56)

Goods is neutral, to be used for salvation through almsgiving when valued with reasoned moderation but a force for damnation when the sole focus of humankind's desires, the more usual role: "If I saue one, a thousande I do spyll" (443). As Jambeck suggests, this capacity of *Everyman* to be read as a drama of the inner being may account for some of its modern appeal.[23] *The Castle of Perseverance*, for example, also dramatizes a process of repentance. Humanum Genus rejects Shrift but is led to repentance by the prodding spear of Penitence and goes into the castle of perseverance to be defended by the seven virtues. What we witnesss is an inner drama; but what we experience is a play in which Humanum Genus is displaced from the center of the action by powerful external forces for good and evil. In *Everyman* the issue is determined by Everyman's misreadings of the world he occupies. The play's theatrical strategy denies the determinism of the *Castle*; responsibility is shown, both morally and dramatically, to rest with the individual.

In turning to Good Deeds, therefore, Everyman is also moving further into his own mind, having freed it from the preconceptions that are immediately present in his material environment. With the change of allegorical mode, the play has reached a point of transition. Good Deeds "exists" only in Everyman's past. Paradoxically, she is called to mind perhaps by Goods' reference to alms-deeds, that is, active charity. Hidden in the ground, she is also buried deep in the memory of Everyman. She directs him to Knowledge, who can instruct Everyman more clearly. Whereas Good Deeds is particular to Everyman, taking a different form in each individual, Knowledge is both individual and collective.[24] She is what Everyman already knows, the way to salvation. As Everyman is definable in terms of his social station and values, he is also definable in terms of his Christian upbringing; he is Every-Christian-man. But Knowledge is also the collective knowledge of Christendom, from which Everyman's particular knowledge itself derives, and she can therefore survive him in a way comparable to that of the "social" allegories. She is the link to the guardian of that collective knowledge, the institution of the church, and hence leads Everyman out from one social construct, his secular world, into another, that of church sacraments, rituals, and worship.

The Theater of Salvation

The House of Salvation where the holy man Confession dwells constitutes a new theatrical space, invitingly present from the start. I have accepted that God's throne might be located above it, providing both the high place and an appropriate proximity to what is clearly construed as a church beneath. The entry into this structure is an act of withdrawal from the theater of society, a rejection of the values of the surrounding community, similar to Humanum Genus's entry into the Castle of Perseverance. Within this specifically designated space—perhaps an open-sided scaffold—Everyman enters a new kind of drama, a series of ritualized and formalized acts that are prescribed for him and undertaken unquestioningly under the direction of Knowledge. This is a different kind of allegory; familiar rituals and their associated symbolic objects, to which value has been arbitrarily attributed, are here translated into dramatic actions and stage properties and require authoritative explanation in order to make sense of the otherwise meaningless actions.

Within this context, physically and symbolically close to the actor-God, Everyman's memory reaches beyond his personal history of wrongdoing to retrieve the knowledge that God required at the outset: "To remember thy Sauyour was scourged for the / With sharpe scourges, and suffred it pacyently" (563-64). This extension of memory is accompanied by an act of prayer to God which introduces a new voice of adoration into the play:

> O eternall God / O heuenly fygure,
> O way of ryghtwysnes / O goodly vysyon,
> Whiche dyscended downe in a vyrgyn pure
> Bycause he wolde euery man redeme,
> Whiche Adam forfayted by his dysobedyence:
> O blessyd God-heed, electe and hye deuyne,
> Forgyue me my greuous offence! (581-87)

This Latinate high-style appropriate to its high subject and purpose reflects in its formality the formal action of the speaker before God, and signals the ritualistic mode of the scourging, and subsequently the administration of the sacrament and the anointing. Everyman's memory now reaches into divine history, to Fall and Redemption. He has been called back to the opening vision given by God, the collectively available redemption, and the distinction of the individual and the generality of humankind has again been dissolved. He can now be "mery and glad" (623).

Everyman's unhappiness has been repeatedly restated by him as each of his friends in society deserted him. His exchange with Kindred emphasizes the recurring issue:

EUERYMAN
    Alas, that euer I was bore!
    For now shall I neuer be mery,
    If that you forsake me.
KYNREDE
    Ah, syr, what ye be a mery man!
    Take good herte to you, and make no mone! (348-52)

The self-focused joviality of the speaker not only contrasts with Everyman's growing misery, but that misery actually feeds the sense of joviality, as Everyman becomes the object of amusement in his mistaken readings. The sneering laugh of Goods, "I am gladde; I must nedes laugh, I can not be sadde" (455-56), is the most deriding and cruel. Everyman is made the more wretched by what are in effect stage-directions indicating the disposition of the actors toward him. He in turn, by his indifference, has caused distress to his Good Deeds, as her reproachful response implies: "If ye had parfytely chered me" (501) (*MED, cheren,* 1[a] "To cheer [sb] up"; 3. "To treat hospitably"). Knowledge's exhortation therefore sharply reverses the situation that has so far obtained. Now, with the arrival of Good Deeds beside Everyman a new language of tender affection is introduced, intensified by the cumulative appellations of Good Deeds, by the mutual use of the possessive pronoun, and accompanied by Everyman's tears of happiness:

GOOD DEDES
    Eueryman, pilgrim, my specyall frende,
    Blessyd be thou without ende. . . .
EUERYMAN
    Welcome, my Good Dedes! Now I here thy voyce,
    I wepe for very swetenes of loue. (629-35)

After the sequence of scornful rejections, Everyman has at last found the loving security and support he sought.

    After his investment with his new "costume," the "garment of sorowe," glossed as "Contrition" (643-45), Everyman is ready to leave the House of Salvation, but he will return to receive the sacrament and extreme unction from Priesthood (750ff). This episode has occasioned some debate. The words *go* (707) and *yonder I se Eueryman come* (769) may suggest that Everyman goes from the audience's view after the speech of Five Wits (749), constituting, incidentally, the only infringement of unity of action in the play. It is at this point that the much discussed digression upon the authority of the priesthood between Five Wits and Knowledge occurs. The dialogue is in two parts—the praise of the power of the priesthood to Everyman, and then, in his absence, a criticism before the audience of the shortcomings of priests who lead lives of public scandal. Possibly the administration of the sacrament and the anointing are carried out in full view of the audience in a mimetic action within the stage of the House of Salvation while the dialogue between the two allegorical characters proceeds outside.

This section provides a further example of calling to memory, the need to remember the role of the church in the scheme for salvation, as evidenced in the comment on the sacraments: "These seuen be good to haue in remembraunce" (726). The sacraments are reminders of God's grace to humankind and also the pathways to redemption. The speeches also stress a distinction between the office of priesthood, as allegorized within the theater of salvation and sacramentalized within the church, and the particular holder of that office in society. The ability to separate the role in the play from the actor occupying it becomes a means of understanding the distinction between the individual priest and the power which that office within the church confers upon him.

The Theater of the Body

As Everyman prepares to leave the House of Salvation for the first time, he is instructed by Good Deeds to accept as companions Discretion, Strength, and his Beauty, and by Knowledge to accept Five Wits (657-69). These new companions are called onto the stage by a conscious act of mind:

KNOWLEGE
    Also ye must call to mynde
    Your Fyue Wyttes as for your counseylours.
GOOD DEDES
    You must haue them redy at all houres.
EUERYMAN
    Howe shall I gette them hyder?
KNOWLEGE
    You must call them all togyder,
    And they wyll here you in-contynent. (662-67)

Their coming heralds the final theater of the play, in which the action shrinks to that of the body. The changing designation of the playing space interconnects the two realms that Everyman inhabits, his social world of men and the world of his own body. It is difficult to understand how these different attributes might have been represented on the stage; possibly some form of costume incorporating symbolic designs could have been worn. Their gathering around him, however, marks the reconstitution of the body of the redeemed as a help and comfort in the world (676), instead of the seat of fleshly desires which work to damnation. Symbolically, this is a moment of rebirth; dramatically, it is emblematized in the return of Everyman from the House of Salvation to the outer acting area, where these qualities make up his defense against the temptations that once beset him.

The heedless confidence of the gallant on his first entry into the playing space is paralleled now by his newfound confidence in his own self-sufficiency as he reenters; he thanks God

> that I haue hyder brought
> Strength, Discrecyon, Beaute, and V Wittes. Lacke I nought.
> And my Good Dedes, with Knowlege, clere.
> All be in company at my wyll here.
> I desyre no more to my besynes. (679-83)

Everyman has found a kingdom that responds to his will to replace the one that worked in willful independence of him.

He asserts this control by making his will, an action that has both social and literary associations.[25] Everyman is now reconstituted in his youthful prime. For the first time his words embrace the audience as well as his newfound friends as spectators, casting them as witnesses to the will:

> Now harken, all that be here,
> For I wyll make my testament
> Here before you all present. (696-98)

The making of a will was a necessary preparation before embarking on a physical journey, but it is also the prudent act of any whose death is approaching. Everyman's will is a product of his newfound Discretion in the world and constitutes a significant piece of stage-business, a model in itself. Perhaps surprisingly, the will does not follow the usual formula of bequeathing soul to Christ and body to church or making provision for funeral expenses. Its concern is with the distribution of the Goods to which Everyman spoke earlier. Here half the money will go to alms-deeds and the other half to paying debts and making other restitution, thereby reclaiming authority over the still-visible Goods who had gloated over his fate. The will, like the books of account, may be displayed; it is presumably entrusted to Knowledge. It is from this point that Everyman properly embarks upon his journey.

Returning from Priesthood, Everyman carries a crucifix (778). Whereas previously he had been reluctant to undertake his journey, he is now positively eager ("let vs go with-out longer respyte" [776]) and expresses weariness with life itself ("Frendes, let vs not tourne agayne to this lande" [790]). With Knowledge, Good Deeds, and bodily qualities he sets off for the grave which, we assume, had been vacated previously by Good Deeds and which is now literalized. The journey to the grave is evidently what the bodily qualities understood by his request to "folowe me" (779), for at the graveside they abandon him. This enacts the aging process, which carries the young man from youth to senility. The attributes leave him as they leave an aging man—first Beauty, then Strength, then Discretion, and finally his Five Wits. They are conscious of the appropriate sequence, suggesting an unstated inevitability about their departure. Strength comments that this is the appropriate time for him to leave: "Ye be olde ynoughe, I vnderstande, / Your pylgrymage to take on hande" (817-18). Discretion says that he must leave after Strength (834-35), and Five Wits follows the others (846). The dramatization of the aging process transforms the play into a "life of Humankind" format, which realizes the physical and mental degeneration of the aged in terms of a visible social isolation. Everyman is again threatened with loneliness, the more acute because of his earlier confidence and because he—and we through him—has experienced such isolation before. Again his sense of security has proved delusory, and a mistaken value has been projected upon autonomous characters. The parallel is emphasized by Good Deeds: "Beaute, Strength / and Dyscrecyon do man forsake, / Folysshe frendes and kynnesmen that fayre spake" (871-72).

The play concludes by returning the audience from the play world to the everyday world. Everyman first offers himself to the audience as example ("Take example, all ye that this do here or se" [867]). This is then taken up by Knowledge, who steps out of her allegorical role to become at one with the audience: "Now hath he suffred that we all shall endure" (888). Next the Angel turns from addressing the soul to addressing the audience: "Now shalte thou in to the heuenly spere, / Vnto the whiche all ye shall come" (899-900). Presumably the Angel is responsible for leading the soul to the *locus* of heaven. Finally the Doctor addresses "Ye herers, take it of worth, olde and yonge" (903) and urges their assent to the final prayer: "Therto helpe the Trynyte! / Amen, saye ye, for saynt charyte" (921-22). These prayers seem to be made against the tableau of heaven, with Knowledge standing at the grave.

The tightly controlled structure of *Everyman* sets it apart from the looser structures of our longer fifteenth-century morality plays. It would be a mistake, however, to overstress its atypicality. The effectiveness of the play lies not in any one unique feature, but in the skillful allusions to a range of different kinds of drama and allegory, all familiar and established. De Vocht's claim for its priority over *Elckerlijc* may no longer be accepted, but he rightly pointed to *Everyman*'s comfortable accommodation into the existing traditions of English drama and devotional writing: "*Everyman* is as intimately connected with English Literature as any literary document of the period" (1967, 211). It was perhaps as much the recognition of that compatibility as of the appropriateness of its propagandist theme that led to its translation. At the same time, however, the play imaginatively exploits those resources and extends our understanding of the term "morality play."

Notes

1. Arnold Williams, *The Drama of Medieval England* (East Lansing: Michigan State University Press, 1961), 160. On Poel's revival, see Robert Potter, *The English Morality Play: Origins, History and Influence of a Dramatic Tradition* (London: Routledge, 1975), 1-5.
2. A. C. Cawley, ed., *Everyman* (Manchester: Manchester University Press, 1961), xv-xvi. All quotations are from this edition.
3. Alan J. Fletcher, "*Everyman*: An Unrecorded Sermon Analogue," *English Studies* 66 (1985): 297; Thomas J. Jambeck, "*Everyman* and the Implications of Bernardine Humanism in the Character 'Knowledge,'" *Medievalia et Humanistica* 8 (1977): 103-23.
4. Henry de Vocht, "*Everyman*": *A Comparative Study of Texts and Sources* (Louvain: Librairie Universitaire, 1947); E. R. Tigg, *The Dutch "Elckerlijc" is Prior to the English "Everyman"* (London: privately printed, 1981). For a translation of *Elckerlijc*, see Adriaan J. Barnouw, *The Mirror of Salvation* (The Hague: Nijhoff, 1971).
5. See Barnouw, *The Mirror*, xiv-xvi; R. P. Meijer, *Literature of the Low Countries*, 2d ed. (Cheltenham: Thorne, 1978), 54-56.
6. W. W. Greg suggests that probably some ten editions may have been produced (*Everyman*, Materialen zur Kunde des älteren Englischen Dramas 20 [Louvain: Uystpruyst, 1910], 35n2). The four extant editions are described by Cawley (*Everyman*, ix-x).
7. Cawley, *Everyman*, xix-xx; David Bevington, *Tudor Drama and Politics: A Critical Approach to Topical Meaning* (Cambridge: Harvard University Press, 1968), 35.

8. C. J. Wortham, "*Everyman* and the Reformation," *Parergon* 29 (1981): 23.

9. E.g., Play 5 in the *Chester Mystery Cycle*, ed. R. M. Lumiansky and David Mills, EETS supp. ser. 3 (London: Oxford University Press, 1974). See also the use of the figure of Contemplacio in The "*Mary*" *Play from the N-Town Manuscript*, ed. Peter Meredith (London: Longmans, 1987).

10. Most significantly, Hebrews 11:9-16.

11. Cf. Matthew 20:1-9, John 9:4, etc.

12. Dennis V. Moran, "The Life of *Everyman*," *Neophilologus* 56 (1972): 325.

13. See particularly Carolynn Van Dyke, "The Intangible and Its Image: Allegorical Discourse and the Cast of *Everyman*," *Acts of Interpretation: The Text in Its Contexts 700-1600: Essays on Medieval and Renaissance Literature in Honor of E. Talbot Donaldson*, ed. Mary J. Carruthers and Elizabeth D. Kirk (Norman, Oklahoma: Pilgrim Books, 1982), 311-24. On the general judgment, see particularly Matthew 20 and 21; on the individual judgment, Hebrews 9:27.

14. Douglas Cowling, "The Angels' Song in *Everyman*," *N&Q* 85 (1988): 301-3.

15. Cf. Matthew 18:23-30, Romans 14:12, 1 Peter 4:1-8.

16. *Chester Mystery Cycle*, play 11, "The Purification," lines 1-118; *Mankind* (Mark Eccles, ed., *The Macro Plays*, EETS 262 [London: Oxford University Press, 1969], 176), lines 679-86. On books in the "Doomsday" plays, see, for example, Towneley play 30, "The Judgement," lines 134-42; *Chester Mystery Cycle*, play 24, lines 549-564+Latin. The underpinning biblical text is Revelations 20:12.

17. Meredith, The "*Mary*" *Play*, lines 1215-22.

18. Tony Davenport, "'Lusty Fresch Galaunts,'" *Aspects of Early English Drama*, ed. Paula Neuss (Cambridge: Brewer, 1983), 112.

19. See David Bevington, *From Mankind to Marlowe* (Cambridge: Harvard University Press, 1962), 50-51.

20. Ian Lancashire, ed., *Two Tudor Interludes: "The Interlude of Youth": "Hickscorner"* (Manchester: Manchester University Press, 1980), 48.

21. On doubling in the play, see John W. Velz, "Episodic Structure in Four Tudor Plays: A Virtue of Necessity," *Comparative Drama* 6 (1972-73): 88-90.

22. William Munson, "Knowing and Doing in *Everyman*," *ChR* 19 (1984-85): 255.

23. Jambeck, "*Everyman*," 120.

24. The exact reference of "Knowledge" has been much debated. Among suggestions are: "both self analysis and its product" (Allen B. Goldhamer, "*Everyman*: A Dramatization of Death," *Classica et Medievalia* 29-30 [1968-9]: 610); "*Everyman*'s experience of the world, his awareness of sin, and his understanding of God's mercy and grace" (Moran, "The Life of *Everyman*," 326); "'contrition' or, better, 'acknowledgement of one's sin'" (Lawrence van Ryan, "Doctrine and Dramatic Structure in *Everyman*," *Speculum* 32 [1957]: 728).

25. See Eber Carle Perrow, "The Last Will and Testament as a Form of Literature," *Transactions of the Wisconsin Academy of Sciences, Arts and Letters* 17 (1914): 682-753.

"My Name is Worship": Masquerading Vice in Medwall's Nature

John A. Alford

The first known example of masquerading vice in a morality play appears in the work of "the first positively known English dramatist," Henry Medwall's *Nature* (ca. 1500):[1]

PRIDE

>My name is Worship.

MAN

>Worship? now, surely,
>The world told me it was my destiny
>To come to Worship [ere] I die.

PRIDE

>Truly, I am the same.[2]

Pride's assumption of the name Worship is only the first in a series of virtuous pseudonyms taken by the vice figures in this play in order to deceive Man or, as one of them says, "to blear his eye" (81). Pride's retinue, the rest of the seven deadly sins, all follow his lead. Covetousness misrepresents himself as Worldly Policy; Wrath, as Manhood; Envy, as Disdain; Gluttony, as Good Fellowship; Sloth, as Ease; Lechery, as Lust (that is, "vigor, energy, life" [*MED*, 4(A)]). This simple ploy works to perfection, partly because the vices craftily take the names of near-doubles (Sloth *looks* like Ease), and partly because Man himself is so undiscerning—as if he actually wished to be deluded.

Medwall's *Nature* is a watershed in the history of English theater. As Tucker Brooke observes, somewhat peevishly, the use of aliases "was repeated *ad nauseam* in later interludes" (not to mention the countless plays in other genres where it served as the virtual trademark of villainy).[3] As in *Nature*, Wrath takes the name of Manhood in *Albion*

151

Knight (1537-65) and in Wager's *The Longer Thou Livest* (1560-68). Again, following *Nature,* Covetousness disguises itself as Policy in *Respublica* (1553) and *Enough Is as Good as a Feast* (1560-69), as Frugality in *New Custom* (1559-73), and then as Careful Provision in *The Conflict of Conscience* (1575-81). Idleness appears as Honest Recreation in Merbury's *A Marriage between Wit and Wisdom* (ca. 1579).[4] These are only a few examples of the device. "To cite the plays in which it exists," Bernard Spivack claims, "would be tantamount to a roll call of almost the entire morality drama."[5]

The extraordinary success of Medwall's innovation calls for an explanation. After all, a device is not "repeated *ad nauseam*" over the course of a century unless it expresses an important truth or answers to some deeply felt need in the audience. A. P. Rossiter, one of the few critics to offer an explanation, sees the figure of masquerading vice as a product of social conditions:

> We met this [figure] first in *Nature.* But though there is a hint for it in Prudentius [*Psychomachia*], where *Avaritia* calls herself *Parsimonia* (i.e. Greed alias Economy), one reason for its steady persistence in the drama until it becomes stock-in-trade of equivocating villainy is the moral confusion which the Renaissance and Reformation caused, and which the "moral" interlude did much to increase. The contemporary confusion, with its atmosphere of "propaganda" and misrepresentation, made the equivocator the logical symbol for the spokesmen of the other side.[6]

Undoubtedly, the political and religious climate of the sixteenth century made audiences especially receptive to the device of double-naming. Yet Rossiter's explanation underplays the importance of both earlier "moral confusion" and earlier literary tradition. Tudor playwrights inherited considerably more than a "hint" of the device. It was, after all, a convention "in all moral allegory."[7] Thanks largely to Gregory the Great's virtual rewriting of the *Psychomachia* in his treatises and commentaries, the device was extended from *Avaritia* to all the other sins. In his *Pastoral Care,* for example, Gregory warns those entrusted with the cure of souls that "vices commonly masquerade as virtues": "Often, for instance, a niggard passes himself off as frugal, while one who is prodigal conceals his character when he calls himself open-handed. Often inordinate laxity is believed to be kindness, and unbridled anger passes as the virtue of spiritual zeal. Precipitancy is frequently taken as efficient promptitude, and dilatoriness as grave deliberation."[8] In his massive commentary, the *Moralia in Iob,* Gregory gives even freer rein to his penchant for listing the aliases of sin.[9] But the

the prize must go to the fourteenth-century Augustinian friar Henricus de Frimaria who, acknowledging his debt to Gregory, devotes an entire treatise (*Tractatus de occultatione vitiorum sub specie virtutum*) to the names under which the vices attempt to pass themselves off as virtues.[10] In English literature the most familiar and profound expression of the Prudentian-Gregorian theme, during the Middle Ages, is *Piers Plowman* (where Lady Meed, a lineal descendant of *Avaritia*, confuses vice and virtue under the double meaning of her name, "bribery" and "just reward"[11]), and, during the Renaissance, Spenser's *Faerie Queene*, especially in the figure of "false *Duessa*, now *Fidessa* hight" (I.ii.44).

Clearly there was a vital literary tradition of masquerading vice long before Medwall and other sixteenth-century playwrights transformed the figure into a popular stage villain. This fact does not rule out the "moral confusion" of the times as a contributing cause of the figure's appeal, of course, but it does argue for shifting the focus of the question. Instead of asking why the vice's theatrical debut proved so successful, we might learn more by asking why it was so long delayed.

Part of the answer can be found in the tentative efforts of playwrights before Medwall to adapt the convention to the stage. As far as I know, the earliest example is the *Ludus Coventriae* or N-Town cycle (1400-1450), in which Lucifer gives each of the deadly sins a new name:

> I haue browth ȝow newe namys, and wyl ȝe se why
> Ffor synne is so plesaunt, to ech Mannys intent
> Ȝe xal kalle pride oneste and naterall kend lechory
> And covetyse wysdam there tresure is present.
> Wreth manhod, and envye callyd chastement
> Seyse nere sessyon lete perjery be chef
> Glotonye rest let Abstynawnce beyn Absent
> And he þat wole exorte þe to vertu put hem to repreff.[12]

What is so striking about the use of aliases in this scene is that the convention is not acted out. Lucifer merely assigns the false names. We never witness Wrath disguised as "Manhood" or Covetyse pretending to be "Wysdam." The story is the same in fifteenth-century morality plays. In *Wisdom* (1461-85) we hear that Covetyse, again, "ys clepede wysdam"—while the proud are denominated "curtely personys," and lechery "no more þan drynke atawnt"—but we never see this perverse nomenclature actually performed.[13] In the "hybrid" morality *Mary Magdalene* (1480-90), Pride assumes the form of a gallant named

Curiosity, but there is no intent to deceive: "curiosity" is more a nick-
name than a pseudonym, a species, in fact, of pride.[14] In *Everyman*
(1480-1500) Fellowship reveals his true nature as he abandons the title
character on the verge of death—

> And yet if thou wilt eat, and drink, and make good cheer,
> Or haunt to women, the lusty company,
> I would not forsake you while the day is clear—

but this confusion of "fellowship" with drunkenness and lechery is
never dramatized.[15] In short, fifteenth-century playwrights were able to
describe but not, apparently, to *show* vice in the act of impersonating
virtue. Their treatment of the convention remained essentially literary.

We may surmise that adapting the convention to the theater proved
to be no easy task. For one thing, playwrights (and playgoers) were
occupied already with the problem of impersonation at the most basic
level—the actors themselves pretending to be "someone else." This was
challenge enough. Indeed, the use of disguise in any form of drama,
not in the morality alone, was rare before the Tudor period.[16] The
device presumes the kind of artistic self-consciousness fostered during
the sixteenth century by the growth of professionalism in the theater
and the rise of coterie audiences in the larger households, in the
schools, and at court. It is, we may say, metatheatrical. As with other literary conventions transferred to the stage (for example, the embedded
narrative recast as the play-within-a-play), the use of pseudonyms calls
attention to the nature of the medium itself. Playwrights could not
incorporate this literary device without its becoming in its new context
a commentary on, a re-exemplification of, the essential dramatic act of
impersonation. When Pride disguises himself as Worship in Medwall's
Nature, he is imitating the actor who plays him. He *is* an actor. His purpose is to fool Man even as that of the player who gives him voice and
motion is to "fool" the audience. After Medwall, the use of onstage disguises proliferates and becomes ever more complicated, until it reaches
its probable limit in the piled-up impersonations of *As You Like It*—a
boy-actor pretending to be a girl (Rosalind) pretending to be a boy
(Ganymede) pretending to be a girl (Rosalind). The ubiquity of the
device in sixteenth-century drama testifies not only to the audience's
keen interest in questions of personal identity (very much in flux since
the social upheavals of the late Middle Ages) but also to their newly
acquired sophistication as playgoers.

To elaborate on dramatic disguise as a self-referential device would
take us too far from our subject, but a few examples from later sixteenth-century moralities may help to put Medwall's achievement in

perspective. His introduction of masquerading vice, in an art form that is itself a masquerade, changed the audience's relation to the play. It not only called attention to the ludic nature of the performance, it also extended the action to include the audience as players, and not merely spectators, of the game. Normally, as spectators, we are encouraged to forget the identity of the person behind the mask—to believe that the figure we are watching on stage is not Laurence Olivier, say, but Richard III himself. In the case of masquerading vice, however, the focus is all on the true identity of the malicious "actor." We are invited to guess his name. Often the invitation is explicit, as in this scene from *The Trial of Treasure* (1567), where an unidentified vice addresses the audience directly:

> I can remember, I am so old,
> Since Paradise gates were watched by night;
> And when that Vulcanus was made a cuckold,
> Among the great gods I appeared in sight.
> Nay, for all you smiling, I tell you true.
> No, no, ye will not know me now;
> The mighty on the earth I do subdue.
> Tush, if you will give me leave, I'll tell you how;
> Now, in good faith, I care not greatly,
> Although I declare my daily increase;
> But then these gentlewomen will be angry,
> Therefore I think best to hold my peace:
> Nay, I beseech you, let the matter stay,
> For I would not for twenty pounds come in their hands;
> For if there should chance to be but one Dalila,
> By the mass, they would bind me in Samson's bands!
> But what, mean I first with them to begin,
> Seeing that in all men I do remain?
> Because that first I remained Eve within,
> And after her Adam, and so forth to Cain.
> I perceive by your looks my name ye would know;
> Why, you are not ignorant of that, I dare say;
> It is I that do guide the bent of your bow,
> And ruleth your actions also day by day;
> Forsooth, I am called Natural Inclination. . . .[17]

Though delivered by a single actor, these lines actually constitute a kind of dialogue, with the audience's part written into the speaker's pretended responses to their doubts ("Nay, for all your smiling, I tell you true"), their interruptions ("Tush, if you will give me leave, I'll tell you how"), their pleas to continue ("I think best to hold my peace: Nay, I beseech you, let the matter stay"), and their requests for identification ("I perceive by your looks my name ye would know").

Quite common in sixteenth-century moralities, this sort of guessing game translates into dramatic terms the literary convention of "delayed identification" in order to test the audience's moral sensitivity or ability to recognize a particular vice or virtue (usually a vice) when it sees one.[18] As a mixed medium, however, drama can test the audience in more than one way. In *The Trial of Treasure*, Natural Inclination relies on words alone; but in *The Contention between Liberality and Prodigality* (1567-68), the principal vice challenges the audience to guess his identity not from "words" but from such visual clues as "attire":

> In words to make description of my name,
> My nature or conditions, were but vain;
> Sith this attire so plainly shows the same,
> As showed cannot be in words more plain.
> For lo, thus roundabout in feathers dight,
> Doth plainly figure mine inconstancy:
> As feather, light of mind; of wit as light,
> Subjected still to mutability,
> And for to paint me forth more properly,
> Behold each feather decked gorgeously
> With colours strange in such variety,
> As plainly pictures perfect vanity.
> And so I am, to put you out of doubt,
> Even vanity wholly; within, without:
> In head, in heart: in all parts roundabout.[19]

The difference between the ways in which Natural Inclination and Vanity identify themselves—one verbally, the other visually—is a function or extension of the difference in their natures. As an instance of personal history ("I can remember . . . that first I remained Eve within, / And after her Adam, and so forth to Cain"), Natural Inclination's speech emphasizes the transmission of original sin from generation to generation. Vanity, on the other hand, is identified more appropriately by its "attire," because the vice itself is preoccupied with appearances. The feather image is especially good. It suggests a wide range of associations and, in contrast to words once spent, remains an ever-present reminder to the audience of lightness "of mind" and "of wit," "inconstancy," "mutability," "vanity." The image is part of the iconography of vanity; it is, as art historians might say, an "attribute" of the vice. Over time audiences learned to interpret such attributes as clues to the real character of the *dramatis personae*. When Tom Tosspot appears on stage with a feather in his hat (*Like Will to Like*), the audience has good reason to suspect that this figure is given to vanity, even before Nichol Newfangle says, "Methink, by your apparel you have had me in regard."[20]

The development of a verbal and visual rhetoric of masquerading vice was essential to the rise of this figure as a dramatic convention. Without such clues as telltale language, gestures, "attributes," costumes, and the like, audiences often had no means of identifying the vice or, if they had, no means of keeping alive throughout a performance the subtle differences between what this figure pretended to be and what he actually was.

Before examining this rhetoric more closely in *Nature*, however, I must note one of the main obstacles to its recovery. Most readers have never seen any Tudor moralities in performance. Although we may appreciate the force of perennial caveats such as Roy MacKenzie's (1914)—"No criticism of the Moralities can be definitive which ignores the fact that they were presented to contemporaries as acted performances"[21]—we continue to experience these plays primarily as written texts. We have no choice. Nor can the lack of performance opportunities be replaced by visualizing the action in our mind's eye. We may try to move imaginatively from page to performance, but we cannot suppress the page or what we have learned from it. Take, for example, the passage with which this essay begins: "*Pride*. My name is Worship. . . ." The reader is not fooled. Whatever name the speaker may give out, the rubric has identified him already as Pride. In order to illustrate how delayed identification works in *The Trial of Treasure* and *The Contention between Liberality and Prodigality*, as I tried to do earlier, it was necessary to strip away the stage directions—in the first instance, "*Enter Inclination, the Vice*," and in the second, "*Enter* VANITY *solus, all in feathers.*" Audiences were not given such information; they had to purchase the insight by dint of their own observation and thought. In cases like these, therefore, to *read* a morality play is necessarily to frustrate one of its purposes. The reader is not tested, is not joined with the protagonist in a brief but salutary ignorance and, knowing the identity of all the characters from the start, is probably less sensitive to the verbal and visual clues intended to reveal their true nature.

Even so cogent a critic as Joel Altman unwittingly permits his reading of *Nature* to interfere with his judgment of its moral purpose.

Nature is a humanist morality play. . . . Although Man takes these Vices at their word [Pride as "Worship," etc.] and is misled into following evil counsel, the audience is always alerted to their true identity so that it may observe their techniques of deception in operation. . . . But beyond its genial admixture of doctrine and solace, one is struck chiefly by the fact that it is a profoundly reassuring play. . . . Its comic form suggests that our life, too, can have a happy ending if we are careful and, like the hero of the play, finally make the correct choice. For while Pride may disguise himself as "Worship," and Wrath as "Manhood," this only warns us that vigilance is necessary; it does not suggest that the choice itself is ultimately problematic.[22]

Altman's optimistic assessment rests, in part, on his experience of the play as a text rather than as a performance. Consider his claim that although Man is misled by the vices, "the audience is always alerted to their true identity." A spectator might object, "*at what point?*" When Pride first takes the stage, he is identified only as "a well-drawn man . . . well-taught . . . well-apparelled" (66). Readers know his name from the stage direction, but spectators are no more privy to this figure's "true identity" than Man himself. For 130 lines the audience is forced to play a guessing game. The playwright does not keep us in the dark so long as he does Man, but long enough to let us feel for ourselves the nature of his predicament. And what if we fail to recognize the vice's identity before he reveals it? Can we then be as sanguine as Altman about the play's purpose? What basis would we have for believing that "vigilance" alone is enough to distinguish Pride from Worship? As I mean to show presently, the whole point of the masquerade is that vigilance is *not* enough.

So far I have argued that the appearance of masquerading vice during the Tudor period was determined as much by the nature of the dramatic medium itself as by any external factors such as the "moral confusion" of the age. Adapting the literary convention to the stage required time. Reading a text and watching a play are very different kinds of experiences, and until an adequate *dramatic* rhetoric had been developed the figure of masquerading vice could not express itself. Certainly the fourteenth and fifteenth centuries had their share of moral confusion. What they did not have, what only the more advanced dramaturgy of the next century could provide, was an effective means of translating the emblem of that confusion from page to performance.

•   •   •

In order to assess Medwall's contribution to a dramatic rhetoric of vice, let us begin with an overview of his play. *Nature* was presented originally in two installments, presumably because its length would have taxed the strength (or patience) of Medwall's patron, John Morton, archbishop of Canterbury. In part one, Man sins and repents; in part two, the pattern is repeated. The structure is very similar to that of earlier moralities, such as *The Castle of Perseverance*.[23] What gives this slight plot its chief interest is the allegorical analysis of the motives that drive Man to behave as he does. In the opening scene Nature introduces Man to the two faculties that will guide him on his "long voyage . . . through the world":

> Lo! here Reason to govern thee in thy way,
> And Sensuality upon thine other side.
> But Reason I depute to be thy chief guide. (46)

So Nature ordains—but Sensuality has other ideas: "What, lady Nature!" he protests, "Ye know right well that I ought *naturally* / Before all other, to have of him the [care]."[24] Reason objects that Sensuality, though natural in man, "causeth him to fall . . . and maketh him bestial," and puts himself forward as the God-like faculty that allows Man to discern "Sufficient difference betwixt good and bad" (52-53). Dismayed by their quarreling, Man cries, "O, blessed Lord! what manner strife is this / Atwixt my reason and sensuality. . ." (55). Man's cry defines the basic conflict of the play, which is soon a fullblown psychomachia. Sensuality's "troops" enter the field seriatim rather than all at once (Worldly Affection, then Pride, Bodily Lust, Gluttony, Sloth, [Covetousness], Envy, and Wrath), a practical necessity for a limited cast[25] but also an effective illustration of how one sin leads to another—a dramatization of Gregory's "psychological concatenation of the vices."[26] On the other side, a lone combatant for most of the play, Reason fights on, his battle plan limited mainly to preaching virtue and warning against the sleights of vice. Caught between the two sides, Man asserts, "I [have] free election / To do what I will, be it evil or well" (47), but whether he knows the difference is not always clear. He much prefers the merry company of the vices (all disguised as virtues) to the sober friendship of Reason, who is plotting, he complains, "to bring me in captivity" (104).

But Reason prevails in the end. In *Nature I* the action is hurriedly brought to a close in the last several dozen lines as Man, spurred by Shamefacedness, abruptly vows to mend his ways, but in *Nature II* his conversion takes up nearly one-third of the play. Warned by Age of his approaching death, Man resolves to leave Sensuality (and his company) and to follow Reason for the rest of his life. Reason, now Man's physician, prescribes a regimen of "contraries" to cure the wounds of sin: against pride, Man must practice meekness; against wrath and envy, patience and charity; against covetise, alms-deed; against gluttony, abstinence; against lechery, chastity; against sloth or idleness, "good business."[27] This regimen is played out in a masque-like parade of the virtues, during which each announces itself by its right name ("I am called Charity," etc.) and then describes its remedial powers against the corresponding vice.[28] Thus is Man prepared for Repentance, who leads him to contrition, confession, and satisfaction (traditionally the three stages of the sacrament of confession). The play ends with Reason's reassuring words that Man is now "fully the child of salvation!"

In its thematic development *Nature* is thoroughly medieval. All of its ideas can be found, for example, in *Piers Plowman*; and it is quite misleading to characterize the play, as critics often do, as "humanist" drama.[29] What does separate the play from earlier moralities on the same theme is Medwall's treatment of the vices. Not only do they act out for the first time the convention of the virtuous pseudonym, but the ruse itself is made to stand for a complete psychology of sin. In *Nature* the name changes are less a device than an *idea* that pervades every aspect of the play. Man believes that Pride is really "Worship" and Gluttony nothing more than "Good Fellowship" because he wants to believe it. Their disguises represent man's own powers of rationalization. *Nature* is "a profoundly reassuring play" only if one forgets that it is an allegory. It is inaccurate to say, as Altman does, that Man "is misled into following evil counsel." Pride and Sloth and Lechery are not autonomous agents out to deceive Man; they are aspects of his own will. The play is a study in self-deception.

The rhetorical means developed by Medwall for conveying Man's willful ignorance are both verbal and visual. First, the verbal. The vices' duplicitous speeches, really expressions *in extenso* of their double names, objectify Man's self-serving ability to turn a vice into a virtue—or, if it suits his desire, a virtue into a vice. He accepts the World's sophistical argument that *not* to "follow the guise that now-a-day goeth . . . is but vanity" (58), as well as Sloth's perverse suggestion that the motive for hard work is actually covetousness:

> Your body laboureth as doth an hackney
> That beareth the burden every day,
> That pity it is to see;
> And your mind, on that other side,
> Is never idle, nor unoccupied.

> I wis it grieveth me
> To see you demeaned that wise:
> I trow ye be set all on covetise! (103)

The vices habitually speak in this way, inverting reason or the natural order of things. They call Man their "master" and themselves his "servants," when in fact the relationship is just the reverse.

Mistranslation is another instance of the same process. When Pride announces that Worship is the name he usually goes by, Sensuality responds,

> Worship, now, in faith, ye say true;
> Ye be *radix viciorum*—root of all virtue. (70)

When Bodily Lust proposes to Gluttony that they visit a local prostitute, Gluttony notes,

> They say she is *innupta mater*,
> Hardely an holy woman. (108)

Man himself joins the game. When he cannot think of a Latin euphemism for bald English *stew* (brothel), he asks Bodily Lust, "*Quid est Latinum propter le stewys?*"—though he is quick to deny that modesty is the cause, "Nay, nay. . . . I am as wanton as ever I was" (94). Elsewhere, on the same subject, he engages Sensuality in an extended "mistranslation" of Margery's new calling:

SENS.
> She hath entered into a religious place,
> At the Green Friars hereby.

MAN.
> Yea, has'e?
> Alack, good little wench!
> Is it an house of strait religion?

SENS.
> Yea, as any that ever was bygone
> Sith the world stood.

MAN.
> Be they close nuns as other be?

SENS.
> Close, quod a? nay, nay, parde!
> That guise were not good—
> Ye must beware of that gere!

Nay, all is open that they do there;
As open as a goose eye!

MAN.

And cometh any man into their cells?

SENS.

Yea, yea, God forbid else!
It is free for everybody;
And, beside all this, they be
Ex omni gente cognite. (92-93)

Margery herself knows how to wield a euphemism when necessary. Bodily Lust reports that when he applied to her the previous night on behalf of his master, Man, she turned him away with the excuse that everyone in the house was "asleep."

MAN.

How knowest thou whether they be asleep or no?

BOD. LUST.

Marry! she herself told me so
When I rapped at the door.

MAN.

It seemeth she was not asleep then.

BOD. LUST.

No! she was abed with a strange man. (97)

Still another expression of the vices' habit of turning language inside out is their slips of tongue. Gluttony is the most prone to this, owing, we may assume, to a constant state of inebriation. In one instance he seems unable to get his pronouns in order:

GLUT.

Sir! my fellow, Ease, commandeth me to you.

MAN.

Commandeth thee to me?

GLUT.

You to me!

MAN.

Me to thee!

GLUT.

Commandeth you to him, I would have said. (113-14)

Especially significant is Gluttony's reaction to the effects of Reason's "diet" on Man:

GLUT.
> His diet, quod a! it may be, verily:
> For ye be haltered marvellously—
> Altered, I would say. (107)

Gluttony's slip evokes the traditional image of reason as "haltering" or reining in bestial sensuality,[30] and subtly reawakens Man's fear, expressed earlier, that Reason is out "to bring me in captivity; / And to take from me my liberty" (104).

In developing a verbal rhetoric of vice, Medwall was also able to draw on a wide range of linguistic resources not available to nondramatic artists. The printed page does a poor job of communicating such important signs of meaning as voice quality (tone, pitch, inflection, volume), pacing (slow, fast), significant "noises" (a shriek, a clearing of the throat), and all the other oral devices that linguists have so inelegantly dubbed suprasegmental phonemes. The page cannot adequately convey Gluttony's slurred speech, or Pride's bombast, or Bodily Lust's insinuating tone. Of course, playwrights before Medwall had exploited the unique resources of speech. The ranting of Herod and the high voice of Pilate, for example, made these characters among the most popular of the medieval cycle plays.[31] Laughter is especially suited for dramatic purposes. Although it is not uncommon to find imitative sounds of laughter in written texts (one thinks, for example, of Alisoun's history-making "Tehee" in *The Miller's Tale*), we are far more likely to get a bare report: "she laughed." In a performance we hear the laugh itself. As V. A. Kolve observes, laughter is "a phenomenon not restricted to the drama, but the drama may reasonably be regarded as its *locus classicus*."[32] Yet late medieval playwrights (though certainly they tried to provoke laughter) do not seem to have given much thought to the expressive possibilities of laughter on stage; at least, the surviving manuscripts provide little evidence that they did.[33] Medwall is one of the earliest playwrights actually to write laughter into the dialogue of a play.[34] Significantly, it is the vices who laugh. In his initial appearance on stage (after calling attention to his scarlet gown and satin stomacher) Pride says,

> Some men would think that this were pride;
> But it is not so—ho, ho, abide! (68)

Just imagining the sensation that Man's fancy new apparel will cause among the town gallants makes Worldly Affection laugh:

> Ha, ha, ha! now by the Mary Virgin!
> This will set him on a merry pin. . . . (77)

Medwall did not invent the vice figure, but he made him laugh. In fact, in the subsequent history of the morality play, laughter becomes his trademark. As Spivack says: "No stage direction of the moralities is more common than that one which documents his hilarity: 'Here cometh in Crafty conueyaunce [and] Cloked colusyon with a lusty laughter' or 'Enter Inclination, laughing' or 'Here cometh enuye runnynge in Laughyng' or 'Here entereth Nichol Newfangle the Vice laughing.' And if one monosyllable can be said to be more frequent than any other in the moralities, it is the interminable 'ha, ha, ha' of the Vice's laughter, as he brays out to the audience the triumph of his guile" (1958, 163). Like his false name and his incongruous speech, the vice's laughter is a perversion. Its signification is not mirth or the ebullience of shared feelings but the very opposite—hurt, spite, hatred of community. The most hilarious character in *New Custom*—

> What? ha, ha, ha; I cannot tell for laughing—

is Cruelty.[35]

Although Medwall was not the first to exploit the verbal resources we have been discussing, he was mainly responsible for their consolidation in the drama. The changing of names, the mistranslating and misunderstanding, the mangling of words, the slips of tongue, the punning, the laughter—with *Nature* these became the stock elements in a distinctive rhetoric of vice.[36] Before Medwall, they occur sporadically; after Medwall, there is hardly a morality play that does not make use of most or all of them.

Equally important was Medwall's contribution to a *visual* rhetoric of vice, so that what audiences heard was reinforced by what they saw. The main component in the visual rhetoric of *Nature* is costume.[37] No previous literary or dramatic work uses dress so effectively to convey its ideas. Early in the play a "well-apparelled" figure appears on the stage and describes every detail of his lavish getup—the "colour of scarlet red," the "soft wool," the "stomacher of satin," the "short gown, with wide sleeves," "side hair half a wote beneath mine ear," a dagger purchased "at the mart," along with "a sword or twain," and so forth (66-69). The speech has the character of a rhetorical *descriptio*: we find similar inventories of dress in literary sources, such as *Sir Gawain and the Green Knight* and Chaucer's *Book of the Duchess*. But in length this speech, which covers some four dozen lines, has no precedent in the theater. Why does the audience need to be *told* what it can plainly see for itself? The speech is partly an exercise in self-definition, but it also serves to educate spectators to the ways in which apparel is used in the play. The speaker himself invites the audience to guess his identity on the basis of his clothing:

> How say ye, sirs, by mine array?
> Doth it please you, yea or nay?
> In the best wise, I dare well say!
> By that ye know me awhile. . . . (67)

As noted already, this game of "delayed identification" goes on at some length. Not until 130 lines after his appearance on stage does the figure give his name: Pride. Medwall thus constrains us to focus our attention initially on the *res* rather than the *nomen*, which, as he demonstrates throughout the play, is often untrustworthy. Indeed, no sooner has Pride revealed his name to Sensuality than he adds immediately, "But I am cleped Worship, commonly, in places where I dwell" (70).

Medwall's treatment of Pride's clothing, though grounded in the traditional iconography of the vice, was sufficiently novel to inspire a host of imitations, such as the treatment of Vanity in the anonymous *Contention between Liberality and Prodigality*. His originality shows more clearly, however, in the way he extends the image to embrace Man, whose own clothing undergoes several changes in the course of the play to signify changes in his moral condition. Something of this sort had been attempted in *Mankind*—the title hero's jacket is progressively shortened as he falls under the influence of New Guise and his no-good companions[38]—but Medwall carries the device to unprecedented length. It is the leitmotif of the play. When Man first appears on the scene, The World reacts with mock astonishment, "O, benedicite! Ye be all naked!"

MAN.
> I thank you; but I need none other vesture;
> Nature hath clothed me as yet sufficiently.
> Guiltless of sin, and as a maiden pure,
> I wear on me the garment of innocency. (57)

"The garment of innocency," The World points out reasonably enough, is inadequate protection against the elements ("this is not paradise" [57]), but then his argument slides into sophistry as he turns virtue into vice, innocence into vanity. Whoever lives in the world, he argues,

> must himself apply
> To worldly things; and be of such condition
> As all men be; and leave each fond opinion
> That is not approvable of wiser men than he;
> To take such way it is but vanity.
> Take this garment! man, do as I you bid! (58)

As soon as Man puts on his new garment, The World exclaims, "You be a goodly one. . . Worth a thousand that ye were beforne." The message is clear. Man's "worth" is all invested in his clothing, that is, in how he appears to the rest of the world. In himself he is nothing. This is the recurring theme of his education. The lesson is reinforced by Pride, who, playing on Man's anxious need for approval, first flatters him that "all men . . . give you a praising good" (73), and then ridicules his new clothing for being more than two days out of fashion:

> But, in faith! I like not your array;
> It is not the fashion that goeth now-a-day,
> For now there is a new guise.
> It is now two days agone
> Sith that men began this fashion,
> And every knave had it anon;
> Therefore, at this season,
> There is no man that setteth thereby
> If he love his own honesty. (76)

Pride's appeal to Man's "honesty" gains ironic force as he launches into an enthusiastic description of the new gown he has in mind for his client, "a gown / That all the gallants, in this town, / Shall on the fashion wonder" (77). The whole purpose of this vice-turned-couturier ("I have none other study a-days / But how I may new fashions find") is empty show. His life's motto? "Clothes make the man." Since Man lives at this same level of profundity, the vices' first reaction to his new apparel is all that he could have hoped for: they do not recognize him. "Why?" he asks, "Because I have changed mine array?" Gluttony protests, "Nay, nay! That is not the thing / That can deceive me."[39] Gluttony has no trouble at all seeing through the alterations of vice. In the morality tradition vice always recognizes vice.[40] What confuses him temporarily—"the thing," he hints, "that can deceive me"—are the alterations of virtue. "For ye be haltered marvellously—Altered, I would say. . . . Ye look now as it were a ghost," Gluttony declares, as he takes in the effects of the diet prescribed by Reason (107). Man's final change of clothing occurs near the end of the play as he sheds Pride for Meekness. As part of his penance Meekness tells him, "Thou must, before all thing, set little prize / By thine own self; and take no heed / Whether the people do thee praise or despise. . . . / And use none array that staring is to sight!" (124). "From this day forth," Man announces, "I will set them aside"; and at this point we may assume (though rubrics are lacking) that he removes his excessive finery on the spot as a sign of true penitence.

There are several points to be made about Medwall's handling of costume. The relation between Pride and Man, rhetorically speaking, is chiastic. Pride changes his name but not his clothing; Man changes his clothing but not his name. In both cases the intent is to deceive, however, and Medwall's equation of the two kinds of change paves the way for their conflation by subsequent playwrights. Medwall suggests the linkage of names and clothing in a couple of ways. For one thing Sensuality's report that the vices have changed their names is followed immediately by Pride's announcement that he must leave to "make some provision / Of garments after the new invention" (83). For another, the word itself that is used to describe the vices' change of names is a term of clothing: "And Covetise, to eschew all blame, / Doth his name *disguise*, / And calleth himself Worldly Policy" (81). To "disguise" originally meant "to dress in newfangled, elaborate, or showy attire" (*MED* 1[a]) and somewhat later "to transform . . . in outward appearance" (*MED* 2c.[a]). Both meanings were current in Medwall's day (and indeed the costume dramas or *tableaux vivants* so popular throughout the sixteenth century were called "disguisings"). By his showy attire Pride is "disguised" in one sense of the word, and then in another by his adoption of the pseudonym Worship. In this instance semantic change reflected historical change. During most of the Middle Ages the relation between dress and status was constant, but in the late fourteenth century clothes ceased to be a reliable badge of identity. Moralists condemned the change, preachers railed against it from the pulpit, Parliament even called for "the reformation of excessive array."[41] A contemporary observer sums up the feeling behind these reactions:

> [T]he elation of the inferior people in dress and accoutrements in these days [is such] that one person cannot be discerned from another in splendour of dress or belongings, neither poor from rich, nor servant from master, nor priest from layman, but everybody tried to imitate the other, till the magnates had to decide on a remedy.[42]

What the "magnates" did was pass a law, in fact a series of laws (beginning in 1363) that attempted to regulate dress according to one's annual income. But parliamentary efforts to legislate a dress code for the nation proved to be unenforceable. Such efforts only contributed to the belief that clothes do, indeed, make the man.

Medwall's use of fashion in *Nature* signals a major advance in the iconography of the theater. From the beginning playwrights had garbed *dramatis personae* in clothing appropriate to their gender, status, occupation, and so forth.[43] In this they reflected social custom. With its collapse, however, they were free to employ costumes as more arbitrary signs. The failure of sumptuary legislation is personified, so to speak, in the classless dandies of *Mankind*, New-Guise and Nowadays. Yet the dramatic connection between clothing and identity remains relatively stable throughout the fifteenth century. Even in *Nature* the clothing of both Pride and Man is presented as an accurate sign of the inner reality, but it is now a sign contaminated by its brush with the convention of false names. Subsequent playwrights came to realize that apparel could be used to *question* as well as reinforce a character's speech and behavior. In Skelton's *Magnificence* (1513-16), clearly influenced by Medwall's example, the vices change both their names and their clothing. Courtly Abusion disguises himself as a courtier "Properly dressed, / All point-device," and then asks his fellow vice Fancy, "But what shall I call my name?" Fancy replies, "Cock's heart, turn thee, let me see thine array. . . . Mary, Lusty Pleasure, by mine advice, / To name thyself."[44] In Bale's *King John* (1530-36), changes of name and costume work together to further the author's anti-Catholic propaganda. Private Wealth dresses as a cardinal (Pandulphus), and then just seventy-eight lines later, as Nobility.[45] As Glynne Wickham observes, "Bale thus succeeds in equating Nobility with Private Wealth in a way that spectators can remark with their eyes. . . . [W]hat these characters then say becomes instantly recognizable as the hypocritical and seditious cant that Bale intends it to be. In short, visual and verbal image are here so juxtaposed as to contradict each other flatly."[46] Since Wickham offers a generous survey of the use of changed names and costumes in the Tudor morality, there is no need to multiply examples here. I will simply quote from his excellent conclusion on the device: "It was a technique that depended in very large measure on the willing collaboration of spectators who were as well trained in the theatrical iconography of stage costume and disguise as were the play-makers and the actors themselves, and who entered a playhouse expecting to 'read' a play with their eyes as well as with their ears" (1981, 109).

•   •   •

Medwall's efforts to create a definitive rhetoric or "theatrical iconography" for masquerading vice were guided by the traditional meaning of the convention. From the beginning this figure had stood for the human will's elastic ability to rationalize its own wicked desires. The crucial question raised by Avarice's temporary triumph in the *Psychomachia* is why were the virtues fooled in the first place? Prudentius's answer is quite extraordinary. If the virtues could not tell Avarice from Thrift, it was because they had not totally extinguished the "lust for gain" in themselves (*Psychomachia*, 321). At some level they *wanted* to confuse the two. "The psychology of this may not seem to us profound," C. S. Lewis remarks, but "we must remember how rarely we find in classical literature any adequate recognition of the great fact of self-deception."[47] In Gregory's drama of the internal warfare, as we have seen already, "the great fact of self-deception" assumes the central role. Man's natural concupiscence invites the shading of every vice into a virtue. The casualty is self-knowledge. Gregory warns that choleric people often "think that the goad of anger is zeal for righteousness; and when vice is thought to be virtue, guilt accumulates without apprehension"; that the impatient "hardly recognize the evil they have done"; that talkative people, always chattering, dissipate "the power to return inwardly to self-knowledge."[48] Self-deceived, the sinner has no motive for reform. One of a pastor's weightiest responsibilities, therefore, is to lead his flock to recognize their sins *as sins*. They must be taught to examine their consciences carefully. The most effective instrument is penitence, which Gregory describes, characteristically, as a medical procedure. "These vices which the old enemy hides under the semblance of virtues," he says, "are very minutely examined by the hand of compunction."[49] In Gregory's view of sin, the vices' masquerade and man's penitence are opposing attitudes or states of mind. If the disguises of vice are really the products of a corrupt will seeking to rationalize its own desire, then only a penitent will seeking to fulfill the divine purpose can adequately defend against them. The Gregorian scheme serves as the psychological basis of Langland's great poem. Throughout *Piers Plowman* the Will's search for "truth" is linked with a nearly unbroken procession of ambiguous sins; and in the final apocalyptic scene, a reprise of the *Psychomachia* itself, the triumph of the deceitful vices is built on the failure of penitence. The "hand of compunction" has ceased to do its job. Instead a false confessor named Friar Flatterer, like a physician probing a wound, "gropeþ Contricion" and then administers "a plastre of a pryuee paiement."[50] So easy are the friar's prescribed penances that, over time, "Contricion hadde clene foryeten to crye and to wepe." Contrition is no longer contrite. Like masquerading

vice itself, he is now a *nomen sine re*, the last and most fateful in a long
succession of empty signifiers in the poem.[51]

When Medwall adapted the convention of the virtuous pseudonym
to the stage, he borrowed a history as well—a penitential context. The
masquerade of sin is more than a clever device. It is an emblem of the
psychological matrix out of which the entire play develops. As I said
before, *Nature* is a study in self-deception. Nowhere is this point made
more explicitly than in the final scene of the play, constructed, as tradition would have it, on the medical imagery of penitence. Reason,
man's physician, prescribes the treatment for his "sores":

> But do as I shall tell thee, and have no dread;
> And, for to give thee medicines most according
> Ayenst thy sores, do by my rede.
> Look! what disease is hot and brenning
> Take ever such a medicine as is cold in working;
> So that the contrary, in all manner of wise,
> Must heal his contrary, as physic doth devise. (121-22)

Reason's prescription is an elaboration of the principle he enunci-
ated at the beginning of the play (part two), "*Quia contraria contrariis
curantur*," an elaboration indeed of his very name—in Latin, *ratio*,
"order, symmetry." Against pride, as we noted earlier, Man must practice meekness; against wrath, patience; and so forth. "But how shall I
know them?" Man anxiously inquires. Reason's response lays bare the
epistemological ground of the play: "Thou shalt know them at the
first meeting. / Of contraries there is but one learning" (123). The
meaning here is so apparent that we are liable to overlook the
enabling presumption that Man *already knows the sins for what they are.*
He is not fooled in the least. After all, the vices never had any independent existence. Pride and his confederates are only the projections of Man's will; and their "disguises" merely his own
rationalizations. Once Man turns his mind to penitence, the vices
have no further role in the play. The action reflects standard penitential doctrine. "For if the heart feels true sorrow," Gregory had taught
long before, "the vices have no tongue against it. And when the life of
uprightness is sought with an entire aim, the fruitless prompting of
evil is closed up."[52]

If merely the recognition of sin were the issue in *Nature*, it might
be true, as Altman supposes, that Man "is misled into following evil
counsel" and that his error "only warns us that vigilance is necessary."
Because perception is colored by desire, however, vigilance is not
enough. Man cannot see what he does not wish to see. This became

the central fact in the psychology of masquerading vice, though subsequent playwrights recognized that willful ignorance is a matter of
degree. One of the questions raised in Wager's *The Longer Thou Livest
The More Fool Thou* (1560-68), for example, is whether the masquerade is even necessary in extreme cases like those who "had lever to
folly and idleness fall / Than to harken to sapience." Wrath says to his
fellow sins that Moros, the central character, is such a fool that "Little
needeth this device":

> To be called by our names is as good.
> Doth he know what Idleness doth mean?
> Knoweth he Incontinency to be lechery?
> He discerneth not clean from unclean;
> His mind is all set on foolery.[53]

Like Moros, Medwall's protagonist also has a mind "set on foolery,"
but the causes are different. Moros is represented as the product of
parental neglect and bad schooling, one of those "many past cure /
That nothing can their crookedness rectify" (lines 47-48). Self-knowledge is impossible. Penitence is out of the question. At the end of the
play Moros is carried off by Confusion to "eternal fire / Due for fools
that be impenitent" (lines 1849-50). By contrast the central figure in
Nature is more representative of humankind, and the cause of his sickness, more general. In lording it over his servants, in posing as a
lady's man, in seeking to impress the town gallants by his wardrobe,
Man is motivated—so the allegory suggests—by pride. Yet something
more is involved. What really tempts Man, as we can infer from his
sense of personal inferiority ("every man is fresher than I") or his
consuming eagerness to change his appearance ("let us go to see my
new apparel"), is the allure of a new identity (76, 105). His response
to the failure of his own servant Gluttony to recognize him is a definitive moment: "Why? Because I have changed mine array?" (107). The
question rings with a pathetic hope. Man wants to be someone other
than himself. When in the end he turns to penitence at the prompting of Age, the import is not only that he has redirected his will but
also that he has acknowledged finally who and what he is.

● ● ●

The dramaturgical importance of *Nature* has yet to be acknowledged. F. P. Wilson's assessment of the play is a fair sample of critical
opinion: "As the author of *Nature*, Medwall would barely merit a mention in the history of our drama, but as the author of *Fulgens and*

Lucrece, the first purely secular English play that has survived, he is a significant figure."[54] *Nature* may appeal less to our modern (and "secular") taste than *Fulgens*, but its influence in the history of English drama was far greater. The play not only transformed the morality—redefining the traditional psychomachia as a *collusion* rather than an assault, a masquerade in which man is seen to be a full and willing participant—but it probably helped to keep the genre alive for another hundred years. More important, even after allegorical drama had run its course, the stage career of its popular villain continued to prosper. Masquerading vice did not fade with the dramatic vehicle that had made him a star. He simply evolved into something else. Still misrepresenting himself as virtuous, still plying his sophistries, still misconstruing words and events in order to deceive, he is reincarnated as Shakespeare's Iago, Richard III, and even Sir John Falstaff, who was, as Bernard Spivack first recognized, "originally a personification, or a set of cognate personifications, to whom, because he was too theatrically attractive to die with the dramatic convention to which he originally belonged, Shakespeare gave a local habitation and a name."[55]

Notes

1. The quotation is by Tucker Brooke, in Albert C. Baugh, ed., *A Literary History of England* (New York: Appleton-Century-Crofts, 1948), 358.
2. John S. Farmer, ed., *"Lost" Tudor Plays* (London: EEDS, 1907), 73 (original reading *or* changed here to *ere* for clarity). All subsequent quotations from *Nature* are from this edition (cited by page number).
3. Baugh, *A Literary History*, 359.
4. The dates are taken from Bernard Spivack's appendix, "Bibliography of Morality Plays," in his *Shakespeare and the Allegory of Evil* (New York: Columbia University Press, 1958), 483-93.
5. Spivack, *Shakespeare and the Allegory of Evil*, 159.
6. A. P. Rossiter, *English Drama from Early Times to the Elizabethans* (New York: Barnes and Noble, [1950] 1967), 134-35. For the *Psychomachia* see H. J. Thomson, trans. *Prudentius*, Loeb Classical Library (Cambridge: Harvard University Press, 1949), 274-343.
7. F. P. Wilson, *The English Drama 1485-1585*, The Oxford History of English Literature (Oxford: Oxford University Press, 1969), 22. The figure may be seen as the product of allegorical discourse itself. Beginning with the account in Genesis, sin has always been identified with deception; and it is only natural that in the context of allegory, a literary mode based on the very idea of *naming*, such deception should take the form of a false name. Moreover, equivocation has always been an inseparable part of the idea of allegory, defined broadly by the ancients as "saying one thing and meaning another"; and in classical discussions of allegory

as a trope we can discern already the outlines of Medwall's personification of Pride / Worship. "An allegory is drawn from a contrast," says the *Rhetorica ad Herennium* (IV.xxxiv.46), "if, for example, one should mockingly call a spendthrift and voluptuary frugal and thrifty" (trans. Harry Caplan, Loeb Classical Library [London: Heinemann, 1954], 345). Similarly Quintilian in the *Institutio oratoria* (VIII.vi.57): "Further, we may employ *allegory*, and disguise bitter taunts in gentle words by way of wit, or we may indicate our meaning by saying exactly the contrary" (trans. H. E. Butler, Loeb Classical Library [Cambridge: Harvard University Press, (1921) 1986], 333). This understanding of allegory—what normally we would call irony—survives in the rhetorical manuals of the Middle Ages. John of Garland's *Parisiana poetria* (ca. 1231-34), to cite only one instance, is particularly suggestive of equivocating vice: "By Allegory a miser is called a philanthropist, or vice versa. Here a dog—no, a wolf—goes about, passing for a shepherd; he is bent on tearing apart the flock" (trans. Traugott Lawler [New Haven: Yale University Press, 1974], 129).

8. *Pastoral Care*, trans. Henry Davis, in Ancient Christian Writers No. 11 (Westminster, Maryland: Newman Press, 1950), 78.

9. See, for example, his comment on the armor of Behemoth (the devil) in Job 40:13:

> *His cartilage as plates of iron.* For what but his simulation is understood by cartilage? For cartilage presents the appearance of bone, but it has not the strength of bone. And there are some vices which present an appearance of rectitude, but which proceed from the weakness of sin. For the malice of our enemy clokes itself with such art, as frequently to make faults appear as virtues before the eyes of the deluded mind; so that a person expects, as it were, rewards, for the very conduct for which he deserves to meet with eternal punishment. For cruelty is frequently exercised in punishing sins, and it is counted justice; and immoderate anger is believed to be the meritoriousness of righteous zeal. . . . Frequently negligent remissness is regarded as gentleness and forbearance. . . . Lavishness is sometimes believed to be compassion. . . . Tenacity is sometimes considered frugality. . . . The pertinacity of the wicked is often termed constancy. . . . Inconstancy is often regarded as tractability. . . . Sometimes incompetent fear is believed to be humility. . . . Sometimes haughtiness of voice is counted freedom for the truth. . . . Sloth is frequently looked upon as a maintenance of peace. . . . Restlessness of spirit is frequently termed a watchful solicitude. . . . Slowness in promoting goodness, is counted judgment. . . . Since, therefore, error is corrected with more difficulty, when it is believed to be a virtue, it is rightly said, *His cartilage as plates of iron.* (*Morals on the Book of Job,* in A Library of Fathers of the Holy Catholic Church [Oxford: Parker, 1850], 4:544-46)

10. The treatise begins, "Est via que homini videtur recta, nouissime autem illius. . . (Prov. 14.12). Nam secundum beatum Gregorium III° Moralium multa sunt vitia que sub specie virtutum"—quoted in Richard

Newhauser, *The Treatise on Vices and Virtues in Latin and the Vernacular,* Typologie des sources du moyen âge occidental, fasc. 68 (Turnhout: Brepols, 1993), 46. I am grateful to Professor Newhauser for calling this treatise to my attention. A brief biographical notice of Henricus, also known as Henricus de Urimaria, appears in Johannes Trithemius, *Liber de Ecclesiasticis Scriptoribus,* included in J. A. Fabricius, *Bibliotheca Ecclesiastica* (Farnborough, Hampshire: Gregg, [1718] 1967), 141.

11. The standard history of venal satire, J. A. Yunck's *The Lineage of Lady Meed* (Notre Dame: University of Notre Dame Press, 1963) fails to note the *Psychomachia* as an important source of personifications of avarice.

12. Lines 109-16. Ed. K. S. Block, EETS, e.s. 120 (London: Oxford University Press, 1960), 228.

13. *The Macro Plays,* ed. Mark Eccles, EETS 262 (London: Oxford University Press, 1969), 133-34. It should also be noted, although no masquerade is involved, that the three principal figures in this play are renamed after their fall: Mind becomes "Maintenance," Understanding "Perjury," and Will "Gentle Fornication."

14. *The Digby Plays,* ed. F. J. Furnivall, EETS, e.s. 70 (London: Oxford University Press, [1898] 1967), 73-75. The term *hybrid* is Spivack's to describe plays that combine allegorical and literal characters (*Shakespeare and the Allegory of Evil,* 251-303).

15. A. C. Cawley, ed., *Everyman and Medieval Miracle Plays* (New York: Dutton, 1959), 214. There is disagreement about whether *Everyman* was intended as closet drama only.

16. Probably the most notable instance occurs in the Wakefield *Second Shepherds' Play,* where Mak tries to fool the shepherds by wearing a cloak over his usual dress (*Tunc intrat mak, in clamide se super togam vestitus*) and by adopting an odd southern accent. See *The Towneley Plays,* ed. George England, with notes and introduction by A. W. Pollard, EETS, e.s. 71 (London: Oxford University Press, [1897] 1966), 122-23.

17. *Anonymous Plays,* ed. John S. Farmer (London: EEDS, 1906), 211-12.

18. For earlier literary examples of the convention, see such allegories as *Winner and Waster, Piers Plowman,* and Lydgate's translation of Deguileville's *Pèlerinage de la vie humaine.*

19. *A Select Collection of Old English Plays, originally published by Robert Dodsley in the year 1744,* 4th ed., rev. and enlarged by W. Carew Hazlitt (London: Reeves and Turner, 1874), vol. 8.

20. Hazlitt, *A Select Collection of Old English Plays,* 3:318.

21. Roy MacKenzie, *The English Moralities from the Point of View of Allegory,* Harvard Studies in English 2 (New York: Gordian, [1914] 1966), 263. When MacKenzie wrote this in 1914, the caveat was especially necessary. Criticism did indeed treat these plays as texts to be read. Just three years earlier, for example, Tucker Brooke had filled his book on *The Tudor Drama* (Boston: Houghton Mifflin, 1911) with statements like the following. Of Wager's *Magdalene* he says, "The only readable portion is that which depicts the perversion of Mary by the vices . . ." (113), and of Merbury's *Wit and Wisdom,* he writes, "The poet has managed to get into

the piece enough of irrelevant farce and melodramatic interest to make it tolerable reading" (77).

22. Joel Altman, *The Tudor Play of Mind* (Berkeley: University of California Press, 1978), 13-17.

23. The comparison is often made (e.g., MacKenzie, *The English Moralities*, 70).

24. Farmer, *"Lost" Tudor Plays*, 48 (italics mine). Sensuality stresses repeatedly that he is "natural" and "the chief perfection of [man's] nature."

25. The standard work on theatrical doubling in Tudor drama is David Bevington, *From Mankind to Marlowe* (Cambridge: Harvard University Press, 1962). Covetise does not appear in person, a curious omission, but it is referred to by the other sins and in the concluding parade of the virtues.

26. See Newhauser, *The Treatise on Vices and Virtues*, 120. Gluttony's remark to Bodily Lust makes the "concatenation" explicit: "I must / Sometime follow the wanton lust . . . For hot drinks and delicate refection / Causeth fleshly insurrection" (106).

27. The medical metaphor is familiar to all readers of Shakespeare; cf. Sonnet 147, "My reason the physician to my love, / Angry that his prescriptions are not kept / Hath left me. . . ." The imagery is discussed further in this essay, 169-70.

28. Processions of the sins are quite common (e.g., *Piers Plowman*, Marlowe's *Faustus*); those of the virtues are less so. The treatment of both together in contrasting pairs, as here, is a medieval commonplace. See, for example, the sculptural programs of the cathedrals of Amiens and Paris, in Emile Mâle, *The Gothic Image: Religious Art in France of the Thirteenth Century*, trans. Dora Nussey (New York: Harper, 1958), 98-130.

29. E.g., Altman, *The Tudor Play of Mind*, 13; Brooke, *The Tudor Drama*, 73, and again in Baugh, *A Literary History*, 359. Brooke asserts that the moral theme of *Nature* "is discussed from a purely ethical, not religious standpoint," and that the play's emphasis on reason, bolstered by references to Aristotle, reflects "the new influences in scholarship" (*The Tudor Drama*, 73)—as if the Renaissance discovered reason and the writings of Aristotle. A small dose of Aquinas is needed here. Nobody familiar with medieval theology—or even with more popular works such as Alan of Lille's *De planctu Naturae*, the *Roman de la rose*, or *Piers Plowman*—could make a statement like the following: "Man sins, not because he alienates himself from God, but because he dethrones Reason" (ibid.). It is also difficult to see how any view of repentance that requires the sacrament of confession, as *Nature* does, can be characterized as "purely ethical." For other arguments against the use of "humanist" to describe early Tudor drama, see Wilson, *The English Drama*, 8.

30. For a discussion of the image, see V. A. Kolve, *Chaucer and the Imagery of Narrative: The First Five Canterbury Tales* (Stanford: Stanford University Press, 1984), 237-48.

31. As Arnold Williams has observed, "All English Pilates seem to have been ranters, who boasted of their prowess and threatened the crowd, in the same manner as Herod. . . . So common was the characterization of

Pilate as a raging tyrant that Chaucer could consider 'Pilates voys' an adequate description of the cry of the drunken Miller" (*The Characterization of Pilate in the Towneley Plays* [East Lansing: Michigan State College Press, 1950], 14).

32. V. A. Kolve, *The Play Called Corpus Christi* (Stanford: Stanford University Press, 1966), 124.

33. Kolve makes the distinction between laughter in the audience and among the players, but curiously in a chapter titled "Religious Laughter," he does not mention a single play that calls on an actor to laugh.

34. The issue is not certain. It is hard to say whether the words "A ha!" in *Wisdom* (Eccles, *Macro Plays*, 129) and in *Mankind* (*Medieval Drama*, ed. David Bevington [Boston: Houghton Mifflin, 1975], 925) indicate laughter or not.

35. Hazlitt, *A Select Collection of Old English Plays*, 3 :34.

36. As Lois Potter observes, "Good characters are divided from bad by their ability to understand allegory. The Vices' favourite trick is to take literally the abstract language of a virtuous character" (*The Revels History of Drama in English*, by Norman Sanders, et al. [London: Methuen, 1980], 2:155). Puttenham refers to "conterfaite vices" in his *Art of English Poesy* (1589) as "*Pantomini*"—"and all that had before bene sayd, or great part of it, they gave a crosse construction to it very ridiculously" (quoted in Potter, *The Revels History*, 171-72).

37. Other elements, not discussed here, would include makeup, props, scenery, the symbolic use of color, and so forth.

38. Farmer, *"Lost" Tudor Plays*, 30-32.

39. Farmer, *"Lost" Tudor Plays*, 107. Glynne Wickham states, inexplicably, that the vices fail to recognize Man because of his new clothes. He says it twice. "When . . . Man has put them on, his servants fail to recognize him until Gluttony realizes what has happened" (*Early English Stages 1300 to 1660* [London: Routledge, 1981], 3:94, cf. 101. But Gluttony's remark makes it clear that Man's attire has nothing to do with the confusion.

40. MacKenzie, *The English Moralities*, 193.

41. On Parliament's role, see May McKisack, *The Fourteenth Century 1307-1399*, Volume 5 of *The Oxford History of England* (Oxford: Clarendon, 1959), 346.

42. F. R. H. DuBoulay, *An Age of Ambition: English Society in the Late Middle Ages* (New York: Viking, 1970), 67.

43. The Fleury play of the scene at the Lord's sepulchre (twelfth century) specifies that three brethren of the monastery should be "*prepared and vested in imitation of the three Marys*" (Bevington, *Medieval Drama*, 39); the N-Town passion play directs that the high priest Annas should be "*beseyn after a busshop of the hoold lawe in a skarlet gowne, and over that a blew tabbard furryd with white, and a mitere on his hed, after the hoold lawe* (Bevington, 486); and the author of *Mankind*, perhaps the most original of the early playwrights in his use of clothing, symbolizes the title hero's lapse into sin by having his jacket cut shorter and shorter "after the new guise" (Bevington, 928-29).

44. *The Complete Poems of John Skelton,* ed. Philip Henderson (London: Dent, 1959), 195.
45. *The Dramatic Writings of John Bale,* ed. J. S. Farmer (London: EEDS, 1907), 218, 221.
46. Wickham, *Early English Stages 1300-1660,* 3:104.
47. C. S. Lewis, *The Allegory of Love* (New York: Oxford University Press, [1936] 1958), 71.
48. Davis, *Pastoral Care,* 137, 107, 132.
49. *Morals on the Book of Job,* 1:175.
50. *Piers Plowman: The B Version,* ed. George Kane and E. Talbot Donaldson (London: Athlone, 1975), 679.
51. *Nomen sine re* is the formula established at the beginning of the poem for describing counterfeit identities. One of the questions posed in the B Prologue, in what looks like a coronation, is whether a king whose behavior is *un*kingly can be called a king at all. According to a certain "Goliard" on the scene (lines 139-42), "*Dum rex a regere dicatur nomen habere / Nomen habet sine re nisi studet iura tenere*" ("Since the name of king, *rex,* comes from *regere,* 'to rule,' he has a name without the reality unless he works diligently to maintain the laws"). Medieval political theorists were not slow to appreciate the practical implications of this well-known tag: though law may forbid the deposition of a king, it does not protect the tyrant who merely hides behind the name of king. Langland's use of the *nomen sine re* formula is also political at first, a warning to the newly crowned monarch (presumably Richard II), but it quickly develops into a moral touchstone as the allegory thickens with more and more names.
52. *Morals on the Book of Job,* 1:175-76.
53. *The Longer Thou Livest and Enough Is as Good as a Feast,* ed. R. Mark Benbow (Lincoln: University of Nebraska Press, 1967), 31 (lines 689-94).
54. Wilson, *The English Drama,* 7.
55. Spivack, *Shakespeare and the Allegory of Evil,* 91.

Plays, Players and Playwrights in Renaissance Oxford

John R. Elliott, Jr.

The recent publication of the records of dramatic activity at Cambridge University by Alan H. Nelson has made available a large amount of evidence, much of it appearing in print for the first time, about the extensive part that drama played in the education of Cambridge students, particularly during the high tide of humanism in sixteenth-century England.[1] Beginning in the 1540s drama at Oxford, largely following the model provided by Cambridge, also played an increasingly important role both in college life and in the public life of the university, until by the time of the Stuart monarchs Oxford actually eclipsed Cambridge as a site of innovative theatrical activity in England. Thanks to the stimulus of the Records of Early English Drama project (REED), of which Arnold Williams was a godfather, it is now possible to give a survey of Oxford plays, players, and playwrights during this period, in the light of the considerable new evidence that has come to our attention in recent years.

Drama and the Humanist Curriculum

Drama in Tudor Oxford had no formal faculty, but it still managed to attach itself to the arts curriculum at an early date. In 1512 a bachelor named Edward Watson was admitted to master's status and allowed to teach in the School of Grammar on condition that he write a comedy (*comediam*) and 100 songs (*carmina*) in praise of the university.[2] By 1640, more than 100 years later, this practice had apparently become so widespread that at Christ Church a student named Martin Llewellyn wrote that he had composed a play and presented it to his dean in order to "begge degree," a custom he described as "bringing a Trifle to receive a Hood."[3] In the meantime

179

Christ Church had instituted a requirement that its undergraduates should give annual performances of two comedies and two tragedies, one of each pair in Latin and the other in Greek. Payments for these productions are recorded in the Christ Church treasurer's accounts from 1554 to 1587.[4] Although the accounts after 1587 are lost, it seems likely that the Latin performances, at least, continued well beyond that year, since William Gager, Christ Church's leading humanist playwright, wrote two Latin plays, *Ulysses Redux* and *Hippolytus*, for performance by the students in 1592, and as late as 1598 Francis Meres could still call Gager "one of the best for comedy amongst us."[5]

All of these quasi-curricular plays were in Greek or Latin and reflected the humanist conception of the practical value that drama was thought to have in the training of young men for public life, either in the church or the state. Plays were regarded as a branch of rhetoric, whose educational function was to hone the skills of the future preacher, orator, and statesman in the classical style. In Oxford this educational philosophy was best put by Gager in a letter written in 1592:

> [Plays serve] to practice our own style either in prose or verse; to be well acquainted with Seneca or Plautus; honestly to embolden our path; to try their voices and confirm their memories; to frame their speech; to conform them to convenient action; to try what mettle is in every one, and of what disposition they are of; whereby never any one amongst us, that I know, was made the worse, many have been much the better; as I dare report me to all the University.[6]

The recipient of Gager's letter, John Rainolds of Corpus Christi College, was a vigorous opponent of stage plays, as was Stephen Gosson, another graduate of the same college. In Oxford, however, the objections of such critics fell largely on deaf ears, at least as far as student plays went. The occasional bans by the authorities against play-acting in Oxford were always aimed solely at itinerant professional companies, not at student actors. A letter from the chancellor, the earl of Leicester, to Congregation in 1584, for example, endorsing the reform of various disorders in the university, approved a ban against traveling actors but explicitly exempted student plays from the order. These Leicester declared to be "commendable and great furtherances of learning," and he even recommended that they be "continued at set times and increased, and the youth of the university by good means to be encouraged in the decent and frequent setting forth of them."[7] A similar order from the Privy Council in 1593 was directed only at professional players and made no mention of student plays.[8] There was, in fact, a notable increase in the number of play productions in Oxford during the first two decades of the seventeenth century, at a time when the Puritan opponents of the stage in Cambridge were succeeding in reducing their number there.

The academic plays that Gager and Leicester commended took place principally in those colleges with large numbers of undergraduates to draw on, such as Christ Church, Magdalen, and St. John's. These colleges also had halls large enough to accommodate the audiences, which were not always confined to members of the college. (The modern practice of performing plays outdoors in college gardens during the summer was unknown in Tudor Oxford.) The vast majority of student plays were put on during the Christmas season, beginning sometimes as early as November and often extending to Candelmas or Shrovetide. Since they were considered quasi-curricular, the plays were supported financially and their performances regulated by the governing bodies of the colleges.

Some student plays were written by students themselves, although their names were seldom recorded unless they subsequently presented them to their dons as "degree plays," in the manner of Edward Watson and Martin Llewellyn. Better known, because better documented, are the plays written for student actors by their dons, who tried to maintain their amateur profile by keeping their works unpublished. William Gager was a notable exception to this rule, as was Nicholas Grimald, Oxford's first known playwright, who emigrated from Cambridge to Brasenose and Christ Church in the late 1540s, and who published two Latin biblical dramas under his own name, though he was prudent enough in those troublesome times to have them printed in Germany. The names of many other Oxford playwrights can be recovered from manuscript texts, letters, and diaries:

Robert Burton
James Calfhill
William Cartwright
Richard Edes
William Gager
Thomas Goffe
Nicholas Grimald } Christ Church
Barten Holiday
Leonard Hutten
Toby Mathew
Robert Mead
William Strode

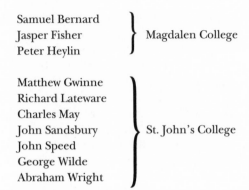

Samuel Bernard
Jasper Fisher   } Magdalen College
Peter Heylin

Matthew Gwinne
Richard Lateware
Charles May
John Sandsbury   } St. John's College
John Speed
George Wilde
Abraham Wright

All of the plays written by these authors, whether Latin classics or humanist dramas on biblical, secular, or allegorical subjects, were written exclusively for the use of student actors, not for any profit that might be gained from either the printed page or the professional stage. Conversely, the student actors never performed any plays written for the professional theaters in London, not even those of Ben Jonson, who was awarded an honorary M.A. by the university in 1619. The only Oxford playwright who did eventually see a professional production of one of his works was William Cartwright, a lecturer in metaphysics at Christ Church. His tragicomedy, *The Royal Slave*, originally performed in Christ Church for the visit of King Charles I to the university in 1636, was revived later in that year at Queen Henrietta Maria's request for a private performance by the Queen's Men at Hampton Court Palace, but only with the university's proviso that Oxford's "costumes" (and presumably the rest of the play's furnishings as well) should not thereafter be worn "upon any mercenary stage."[9] By carefully maintaining the distinction between educational drama and the work of common players, Oxford managed to preserve its humanist theatrical tradition right down to the eve of the Civil War.

College Entertainments

Such was the official face of Oxford drama. It would, however, be a mistake to think that academic plays were the only, or even the main, type of theatrical offering that a member of the university would see during his residence in Tudor-Stuart Oxford. Many plays were put on primarily for entertainment, with the secondary practical purpose of keeping the students occupied during the long Christmas holidays, when travel home was difficult and often limited by college statutes.

The fullest record of such entertainments is a manuscript preserved in the St. John's College library now generally referred to as *The Christmas Prince.*[10] This unique work is an untitled anthology of play-texts with connecting narratives, commemorating the performance of eight different plays by the students of St. John's over the Christmas vacation of 1607-8, on a scale to match the revels of the Inns of Court in London, on which they were clearly modeled. As at the Inns, the individual plays marked the stages of a larger festive occasion, the election, coronation, and reign of a Christmas Prince, or Lord of Misrule, who in this year was a bachelor of arts named Thomas Tucker.

The eight plays began as early as 30 November and continued until Shrovetide. A ninth play whose text was lost before it could be copied is mentioned, as well as three more which were partially written but prevented from performance "by the shortness of time and want of money." Virtually every member of the college was expected to partic-ipate in the festivities, since "it was thought fit that in so public a busi-ness everyone should do something." This left no one to fill the scaffolds that were erected in the hall for the audience, and so the plays were thrown open to the public. Start-up money was raised from the senior members, including William Laud, the future president of the college and archbishop of Canterbury, who contributed 10 shillings, and the balance was paid out of general college funds later on.[11] The actors were principally recent bachelors and undergradu-ates, as were the playwrights, none of whom are named in the com-memorative manuscript. The plays, variously called comedies, tragedies, interludes, "devices," "shows," "mock plays" (i.e., parodies), and "wassails," were performed on a platform in the hall before an audience that consisted mainly of students from other colleges, some of whom behaved in quite unruly fashion. Sword-bearing ushers called "whifflers"[12] were obliged to lock the rowdier of them in the porter's lodge, and to carry out others who had fainted or been tram-pled under the press of people in the crowded hall. On 21 January 1608 students at Christ Church parodied the St. John's offerings with a comedy performed in their own hall called *Yuletide,* described by the St. John's chronicler as "a medley of Christmas sports, by which occasion Christmas Lords were much jested at." A counterattack by the Johnians was contemplated but rendered unnecessary when the Dean of Christ Church issued an apology. On 13 February, after more work for the whifflers, many broken windows, and two stabbings of actors and spectators, the revels finally stopped.

The high spirits on this occasion, always on the brink of anarchy and violence, strike us today as more in keeping with a crowd of football supporters than with a theater audience, yet they seem to have been taken for granted as part of a holiday ritual. Only a single student was disciplined by university officials, the rest of the miscreants being left to the jurisdiction of the Christmas Prince's own mock-court, which devised various imaginative but mainly symbolic punishments for them.[13] On the day after the festivities came to their scheduled end, the president of St. John's, John Buckeridge, proved to be as indulgent as the Christmas Prince himself. Finding the hall "still pestered with the stage and scaffolds," and filled with snow that had blown in through the broken windows, he prorogued the beginning of the Lent term by a week and allowed more plays to be performed in the interim.[14]

This tradition of Christmas revels in the colleges was considerably older than Oxford's more recent investment in the fashionable humanist drama of the Renaissance. It is traceable in the Merton College records back to at least 1486, in references to the annual election of a "King of the Beans" (*Rex Fabarum*), who presided over an exotic cast of characters in a mock Christmas court.[15] And it remained deeply entrenched in the life of the colleges long after the high tide of humanism had ebbed. The diary of Peter Heylin, later chaplain to Charles I, tells us that the custom of electing Christmas Princes was still flourishing at Magdalen College in the 1620s and 1630s,[16] while at St. John's the accounts show regular performances of plays at Christmas, New Year's, Twelfth Night, and Candlemas right up to 1641.

University Plays

The most ambitious dramatic entertainments that Oxford produced, however, came on the occasion of official royal visits, of which there were four between 1566 and 1636. At such times the university as a corporate body became the producer of the plays, with the vice-chancellor and his deputies overseeing their texts, venues, financing, and mode of production, in close consultation with court officials. These "university plays," as they may be called, were all, with one exception, put on in Christ Church hall, both because Christ Church as a royal foundation traditionally acted as host to the sovereign, and because its hall was the largest in Oxford.[17] Actors in these plays were usually drawn from all the colleges combined, although occasionally individual colleges might assume responsibility for the casting of an entire play, as with Magdalen's version of Sophocles's *Ajax* for James I in 1605, or the St. John's production of George Wilde's *Love's Hospital* for Charles I in 1636. The latter was the only occasion when the royal party ventured out of Christ Church to see a play, which was staged at St. John's to celebrate the opening of Archbishop Laud's new Canterbury Quadrangle, a gift of the former president to his old college.[18]

Typical preparations for such a royal visit began with an official letter from the chancellor to the vice-chancellor, informing him of the sovereign's intentions and requesting him to provide suitable entertainment. The letter generally stressed that it was the university as a whole that was providing the entertainment and that each college and hall, as well as each student, with the exception of poor scholars, was to bear an appropriate share of the financial burden. The chief beneficiary of this stipulation was Christ Church, which was exempted from making even a proportional contribution in exchange for the use of its facilities. Delegates were then formed to supervise the plays and to collect the money to pay for them. Presumably the same delegates also made the choice of plays and playwrights, though the surviving records do not indicate what options they were given or what considerations determined their choices. We do know that all of the plays presented to the sovereign between 1566 and 1636, with the exception of Sophocles's *Ajax*, were original plays written by Oxford men, in most cases fresh for the occasion. The expenses for their production far outran those of normal student plays, especially in the seventeenth century when scenery grew more lavish. In 1636 the cost of the plays presented to Charles I totaled £843, which, though only a fraction of the cost of a court masque, was extravagant by Oxford standards.[19]

Our principal information about the plays staged for Queen Elizabeth in August 1566 comes from two eyewitness accounts. One is by a spectator, John Bereblock, a Christ Church don, who wrote in Latin; the other is by an actor in one of the plays, Miles Windsor, an undergraduate at Corpus Christi, who wrote in English. Bereblock says little about the content of the plays, none of whose texts survive, but gives a vivid description of how Christ Church hall was fitted out for the occasion. The walls and ceiling were lined with gold paneling to simulate the opulence of an ancient Roman palace ("veteris Romani palatii").[20] Scaffolds for the audience were placed at one end of the hall and along each of the side walls. Boxes or booths for the more important spectators were built at the top of the scaffolds, while the less privileged ("*populus*") stood on the floor around the stage. This was probably placed at the western, or high-table, end of the hall, though Bereblock's wording is ambiguous on the matter. At the back of the stage a throne, or "state," was placed for Elizabeth, who sat facing the audience. The scenery consisted of classical stage-houses, resembling "splendid palaces," which also served as the actors' dressing rooms. Bereblock seems to have considered the play-texts themselves the least important part of the occasion, since he fails to mention either their titles or their authors.

Miles Windsor's account of the occasion, on the other hand, as one might expect from a member of the cast, concentrates on the texts and the actors.[21] He lists the three plays as follows:

1) *Marcus Geminus*, a Roman history play in Latin by Toby Mathew of Christ Church.
2) *Palamon and Arcyte*, a two-part play in English, based on Chaucer's "The Knight's Tale," by Richard Edwards, formerly of Corpus Christi College and now Master of the Children of the Chapel.
3) *Progne*, a tragedy in Latin by James Calfhill of Christ Church.

Although Windsor, who played the part of Perithous in Edwards's play, appears not to have seen the other two performances, he nevertheless gives a list of the actors who took part in all three plays. The characters they played are not given, but the list includes the name of Toby Mathew, the future archbishop of York, who presumably acted in his own play, *Marcus Geminus*, possibly in the title role.[22] It also includes the name of a nonstudent, a boy actor named Peter Carew, the fourteen-year-old son of George Carew, former dean of Christ Church. Peter was evidently something of a child prodigy, since in addition to playing one of the leading female roles in the plays he also regaled the queen with an oration in Latin and Greek earlier in her visit.[23]

Windsor's most detailed information is naturally about the play in which he himself performed, Edwards's *Palamon and Arcyte*. The main interest of his account lies in the fact that while he was onstage he was close enough to the throne to hear the queen's reactions to the student players. In contrast to her present-day namesake, this Elizabeth was voluble and candid, interrupting the actors and speaking back to them and to the audience. Occasionally she was even cruel, treating her subjects as "abjects" in a way that Richard III might have admired. The chief victim of her wit was an unfortunate young man named John Dalaper, who played a character called Trevatio. This character does not appear in Chaucer's tale, but he was probably the Vice, since the name would appear to come from the Italian *traviare*, "to lead astray or corrupt." The actor became so nervous in the presence of the queen that he went dry and, after exclaiming, "by the Mass and God's blood I am out!," decided in desperation to whistle a hornpipe instead. At this the queen exploded "Go thy way!" and, turning to her secretary, Lord Burghley, said "God's pity what a knave it is." Taking his cue from the queen, Burghley then banished the unhappy Dalaper from the stage with the words, "Go thy ways! Thou art clear out! Thou mayst be allowed to play the knave in any ground in England!"[24]

While this misfortune undoubtedly put an end to the stage career of poor Dalaper, other student actors in *Palamon and Arcyte* fared better at the queen's hands. At the end of the second night of the play the queen spoke appreciative words to the two men who played the title roles, and gave rewards of eight angels each to the two female impersonators: John Rainolds, the future president of Corpus Christi, then seventeen, who played Queen Hippolyta; and the talented Peter Carew, who played Lady Emilia and gained the queen's praise for "gathering her flowers prettily in the garden and singing sweetly in the prime of May."[25]

The queen also intervened in another incident during the play, which involved one of the costumes she had lent the students from the royal wardrobe. These were mainly old cloaks and gowns that had belonged to King Edward VI and Queen Mary, a fact that was apparently well-known to the audience. At the moment in the play when Theseus, Emilia, and Perithous all threw mementos onto Arcyte's funeral pyre, one of the spectators standing near the stage grew alarmed and, grabbing Miles Windsor's arm, exclaimed, "God's wounds, will ye burn the King Edward cloak in the fire?" At this, Edwards the author (who must have been nearby with the playbook), Windsor, and the queen (who must have been given a plot synopsis beforehand) all berated the interrupter, the queen shouting "What aileth ye? Let the gentleman alone, he playeth his part!" Whether this spectator was unusually credulous or just a Cambridge provocateur is not known. It is difficult to believe that the royal cloak would actually have been burned in the performance, but we do know that at least one expensive garment was never returned to the Office of the Wardrobe,[26] and that similarly realistic effects were aimed at in other parts of the play. Theseus's hunting scene, for example, took place outside in the Christ Church quadrangle with live hounds, the sounds of the horns and dogs reaching the queen through the windows and prompting her to observe that "those boys [presumably spectators] are ready to leap out at window to follow the hounds."

In addition, the queen had some more serious problems to cope with during the run of *Palamon and Arcyte* than simply the mistakes of actors and audience. Not long into the performance of part 1, the staircase leading to Christ Church hall collapsed under the weight of the overflow crowd, killing three spectators trying to gain entrance. Windsor, who was again at the center of events, reports that the play was stopped and that Elizabeth dispatched the Lord Chamberlain, Lord William Howard of Effingham, to investigate, along with her own surgeons. On discovering that nothing was to be done for the victims, Lord Howard, demonstrating the *sang-froid* that he was to pass on to his son, Charles, the lord admiral who would defeat the Armada twenty years later, said only, according to Windsor, "Bury them." The play continued, and the queen "laughed full heartily afterward at some of the players," according to Windsor. Thus passed one of the more memorable afternoons in the history of the fledgling Elizabethan theater.

The queen's next official visit to Oxford in 1592 is not as well-documented, since the only surviving eyewitness account of the entertainments is that of a Cambridge "spy," Philip Stringer, who made notes at the time but did not write them up until shortly before his death eleven years later. By that time he had forgotten, or found indecipherable, everything except the titles of the two plays acted before the queen, and his judgment that they were "but meanly performed."[27] Anthony Wood, researching the event many years later, could discover even less: "but what they were or how applauded, I know not."[28] From other evidence, however, we know that one of the plays was Leonard Hutten's Latin comedy, *Bellum Grammaticale*, originally performed in Christ Church as long before as 1581,[29] now fitted out with two new prologues and an epilogue by William Gager. The other was Gager's own play, *Rivales*, another Latin comedy, now lost but first performed at Christ Church in 1583 and revived at Shrovetide, 1592, a few months before the queen's visit.[30] The trotting out of two old plays for the occasion suggests that the arrangements for the visit must have been made at short notice, and the fact that Christ Church expended only a meager £31 "for the stage and towards the plays" suggests that as a consequence they were indeed more "meanly" set forth than in 1566. Beyond the fact that the costumes were borrowed from the Revels Office, and that Christ Church issued special instructions to keep "the hall stairs" in order (small wonder!), we know nothing further about the staging of the plays or about the queen's reaction to them. Possibly because both plays were in Latin, she kept this to herself, even in her farewell speech.[31]

Much more is known about the visit of the newly crowned King James to Oxford thirteen years later. In August of 1605 four plays were presented in Christ Church hall for the royal party, three in Latin aimed at the erudite king and one in English for Queen Anne and the young Prince Henry. Another play was given in Magdalen College hall for Prince Henry alone,[32] while a sixth entertainment, a short "device" called *Tres Sibyllae*, in which the prophecies of the witches to Macbeth were spoken to the king by three little boys outside the gates of St. John's, may have planted the seed of the most famous English play of the following year.

The Christ Church plays of 1605 were a combined showcase for Oxford's classical learning and Inigo Jones's revolutionary neoclassical stage designs. As John Orrell has shown, the three Latin plays chosen for the king were intended to demonstrate the three "kinds" of classical drama as labeled by the Roman architect Vitruvius, whose work Jones was busy introducing into England.[33] *Alba*, one of whose authors was Robert Burton,[34] was a satyr play featuring shepherdesses, hermits, various gods and goddesses, and a magician. Though its text is now lost, a costume list survives indicating its classical pastoral characters, and a member of the audience noted that it made use of a live flock of wild doves.[35] The tragedy was Sophocles's *Ajax Flagellifer*, an obvious choice for Jones, since his Italian edition of Vitruvius gave specific instructions for the staging of this play in a Roman-style amphitheater.[36] The comedy was supplied by Matthew Gwinne of St. John's in the form of an allegory of the four seasons called *Vertumnus* (*The Year About*).

The choice of these works was designed to show off the new perspective scenery that Jones, who had designed his first Whitehall masque only a few months before, was using for plays for the first time in England. The stage, we are told, held five "stately pillars which would turn about"—that is, copies of ancient Greek *periaktoi*—in order to change the scene, erected against a permanent backdrop or, as one tongue-tied spectator called it, a "false wall fair painted."[37] In *Ajax* a different scene was painted on each face of the "pillars," which were rotated by winches located under the stage. The machinery remained in place through the four days of performance, furnishing new scenes for *Alba, Vertumnus,* and the last play, Samuel Daniel's *Arcadia Reformed* (later renamed *The Queen's Arcadia*). Since the stage was steeply raked, the king could not sit on it. Unlike Elizabeth, James and his throne were placed on an "isle" in the center of the auditorium, with his courtiers seated on benches in front, as well as in boxes fastened to the side walls. From here the king and his officials had the best sight lines, though some courtiers complained that they could not now be so well seen by the rest of audience as before, and the king complained that he could not hear. The needs of the new technology prevailed, however, and the king stayed where he was put.

Inigo Jones's scenic innovations were to transform English theater, but in 1605 they had a mixed effect on their first audiences. A Cambridge observer, perhaps predictably, claimed that neither *Alba* nor *Ajax* came up to the standard of comparable plays at his university, and that the king found both of them "tedious."[38] At *Vertumnus*, although he thought it better "penned and acted" than the others, he tells us that the king "fell asleep, and when he awaked, he would have been gone, saying, 'I marvell what they think me to be.'" Even Jones's "rare devices" he dismissed as having accomplished "very little to that which was expected." Oxford officials, equally predictably, gave a more favorable verdict, one of them claiming that the king pronounced himself as "much delighted" with *Vertumnus* "as with any sight of the like nature at any time heretofore presented unto him."[39] Whatever the notoriously impatient king really thought, Oxford had helped to change forever the "sights" that would hitherto be seen at the Stuart court.

Thirty-one years elapsed before the next royal visit to Oxford by Charles I in 1636, the last such occasion before the Civil War. By that time Inigo Jones had become Surveyor of the King's Works, and the splendor of his court entertainments had grown far beyond his early experiments for King James. In Christ Church in August of 1636 he left behind his antique *periaktoi* and instead used the modern Italian style of creating visual perspective by means of wing-flats, hinged shutters, sculpted relieves, and painted backdrops.[40] The plays too were in the now fashionable genre of tragicomedy or romance, rather than bookish adaptations of the classics. The two plays performed in Christ Church were William Strode's *Floating Island* and William Cartwright's *Royal Slave*, both of which used exotic plots as political allegories to extol the benefits of monarchy. Both, too, were in English, as was the third play, performed at St. John's, George Wilde's romantic comedy, *Love's Hospital.* The abandonment of any pretense of "academic" drama was noticeable, and was epigrammatically justified by Cartwright in a couplet in the epilogue to his *Royal Slave:*

> There's difference 'twixt a College and a Court:
> The one expecteth Science, the other Sport.[41]

Not surprisingly, eyewitness accounts of this occasion say nothing about texts or "pen men" but concentrate upon Jones's scenic wonders. Brian Twyne, Oxford's first archivist and another Corpus man, left a long description of the two productions that took place on the "goodly stage made at Christ Church," extolling the splendors of what to him was "the new fashion." Perhaps only an Oxford archivist could have compared Jones's wing-flats to "partitions much resembling the desks in a library." But the rest of his description indicates that his imagination quickly left behind any academic preoccupations to marvel at "the great variety and admiration" of the scenes.[42] For this, as Cartwright knew, was not really an Oxford but a court entertainment.

Although the texts of the royal plays of 1636 were written by Oxford men, the performances themselves were, in every other respect, the product of the king's usual purveyors of court entertainment. The scenery and costumes were provided by the Office of the Works and the Office of the Revels; the music was written by William and Henry Lawes, for performance by the King's Musick and the Children of the Chapel; the actors were coached by Joseph Taylor, the leader of the King's Men at the Globe; and even a set of candelabra was dismantled in Whitehall Palace and reassembled to light the Christ Church stage.[43] Cartwright's *Royal Slave* so closely resembled the court plays favored by the queen that she commanded it to be transferred to Hampton Court and performed by her own company. What she saw both there and in Oxford was not a representative of Oxford culture, but an imitation of the prevailing Stuart court taste. Oxford, with its usual unerring eye for lost causes, had ceased to instruct and bent to flatter the monarch.[44]

Notes

1. Alan H. Nelson, ed., *Records of Early English Drama: Cambridge*, 2 vols. (Toronto: University of Toronto Press, 1989).
2. Oxford University Archives, Register G, fol. 143. Such a stipulation was called a "grace of Congregation," the technical term at Oxford for special conditions or waivers attached to the granting of degrees. "Congregation" was the governing body of the university, composed of all Masters of Arts engaged in teaching. Initially graces were thought of as exceptions to normal degree requirements, but by the late Middle Ages nearly all degrees were awarded by "grace of Congregation" (James McConica, ed., *The Collegiate University*, vol 3 of *The History of the University of Oxford* [Oxford: Oxford University Press, 1983], 6-7).
3. John R. Elliott, Jr., "Degree Plays," *Oxoniensia* 53 (1988): 341-42.
4. R. E. Alton, ed., "The Academic Drama in Oxford: Extracts from the Records of Four Colleges," *Malone Society Collections* 5 (1959): 28-95.
5. E. K. Chambers, *The Elizabethan Stage*, 4 vols (Oxford: Oxford University Press, 1923), 3:317-19.
6. Letter to John Rainolds, 31 July 1592, in Corpus Christi College Archives, MS 352, pages 41-65. I have modernized the spelling and punctuation of this and other manuscript documents.
7. Oxford University Archives, Register L, fol. 242[v].
8. Ibid., fols. 262[r]-262[v].
9. Oxford University Archives, Register R, fol. 138.

10. St. John's College Library, MS 52. The manuscript has been edited by F. S. Boas, *The Christmas Prince*, Malone Society Reprints (Oxford: Oxford University Press, 1922). A facsimile of the manuscript has been published by Earl J. Richard, ed., *The Christmas Prince*, Renaissance Latin Drama in England, first series 11 (Hildesheim and New York: Olms, 1982). Quotations here are from the Boas edition.

11. St. John's College Muniments, MS Acc. V.E. 4, fol. 48 ("Set on for an end of our Christmas sportes, £vj iijˢ").

12. Cf. Shakespeare, *Henry V*: ". . . the deep-mouth'd sea / Which like a mighty whiffler 'for the King / Seems to prepare his way" (V, Chorus, 11-13). The image is of a crowd-controlling usher or marshall at the head of a royal or civic procession. The St. John's manuscript usage (not recorded by *OED*) is the first instance of the word in a theatrical setting, a sense recorded by *OED* in several later seventeenth-century citations, including one by Milton (*OED*, "whiffler": one who carries a *wifle*, or javelin).

13. On college discipline in general, with examples from St. John's, see McConica, *The Collegiate University*, 664-65.

14. Boas, *Christmas Prince*, 152.

15. H. E. Salter, ed., *Registrum Annalium Collegii Mertonensis 1483-1521*, Oxford Historical Society 76 (Oxford: Oxford University Press, 1923), 94.

16. Heylin's diary is printed as part of the introduction (x-xxiv) to J. R. Bloxham, ed., *Memorial of Bishop Waynflete*, Caxton Society 14 (London, 1851).

17. Originally founded by Cardinal Wolsey in 1529 as "Cardinal College," Christ Church was refounded by Henry VIII after Wolsey's fall and called "King Henry VIII College" during his reign. In 1548 it was again refounded and re-christened by Edward VI, in the dual role of college and see of the diocese of Oxford.

18. The production was also paid for entirely by Laud. The expense sheets survive in the Public Record Office, SP / 16 / 348, no. 85.

19. John R. Elliott, Jr., and John Buttrey, "The Royal Plays at Christ Church in 1636: A New Document," *Theatre Research International* 10 (1985): 93-109.

20. Quotations are from Bodleian MS Add. A. 63, fols. 1-22, which was copied no later than 1571 and seems the most authoritative of the three surviving scribal copies. The others are MS Bodleian Rawlinson D. 1071, fols. 1-25, and Folger Shakespeare Library MS V.a.109, fols. 1-24.

21. Corpus Christi College Archives, MS 257, fols. 104-23. For a fuller account of this document, see John R. Elliott, Jr., "Queen Elizabeth at Oxford: New Light on the Royal Plays in 1566," *ELR* 18 (1988): 218-29 and *The Human Stage: English Theatre Design, 1567-1640* (Cambridge, 1988), Plate 28, 121.

22. If so, he set a precedent that was repeated in 1619 when Thomas Goffe both wrote and starred in *The Courageous Turk* in Christ Church; see David Carnegie, "The Identification of the Hand of Thomas Goffe, Academic Dramatist and Actor," *The Library*, 5th ser. 26 (1971): 161-65.

23. Anthony Wood, *History of the University of Oxford,* 4 vols. (Oxford, 1786-96), 2:158.

24. Corpus Christi College MS 257, fol. 118. The sense of this remark is: "You could get the role of a knave in any playing-place in the country," i.e., "you would be a knave wherever you were." See *OED,* "ground" 10.a, 14.a.

25. In his narrative, Windsor says that the actor who played Palamon was named "Lynhame," but this name does not appear in his list of actors, nor does it occur in any other list of Oxford or Christ Church students. The actor who played Arcyte was Brian Baynes, an undergraduate at Christ Church. More than thirty years later John Rainolds acknowledged in print his youthful cross-dressing role, but failed to mention his reward by the queen (see Rainolds, *Th'Overthrow of Stage-Plays* [1599], 45).

26. Janet Arnold, *"Lost from her Majesties back": Items of Clothing and Jewels Lost or Given Away by Queen Elizabeth I Between 1561 and 1585, Entered in One of the Day Books Kept for the Records of the Wardrobe of Robes* (London: The Costume Society, 1980).

27. Philip Stringer, "A Brief of the Entertainment Given to Queen Elizabeth at Oxford," Cambridge University Library MS 34, fols. 3-9. Stringer was a fellow of St. John's College, Cambridge. The purpose of his mission to Oxford was to help his own university prepare for their next visit from the queen. It is not known how many such "spies" were sent to Oxford in 1592 besides Stringer and his companion, Henry Mowtloe, fellow of King's College, to whom he gave his manuscript account. In 1605, however, there were forty of them, whose job was "to view in secret and note the whole event,'" then to record their observations in short-hand "in a table-book" [i.e., a tablet or notebook] (William Fennor, *Fennors Descriptions* [London, 1616], E1ᵛ).

28. Wood, *History of the University of Oxford,* 2:248-49.

29. McConica, *The Collegiate University,* 719.

30. *Bellum Grammaticale* was printed in 1635. The prologues and epilogue added to it by Gager for the queen's visit were printed in Gager's *Meleager* (1593). Also see F. S. Boas, *University Drama in the Tudor Age* (Oxford: Oxford University Press, 1914), 181-83.

31. C. Plummer, ed., *Elizabethan Oxford: Reprints of Rare Tracts,* Oxford Historical Society 7 (Oxford: Oxford University Press, 1887), 271-73. The Christ Church Disbursement Book for 1592-93 indicates that the committee to "oversee and provide for the plays" was not appointed until 17 August, with the queen due to arrive on 22 September (Christ Church Archives, xxii. b. 35, fol. 97).

32. Alton, "The Academic Drama in Oxford," 60.

33. John Orrell, *The Theatres of Inigo Jones and John Webb* (Cambridge: Cambridge University Press, 1985), 30. That the choice of the three "kinds" of plays was made by the court, at Jones's instigation, and not solely by Oxford is shown by a document in the University Archives, containing an order by the delegates responsible for the entertainments for "three plays to be made in Latin, viz., two comedies and a tragedy." The

colleges were left the "choice of actors and pen men to help to pen them" (Oxford University Archives, W.P. gamma / 19 / 1, fol. 2ᵛ).

34. Richard L. Nochimson, "Robert Burton's Authorship of *Alba*," *RES* n.s. 21 (1970): 325-31.
35. See F. S. Boas, ed., "James I at Oxford in 1605," *Malone Society Collections* 1 (1909): 247-59, and Isaac Wake, *Rex Platonicus* (Oxford, 1607).
36. Orrell, *The Theatres of Inigo Jones and John Webb*, 33.
37. Wake, *Rex Platonicus*, 46; trans. in Orrell, *The Theatres of Inigo Jones and John Webb*, 31. Orrell has reproduced the original plan for the auditorium constructed in Christ Church hall by the Office of the King's Works for this occasion in "The Theatre at Christ Church, Oxford, in 1605," *Shakespeare Survey* 35 (1982): 129-40.
38. Cambridge University Library, MS 34, fols. 28-45ᵛ. The account is anonymous, but the author may have been Henry Mowtloe, fellow of King's College, who once possessed the manuscript (see note 27).
39. Anthony Nixon, *Oxfords Triumph* (London, 1605), Fol. E1ᵛ.
40. Orrell, *The Theatres of Inigo Jones and John Webb*, 37.
41. *The Plays and Poems of William Cartwright*, ed., Gwynne B. Evans (Madison: University of Wisconsin Press, 1951), 252.
42. Bodleian Library, MS Twyne 17, page 201. The complete description, as copied by Anthony Wood (*History of the University*, 2:408-9), is reproduced in G. E. Bentley, *The Jacobean and Caroline Stage*, 7 vols. (Oxford: Oxford University Press, 1941-68), 5: 1191.
43. Elliott and Buttrey, "The Royal Plays at Christ Church in 1636," 93-109.
44. A shorter version of this essay was given as a paper at the Seventh International Colloquium of the International Society for the Study of Medieval Theater held at Gerona, Spain, in July 1992. The subject of Oxford plays and players is also treated in my chapter, "College and University Drama," in *The Seventeenth Century*, vol. 4 of *The History of the University of Oxford*, ed. Nicholas Tyacke (Oxford: Oxford University Press, forthcoming), where I have been able to set out some of the evidence at greater length. It is a pleasure to acknowledge the support of my research by the Fulbright Commission for the International Exchange of Scholars, Washington, D.C.

English Chronicle Contexts for Shakespeare's Death of Richard II

Lister M. Matheson

The murder of the king, weapon in hand, struck down (probably with a poleaxe) by Sir Pierce of Exton, in Shakespeare's *Richard II* (1595) is remarkable for several reasons. It shows a decisive aspect of Richard's character that is free of any sense of resignation or passive fatalism—in his last moments the *roi fainéant* becomes a man of action imbued with "desperat manhood" (as a marginal note in Holinshed puts it), who refuses to "go gentle into that good night." Derek Traversi characterizes the murder as "no more than a pedestrian piece of melodramatic writing,"[1] but a consideration of Shakespeare's sources shows that the manner of Richard's death represents a choice among conflicting current accounts and that the language has been carefully constructed. The purposes of the present essay are: first, to suggest that Shakespeare was indebted not only to Raphael Holinshed but also to Edward Hall for his account of Richard's death; second, to trace to its direct textual origins the version of Richard's death chosen by Shakespeare (the texts printed below are generally known, but they have not previously been collected in one location and some of their relationships have been imperfectly recognized); finally, to discuss briefly why Shakespeare chose from those known to him the particular version of Richard's death that he did and the implications of that choice. Three options were open to him: death as a result of forced starvation; death as a result of grief or involuntary starvation; or death at the hands of Sir Piers de Exton, fulfilling directly or indirectly the wishes of Henry IV. A fourth option available to the chroniclers—a profession of ignorance as to the circumstances—can be ruled out for the dramatist.

• • •

Those parts of the relevant scenes in *Richard II*, act 5, that portray the immediate incitement to the murder, its execution, and the murderer's report thereof to Bolingbroke, now crowned as Henry IV, are given here at length to facilitate comparison with the sources.[2]

[Scene iv. *Windsor Castle.*]

Manet Sir Pierce Exton &c. [Servant].

EXTON.

Didst thou not mark the king, what words he spake?
"Have I no friend will rid me of this living fear?"
Was it not so?

MAN.

These were his very words.

EXTON.

"Have I no friend?" quoth he. He spake it twice
And urged it twice together, did he not?

MAN.

He did.

EXTON.

And speaking it, he wishtly looked on me,
As who should say, "I would thou wert the man
That would divorce this terror from my heart!"
Meaning the king at Pomfret. Come, let's go.
I am the king's friend, and will rid his foe.

[*Exeunt.*]

[Scene v. *Pomfret Castle.*]

[*Lines 1-97: Richard meditates on his fate and* "this all-hating world" *(line 66); he converses with one of his former grooms until a keeper enters with food.*]

KEEPER.

My lord, will't please you to fall to?

RICHARD.

Taste of it first, as thou art wont to do.

KEEPER.

My lord, I dare not. Sir Pierce of Exton,
Who lately came from the king, commands the contrary.

RICHARD.

The devil take Henry of Lancaster, and thee!
Patience is stale, and I am weary of it.

[*Beats the Keeper.*]

KEEPER.

Help, help, help!

The Murderers [Exton and Servants] rush in.

RICHARD.

How now! What means Death in this rude assault?
Villain, thy own hand yields thy death's instrument.
    [*Snatches a weapon from a Servant and kills him.*]
Go thou and fill another room in hell.
    [*Kills another.*] *Here Exton strikes him down.*
That hand shall burn in never-quenching fire
That staggers thus my person. Exton, thy fierce hand
Hath with the king's blood stained the king's own land.
Mount, mount, my soul! thy seat is up on high;
Whilst my gross flesh sinks downward, here to die.
            [*Dies.*]

EXTON.

As full of valor as of royal blood!
Both have I spilled. O, would the deed were good!
For now the devil, that told me I did well,
Says that this deed is chronicled in hell.
This dead king to the living king I'll bear.
Take hence the rest, and give them burial here.
                    [*Exeunt.*]

        [Scene vi. *Windsor Castle.*]
[Lines 1-29: Bolingbroke, as King, receives reports of the deaths of Oxford,
Salisbury, Blunt, Kent, and others and passes judgment on the bishop of Carlisle.]
       Enter Exton, with [Attendants bearing] the coffin.

EXTON.

Great king, within this coffin I present
Thy buried fear. Herein all breathless lies
The mightiest of thy greatest enemies,
Richard of Bordeaux, by me hither brought.

KING.

Exton, I thank thee not; for thou hast wrought
A deed of slander, with thy fatal hand,
Upon my head and all this famous land.

EXTON.

From your own mouth, my lord, did I this deed.

KING.

They love not poison that do poison need,
Nor do I thee. Though I did wish him dead,
I hate the murderer, love him murderèd.
The guilt of conscience take thou for thy labor,
But neither my good word nor princely favor.
With Cain go wander thorough shades of night,
And never show thy head by day nor light.

[*Lines 45-52: Bolingbroke protests his sorrow to the assembled lords, vows a pilgrimage to the Holy Land* "To wash this blood off from my guilty hand" *(line 50), and leads Richard's funeral procession offstage. The play ends.*]

Shakespeare's favorite primary source for English history was, of course, the posthumous second edition of Raphael Holinshed's *Chronicles* (1587). This was a modernized version of the edition of 1577, with a continuation to January 1587 and with new material added to the earlier annals by the editors, often from sources already used in the first edition.[3] For the reigns of Henry IV through Henry VIII, Holinshed had used as a major source Edward Hall's *Vnion of the Two Noble and Illustre Famelies of Lancastre and Yorke* (Richard Grafton, 1548, 2nd ed. 1550; John Kingston, ca. 1560).[4] Although Holinshed tones down much of Hall's purple prose and improves the rather prolix style, his work is often so close to the *Vnion*, even quoting verbatim, that it is frequently difficult, sometimes impossible (and for literary study often irrelevant) to determine on purely textual grounds whether Shakespeare was using Hall or Holinshed in particular instances.

The second edition of Holinshed is generally accepted as having provided Shakespeare with the principal historical source material for *Richard II*, with only a general debt to Hall for providing "the moral scheme, the point of departure, and the insistence on the continuity between Richard's reign and Henry IV's"[5] and a few points of historical detail. Accordingly, Bullough (*Narrative and Dramatic Sources of Shakespeare*) and those editions that include sources have printed Holinshed's account as the immediate source of Richard's death. However, a close comparison suggests that Shakespeare was influenced by Hall's account of the murder, perhaps attracted by its more melodramatic flavor.[6] I print Hall's narrative here from the 1550 edition,[7] followed by indications of how Holinshed differs in substance:

[fol. xiiij] For poore Kyng Rycharde, ignorant of all this coniuracion [i.e., the rebellion on his behalf], kepte in myserable captiuite, knowyng nothyng but that he sawe in his chamber, was by Kyng Henry adiudged to dye, because that he, beyng synged and tickeled with the last craftie policie of his enemies, would deliuer hymselfe out of all inwarde feare and discorde, and cleane put away the very grounde whereof suche frutes of displeasure might by anie waie bee attempted againste hym, so that no man hereafter shoulde either fayne or resemble to represente the persone of Kyng Rychartde [*sic*]. Wherefore some saye he commaunded, other talke that he condiscended, many wryte that he knewe nat tyll it was done, and then it confirmed. But howe so euer it was, Kyng Rycharde dyed of a violent death, without any infeccion or naturall disease of the body.

The common fame is that he was euery daye serued at the table wyth costely meate lyke a kyng, to the entent that no creature should suspecte any thyng done contrary to the order taken in the parliament, and when the meate was set before hym, he was forbidden that he should not once touche it, ye not to smell to it, and so died of famyn, which kynd of death is the moost miserable, most vnnaturall, ye and most detestable that can be, for it is ten tymes more painefull then death (whiche of all extremities is the moost terrible) to die for thirst standyng in the riuer, or starue [fol. xiiij, verso] for hunger, besette wyth twentie deintie dysshes.

One writer whyche semed to haue muche knowledge of Kyng Rychardes affayres sayeth that Kyng Henry, syttyng at his table, sore syghyng saied, "Haue I no faytheful frende whiche wil deliuer me of hym whose life will be my death, and whose death will be the preseruacion of my lyfe?" This saiyng was muche noted of them whiche were present and especially of one called Sir Piers of Exton.

This knight incontinently departed from the court with eight stronge persones and came to Pomfret, comaundyng that the esquier whiche was acustomed to sewe and take the assaye before Kyng Rychard should no more vse that maner of seruice, saiyng, "Let hym eate well nowe, for he shall not long eate."

Kyng Rychard sate downe to dyner and was serued without curtesie or assaye; he, muche meruaylyng at the sodayne mutacion of the thyng, demaunded of the esquier why he dyd not his duety. "Sir," saied he, "I am otherwise commaunded by Sir Pyers of Exton, whiche is newely come from Kyng Henry." When he heard that worde, he toke the caruyng knife in his hande and stroke the esquier on the head, saiyng, "The deuell take Henry of Lancastre and the together." And with that worde Sir Piers entered into the chamber wel armed, with eight tall men in harneis, euery man hauing a byll in hys hande. Kyng Rycharde, perceiuyng them armed, knewe well that they came to his confusion, and puttyng the table from hym valiauntly toke the byll out of the firste mannes hande, and manly defended hymselfe, and slewe foure of them in a short space.

Sir Piers, being somwhat dismaied with his resistyng, lepte into the chaire where Kyng Richard was wonte to sitte, while the other foure persones assailed and chased hym aboute the chamber, whiche being disarmed defended him against his enemies beyng armed (whiche was a valiaunt acte), but in conclusion, chasyng and trauersyng from the one syde to the other, he came to the chaire where Sir Pyers stode, whiche with a stroke of his pollax felled hym to the grounde, and then shortly he was rid out of the worlde, without ether confession or receit of sacrament.

When this knyght perceiued that he was deade, he sobbed, wept, and rent his heare, criyng, "Oh Lord, what haue we done? we haue murthered hym whome by the space of two and twenty yeres we haue obeied as kyng and honoured as our souereigne lorde; now all noble men will abhorre vs, all honest persons will disdaine vs, and all poore people will rayle and crie out vpon vs, so that duryng our naturall liues, we shalbe poincted with the fynger, and our posterite shalbe reproued as children of homecides, ye, of regicides and prince quellers."

Thus haue I declared to you the diuersities of opinions concerning the deathe of this infortunate prince, remittyng to your iudgement whiche you thynke moost trewe, but the very truthe is that he died of a violent death, and not by the darte of naturall infirmitie.

When Atropos had cut the lyne of his lyfe, his body was embaulmed and seared and couered with lead, all saue his face (to the entent that all men myght perceiue that he was departed out of this mortall lyfe) and [fol. xv] was conueyghed to London, where in the cathedrall churche of Saincte Paule he had a solempne obsequie, and from thence conueyghed to Langley in Buckynghamshire, where he was enterred, and after by Kyng Henry the V remoued to Westminster, and there entombed honorably with Quene Anne his wyfe, although the Scottes vntreuly write that he escaped out of prisone, and led a verteous and solitary lyfe in Scotlande, and there dyed and is buryed in the Blacke Friers at Sterlyng.

What trust is in this worlde, what suretie man hath of his life, & what constancie is in the mutable comonaltie, all men maye apparantly perceyue by the ruyne of this noble prince, whiche beeyng an vndubitate kyng, crouned and anoynted by the spiritualtie, honored and exalted by the nobilitie, obeyed and worshipped of the comon people, was sodainly disceyued by theim whiche he moste trusted, betrayed by theim whom he had preferred, & slayn by theim whom he had brought vp and norished, so that all menne maye perceyue and see, that fortune wayeth princes and pore men all in one balance. (Hall, 1550[8])

Compare the first paragraph of Hall quoted above and the following section from Holinshed (1587):

> And immediatlie after, king Henrie, to rid himselfe of anie such like danger to be attempted against him thereafter, caused king Richard to die of a violent death, that no man should afterward faine himselfe to represent his person, though some have said, he was not privie to that wicked offense.

[After the account of "forced famine," the 1587 edition adds the following]:

[*Margin: Abr. Fl.* [i.e., Abraham Fleming] out of *Thom. Walsi.* pag. 404, 405.] But *Thomas Walsingham* is so farre from imputing his death to compulsorie famine, that he referreth it altogither to voluntarie pining of himselfe. For when he heard that the complots and attempts of such his favourers, as sought his restitution, and their owne advancement, adnihilated; and the cheefe agents shamefullie executed; he tooke such a conceit at these misfortunes (for so *Thomas Walsingham* termeth them) and was so beaten out of hart, that wilfullie he starved himselfe, and so died in Pomfret castell on S. Valentines daie: a happie daie to him, for it was the beginning of his ease, and the ending of his paine: so that death was to him daintie and sweet, as the poet saith, and that verie well in brefe,

[*Margin:* Corn. Gall.]

> *Dulce mori miseris,*
> *Neque est melius morte in malis rebus.*

[The account of Richard's murder by Sir Piers de Exton is wrongly attributed in the margin to "*Thom. Walsin.*"; this section ends as follows:]

It is said, that sir Piers of Exton, after he had thus slaine him, wept right bitterlie, as one striken with the pricke of a giltie conscience, for murthering him, whome he had so long obeied as king.[9]

The actual substance of both accounts is essentially the same, but Shakespeare combines them verbally:

1) Henry Bolingbroke's "rid me of this living fear," that is, Richard (quoted by Exton in 5.4.2), seems based on Hall's description of Henry's "inwarde feare and discorde," which is further echoed in Henry's phrase "this terror from my heart" (5.4.9) and Exton's "thy buried fear" (5.6.31). The verb "rid" parallels Holinshed at this point, though Hall later relates that Richard "was rid out of the worlde."

2) Exton's speech of self-loathing in Hall, only indirectly indicated in Holinshed, is paralleled in the play by Exton's speech of 5.5.113-18. Exton's prediction in Hall that the murderers and their posterity will henceforth be marked outcasts is picked up by Henry, with a verbal parallel to Holinshed's "giltie conscience": "I hate the murderer. . . . The guilt of conscience take thou for thy labor. . . . With Cain go wander thorough shades of night, / And never show thy head by day nor light" (5.6.40, 41, 43-44).

3) The addition in Holinshed (1587) that records Walsingham's opinion that Richard died from "voluntarie pining of himselfe" may be

echoed earlier in the play when Richard exclaims, "Go to Flint Castle. There I'll pine away" (3.2.209).

•   •   •

Although Hall and Holinshed contained, reasonably handily, the latest historical research and, indeed, much striking language that the playwright took over or adapted, their accounts of the death of Richard II did not exist in a contextual vacuum for their readers and other contemporaries. The essential shape of history that formed the general cultural awareness of sixteenth-century England was already formed before 1548 (or 1577) by a rich tradition of printed and manuscript vernacular chronicles, to which Hall pays halfhearted tribute in his dedicatory preface:

> Sithe the ende of Frossarte, whiche endeth at the begynnyng of Kyng Henry the Fourthe, no man in the Englishe toungue hath eitheir set furth their honors according to their desertes nor yet declared many notable actes worthy of memorie dooen in the tyme of seuen kynges whiche after kyng Richarde succeded: Excepte Robert Fabian and one without name, whiche wrote the common English Chronicle, men worthy to be praysed for their diligence, but farre shotyng wyde from the butte of an historie. (Hall [1550], dedication to Edward VI)

The anonymous "common English Chronicle" is the Middle English prose *Brut*, and Hall is probably referring to one of its printed editions, although he was undoubtedly aware of the many manuscripts, of which more survive than of any other Middle English work except the Wycliffite translations of the Bible.[10]

The *Brut* was first translated into English from Anglo-Norman toward the end of the fourteenth century and originally ended in 1333, to which a continuation had been added to bring the narrative up to 1377; in the course of the fifteenth century the basic English text received various continuations and many individualistic versions of the work were also produced. In 1480 William Caxton made the *Brut* the first printed chronicle of England (under the title of *The Chronicles of England*), and it went through a further twelve editions until 1528. The work was owned and read across a wide social spectrum, by priests, monks, merchants, members of the minor gentry, and members of the nobility.[11] In terms of both content and style, its influence on historians of the fifteenth and sixteenth centuries was pervasive.

The earliest account in English of Richard's death occurs in the standard *Brut* continuation of 1377-1419, which was composed soon after its concluding date (probably before 1422), and presents the forced starvation version:

> And þanne anon deied King Richard in þe castell of Pountfret yn the Northcuntre, for þere he was enfammed vnto the deth be his keper, for he was kept into iiij or v. dayeȝ fro mete and drynke; and so he made is ende yn þis worlde. Yet moche pepil yn Engelond and yn oþir landeȝ saide þat he was alyue meny yereȝ aftir his deth; but wheþer he were alyue or ded, þi hilde hir fals opynyons and beleue þat þay hadde; and moche pepil aftirward comyn to myschif and to foule deth, as ye schulle here aftirwarde. And whanne King Henry wist and knew warly þat he was ded, he lete sere hym yn þe best maner þat he myȝte and closed hym yn lynnyn cloth, alle saue his visage, and þat was left opon þat men myȝt se and know his person from alle oþer men; and so he was brought to London with torchis lyȝt brennyng vnto Saynt Pouleȝ, and þere he hadde his masse and his dirige, with moche reverence and solempnite of seruiȝe. And fro Pouleȝ was brouȝt ynto þe Abbey of Westmynstre, and þere hadde alle his hole seruiȝe ayen; and fro Westmynstre he was ladd ynto Langeley, and þere he was beryed: on whose soule God haue mercy! Amen!
> [CUL MS Kk.I.12, printed in Brie 2: 360/8-26;[12] the conspiracy against Henry IV is revealed only after Richard's death.]

This is the version found in the majority of *Brut* manuscripts that continue beyond 1377 and in Caxton's edition of 1480 and it must have been influential in creating the "common fame" that Hall and Holinshed ascribe to death by forced starvation. The elaboration of the common *Brut* account found in two manuscripts, BL Harley 53 (ca. 1452-53) and Lambeth 6 (a magnificently illustrated, late fifteenth-century volume that must have been owned by someone of the highest standing), is extremely close in wording to Hall, although, as we shall see, it was not Hall's direct source:

> in the first yere of the regne of Kyng Henry the iiij[te], Kyng Richard, which þat was put doune of his Rialte, was in þe Castell of Pountfret vndir þe ward of Sir Robert ["Henry" in Lambeth 6] of Watirton, knyght; and þere he was ich day servet [as] a Kyng aught to be, that he myght se it; but he myght come to non þerof; wherfore sone aftir he deyd for honger in prison in þe same Castell; and so he made his ende.
> [BL MS Harl. 53, printed in Brie 2: 546/3-9; the order of Richard's obsequies and the projected rebellion agrees with the common *Brut* description.]

In 1482 Caxton printed John Trevisa's translation of Ranulph Higden's *Polychronicon* and, like the *Chronicles of England*, the work remained current into the sixteenth century, being reprinted in 1495 by Wynkyn de Worde and in 1527 by Peter Treveris.[13] To bring the *Polychronicon* narrative up to date, Caxton added a continuation from 1358 to 1461 that he named the *Liber ultimus*.[14] This continuation falls into two parts, the latter of which, from 1419 to 1461, is based on the corresponding section of Caxton's *Chronicles of England* (1480). The earlier section, from 1358 to 1419, generally agrees in narrative outline with the corresponding section of the printed *Chronicles*, though occasionally somewhat abbreviated. However, Caxton also uses a variety of sources for additional material: a London civic chronicle, the *Grandes chroniques de France* (perhaps as printed at Paris in 1477 by Pasquier Bonhomme), the *Fasciculus temporum* (perhaps a personal copy of the edition published in 1475 in Louvain by Johan Veldener), an unidentified (but clearly minor) source called the *Aureus de vniverso* and, most important for present purposes, the French *Chronicque de la traïson et mort de Richart Deux*. From the latter Caxton translates several sections of narrative for the reign of Richard II, including a close though slightly condensed account of Richard's murder by Sir Piers de Exton (correctly transferred from Gravesend Castle in Kent to Pontefract Castle in Yorkshire) and the alternative story of voluntary starvation.

It was once thought that Caxton had taken this material from Lambeth MS 84, but the reverse is true.[15] The manuscript is an expanded individual reworking of the *Brut*, first completed in 1479 and then extensively revised after 1482 by the incorporation of material from Caxton's edition of the *Polychronicon*, including the Exton murder and the voluntary starvation version, together with the *Brut* account of forced starvation as found in BL Harley 53 and Lambeth 6 (to which the compiler has appended a quaint vision experienced by Richard). Remarkably, Edward Hall seems to have known this manuscript directly.

To Caxton, therefore, belongs the honor of having first introduced into England the version of the murder portrayed in Shakespeare. Many of the surviving manuscripts of the *Traïson et mort* can be associated with the ducal library of Burgundy,[16] with which Caxton seems to have been familiar during his long residence at Bruges, though it must have been between 1480 and 1482 that he decided to adopt the *Traïson*'s account of Richard's end. The *Liber ultimus* text follows, collated with that of Lambeth MS 84 (designated L):[17]

Whanne [And whan L] Kyng Henry sawe that these lordes [the dukes of Surrey and Exeter and the earls of Salisbury and Gloucester, with several knights and servants of Richard II, all taken and executed] thus hadde rysen, and assemblyd greete peple to haue putte hym to deth, and for to restore Kynge Rychard ageyne to his crowne and to his roy-amme, thoughte [he thoughte L] teschue suche peryls. Anone [And anone he L] commaunded Sir Pyers of Exton that he shold goo strayte to Pountfreyte and delyuer the worlde of Kynge Rychard.

And soo he departed fro the kynge and wente to the castel of Pountfret, wher as Kynge Rychard was in prysonne, the whiche was sette at table for to dyne. And anone after, Syre Pyers cam in to the chambre where the kynge was, and eghte [& he broughte viij L] men with hym and eche man an axe in his hond. Trouth it is whan [And whan (Trouth it is *om.*) L] the kyng sawe Sir Pyers with his felaushippe entre in to the chambre defensably arayed, he shoof the table from hym and sprange in [in to L] the myddes of hem & raughte an axe oute of one of theyr hondes and sette hymself valyauntly at defence. And hymself defendynge, he slowe foure of the eyghte. And whanne the sayde Syre [*om.* L] Pyers sawe the kynge soo defende hym, he was soore abasshed and gretely aferde, and forthwith [*om.* L] sterte vpon the place where as Kyng Rychard was wonte to sytte. And as Kynge Rychard foughte and defended hymself, goynge bacwarde, the sayd Syre Pyers smote hym on the heed with his axe that he fyll to gronnde. Thenne cryed Kynge Rychard, "God, mercy." And thenne he gafe hym yet [*om.* L] another stroke on the heede, and soo he deyde. And thus was thys noble kynge slayne and murthred.

And whanne the kynge was deede, the knyght that hadde thus slayne hym sette hym doune by the deede bodye of Kynge Rychard and byganne to wepe, saynge, "Alas, what thynge haue we doone? we haue putte to deth hym that hath ben oure kynge and souerayne lord two and twenty yere. Now haue I lost myn honour. Ne [*om.* L] I shal neuer come in place but I shal be reproched. For I haue done ageynste myn honour."

After this, the tweluest daye of Marche, was the bodye of the noble Kyng Rychard broughte thurgh London to Powlus, whiche corps [Aftyr this moche peeple in Englonde & other countrees also wolde not beleue þat Kyng Richard was deede, but sayde þat he was alyue many yerys aftyr. Where-for Kyng Herry, whan he wist verryly þat he was dede, he leete cere hym in þe best maner & with dyuers spices & balmes & in a fayre cheste closyd alle in lynyn clothe, saaf his visage, which was lefte opyn þat men myht see & knowe his persone from alle othir men. And thus he was broughte thurgh London to Powlus & his body L] was leyd on a charyotte coueryd with black, and foure baners, wherof tweyne

were of the armes of Saynt George and tweyne of the armes of Saynt
Edward. And there were an honderd men clothed in black, eche
berynge a torche. And the cyte of London hadde thrytty men in whyte,
eche berynge also a torche. And the corps was leyd open the vysage
[and þe visage of þe dede body was leyde opyn L] that euery man
myght see and knowe that it was hys body and that he was soo deede,
for many men byleuyd it not. [L *adds* And from Powlus he was had to
Westmenster & þere he hadde his hole masse & diryge also.] And from
thennes he was caryed to the Frerys at [of L] Langley and there he was
buryed. On whoos sowle God haue mercy. Amen.

The comyn oppynyon of Englysshmen is that Kynge Rychard deyde
not after the maner aforesayd, but that he deyde other wyse: that is to
wete [but þat he deyde & was famynyd & lakkyd bothe mete & drynke,
& yet he was dayle seruyd þere-of lyke a kyng but he myht not towche yt
but only see hyt & þerefor his (*sic: add* hunger) was þe more. And on a
tyme, as he lay on his bed of estaate, hym thouhte þere come a fayre
woman vnto hym and brought a kercherful of white rosys & bestruyd all
his bed therwith, & he fed hym of tho rosys, þat his grete hungre was
withdrawe; & whan he woke, hym thoughte his apyted was wel satysfyed,
& þerby his lyf contynuyd a day or tweyne the lenger. And some sayeth
thus L] that whanne he herde saye that his brother [lordys L] the duc
of Excetre, the duc of Surrey, the erle of Salysbury, and the other
lordes were deede, he was soo angry and soo sorowfull that he swore
that he wolde neuer eete meete, and soo abode foure dayes withoute
etynge, as they saye. And whanne that [*om.* L] Kynge Henry [Herry L]
vnderstode that he wolde not ete, he sent to hym two prelates for-to
comforte him. And whan they were come, he confessyd hym to one of
them, the whiche gaf hym in penaunce that he sholde ete his mete.
And whanne he supposed to haue eten, the meete myght not goo
doune ne auale in to his stomake, for the conduytes of his bodye were
shronken togeder. And thenne sayde the noble Kynge Rychard that it
was done and that he muste nedes deye, and soo he deyde [and soo he
deyde *om.* L]. But certes whether he deyde this waye or that other, cer-
taynly he deyde [dede he is L], and was buryed at Langley. God haue
mercy on his sowle. Amen. And thenne was Kynge Harry peasyly [peas-
bly L] kyng.

Within twenty-five years of Caxton's *Liber ultimus* and the compila-
tion of Lambeth 84, Robert Fabyan completed his *New Chronicles of
England and France*, which also contains the murder by Exton.[18] In 1504
Fabyan completed the bulk of his work, ending with the accession of
Henry VII in 1485, though a later continuation to 1509 is probably also
by him. Fabyan used the prose *Brut* and Caxton's print of the

Polychronicon as major sources, and his abbreviated account of Richard's death appears to have been primarily derived from the *Liber ultimus*, though there are details, here and in the earlier truncated account of a quarrel between Richard and the duke of Gloucester, that suggest that Fabyan was also using the original *Traïson*. He notes very cursorily the notion of famine, commenting "but this [the Exton story] of moost wryters is testyfyed & allegid." Such an assessment is extremely curious, since this is not the clear opinion of his English sources. Perhaps he is giving greater credence to the French account here or perhaps he has misread Caxton's account. Whatever the original circumstances, however, this assessment must have circulated fairly widely, for the *New Chronicles* went through seven printings from its posthumous publication in 1516 to 1559 and was an important and respected source for later sixteenth-century chroniclers. Fabyan's full account, together with his record of Richard's Latin epitaph (later borrowed by Abraham Fleming for the 1587 edition of Holinshed), also given in English translation with a stanza of commentary by Fabyan himself, is as follows:

> [*Margin:* Trucidatur Richardus.] Than it foloweth in the story of kynge Henry, whan he had fermelye consyderyd the great conspyracy agayne hym by the forenamyd lordys and other persones entendyd and imagenyd to his dystruccyon, & agayn releuynge Rycharde late kynge, he, in avoydynge of lyke daunger, prouyded to put the sayd Rycharde out of this present lyfe; and shortlye, after the opynyon of moost wry-ters, he sent a knyght, named syr Piers of Exton, vnto Pountfreyt castell, where he with viii other in his companye, fell vpon the sayde Rycharde late kynge, and hym myserably in his chaumbre slewe; but not without reuengement of his deth: for, or he were fellyd to the grounde, he slewe of the sayd viii iiii men, with an axe of theyr owne; but lastely he was woundyd to deth by the hande of the sayde syr Piers of Exton, & so dyed. After execucyon of which dedely dede, ye sayd syr Piers toke great repentaunce; in so moche that lamentably he sayd, "Alas! what haue we done, we haue now put to deth hym that hath ben ouer soueraygne and drad lorde by the space of xxii yeres, by reason whereof I shall be reprochyd of all honoure wheresoer I after this daye become, and all men shall redounde this dede to my dyshonour and shame." Other opynyons of the dethe of this noble prynce are lefte by wryters, as by waye of famyne & other; but this of moost wryters is testyfyed & allegid. Whan the deth of this prynce was publysshed abrode, he was after opyn vysaged layed in the mynster of Pounfrayt, so yat all men myght knowe and see that he was dede. And the xii daye of Marche folowynge, he was with great solempnyte brought thoroughe the cytie of London to Paulys, & there layed open visaged agayn, to the end that

his dethe myght be manyfestlye knowen, whiche was doutfull to many one, and speciallye to suche as oughte to hym fauoure. And then after a fewe dayes the sayd corps was caryed vnto the freris of Langley and there enterryd; but after he was remouyd by kynge Henry ye v in the firste yere of his reygne, and with great honoure and solempnyte conueyed vnto the monastery of Westmynster, and there within the chapell of seynt Edwarde, honourably buryed vpon the South syde of seynt Edwardys shryne, with this epytaphy vpon his toumbe as foloweth.

Prudens et mundus Richardus, iure secundus
Per fatum victus iacet hic sub marmore pictus.
Verax sermone fuit et plenus ratione,
Corpore procerus, animo prudens vt Omerus,
Ecclesiam fauit, elatos subpeditauit,
Quemuis prostrauit regalia qui violauit.

Whiche versys are thus to be vnderstande, in our vulgare and Englysshe tonge, as foloweth.

Parfyght and prudent Rycharde, by ryght the seconde,
Vaynquysshed by fortune, lyeth here nowe grauen in stone.
Trewe of his worde, and therto well resounde.
Semely of persone, and lyke to Omer as one.
In worldely prudence, and euer the Churche in one
Vp helde and fauoured, castynge the proude to grounde,
And all that wolde his royall state confounde.

But yet alas! thoughe that this metyr or ryme
Thus doth enbelysshe this noble pryncis fame,
And that some clerke which fauoured hym some tyme
Lyste by his cunnynge, thus to enhaunce his name,
Yet by his story apperith in hym some blame.
Wherefore to pryncys is surest memory,
Theyr lyues to exercyse in vertous constancy.

Whan this mortall prynce was thus dede and grauen, kynge Henry was in quyet possessyon of the realme, [etc.; Fabyan goes on to relate the riches found in Richard's treasury, "as wytnessyth Polycronycon"].[19]

As noted earlier, Fabyan and Caxton are named by Edward Hall as two of his principal English sources. For Richard's death, however, Hall returned to the English prose *Brut* for the enforced famine version; remarkably, it appears that Hall's direct source was the unique text of Lambeth MS 84, which, like Hall, calls this the generally accepted version. He then turned to the French *Traïson* for the full Exton story, containing, for example, the episode between Richard and his food-tasting esquire (Shakespeare's keeper). The number of ax blows that fell Richard is reduced to one. A couple of details presumably came from Lambeth MS 84, such as the eight (rather than seven) accomplices and Exton's dismay at Richard's spirited resistance. That Henry IV does not directly order Richard's murder and Exton acts as the result of the new king's transparent hints at the dinner table represents a major innovation, duly reproduced by Holinshed and reflected in Shakespeare.

There has been considerable disagreement whether Shakespeare knew directly the *Traïson* and Jean Creton's mainly metrical *Histoire du Roy d'Angleterre Richard II*, which were only available in manuscript.[20] Peter Ure has argued that even Holinshed knew the *Traïson* only through the partial English translation written in the hand of John Stow in BL MS Harley 6219 and that the French work was not necessarily readily available in England in the late sixteenth century.[21] While it is true that all the surviving manuscripts of the *Traïson* are found in French and Belgian libraries, Caxton, Stow, and Hall certainly, and Fabyan possibly, had access to the text (though the manuscript identified by Benjamin Williams as at least belonging to the type used by Stow is also, interestingly enough, of the same type as used by Caxton).[22] The identification of the language in Holinshed's marginal reference to "an old French pamphlet belonging to John Stowe" suggests that it was the original text rather than the partial translation to which he was referring.[23] The "French pamphlet that belongeth to master John Dee" or "master Dees French booke" to which Holinshed also refers can be identified with Lambeth MS 598, a copy of Creton, in French, which contains Dee's signature and the date 1575.[24] There are some general similarities between Shakespeare and the two French historical works, especially parallels drawn between Richard and Christ, but the evidence is not conclusive whether the dramatist knew these narratives.

Similarly, one can speculate which, if any, of the older English chronicles underlying the sixteenth-century historical writers might have been known to Shakespeare. There is a good chance that he was acquainted with both the immensely popular prose *Brut* (*Chronicles of England*) and the *Liber ultimus* of the *Polychronicon* through one of the many subsequent printings of Caxton's *editiones principes*. Both were standard works, still current though perhaps a little old-fashioned by the late sixteenth century, which provided convenient, basic, and relatively short accounts of Richard's reign and death.

•   •   •

It remains to consider whether Shakespeare made a conscious decision to portray the version of Richard's death that he did. If the comments of Hall and Holinshed regarding popular belief in the various versions are to be taken at face value, Shakespeare has deliberately chosen the most colorful (and melodramatic) but not the commonly accepted account. In effect, Shakespeare would be emphatically disclaiming any pretensions to strict historical accuracy at this point, thus marking his version as an overtly self-conscious literary construct with its own criteria of selection. He would be asserting quite categorically that *Richard II* is a *tragedie*, not a chronicle play.

There would have been a certain circumspect political sense to such a decision, given the topicality and touchiness of the question of deposition. We recall that the deposition scene in *Richard II*, although already written, was omitted from the first three quarto editions and was first published after Queen Elizabeth's death in the fourth edition of 1608.[25] It may have been this play (perhaps with the deposition scene) that the conspirators chose to view on the eve of the earl of Essex's short-lived rebellion in February 1601, in order to put steel in their backbones. In the summer following the failed rising and in the context of continuing Catholic agitation for her dethronement, Elizabeth is reported to have remarked, "I am Richard II. Know ye not that?" Parallels between the reigns of Richard and Elizabeth had been drawn earlier.[26] Richard seems to have enjoyed a vogue as the accepted type of the monarch most likely to be deposed. At her trial in 1586 Mary, Queen of Scots, had compared the proceedings to what had happened to Richard;[27] after Mary's execution Elizabeth sought to disclaim all responsibility.[28] In 1592 a correspondent of Lord Burghley reports "a libel" warning James VI of Scotland of Richard II's fate.[29] There could, therefore, have been sound political reasons to portray an account of Richard's death that was generally accepted to be historically false.

On the other hand, there are reasons for doubting the accuracy of Hall and Holinshed's assessment. Their "common fame" echoes suspiciously the "common opinion" of Lambeth MS 84 (and of Caxton's *Liber ultimus*, although Caxton assigns popular belief to the voluntary starvation story). It may well be that Hall and Holinshed were simply following their sources conservatively, thus reflecting the situation in the fifteenth century before the Exton account was introduced into England. Hall does admit doubt whether Henry ordered Richard's death or not and he does offer "the diuersities of opinions concerning the deathe of this infortunate prince, remittyng to your iudgement whiche you thynke moost trewe, but the very truthe is that he died of a violent death, and not by the darte of naturall infirmitie." His tearjerk-ing, Marlowesque apostrophe to the horrors of death by starvation may suggest that this was the version that he accepted as historical. Holinshed gives the three versions, though he seems to favor the Exton story since the narration of Richard's obsequies follows natu-rally thereupon, with no intervening expression of doubt. The *Myrroure for Magistrates* (1559), Samuel Daniel's *Civil Wars* (1595), and John Hayward's *King Henry the IV* (1599) accept the murder by Exton (though Daniel "will not here defile / My unstained verse with his opprobrious name" and it is left to a marginal note to remark "This Knight was Sir Pierce of Exton").[30] Despite Hall and Holinshed, it would appear that the Exton murder had become the "common fame" in the course of the sixteenth century, though there had also arisen some doubt whether Henry was directly responsible. Shakespeare is, then, simply following the general current belief in his choice of deaths. Shakespeare also reflects sixteenth-century doubts over Henry's direct involvement and responsibility—"some saye he com-maunded, other talke that he condiscended, many wryte that he knewe nat tyll it was done, and then it confirmed" as Hall wrote.

Arguably, there are a number of parallels between the Exton account of Richard's death and the murder of Thomas Becket. Shakespeare's Sir Pierce reports that he takes his cue from Henry's rhetorical question, "Have I no friend will rid me of this living fear?" (5.4.2; cf. Hall, followed by Holinshed, "Haue I no faytheful frende whiche wil deliuer me of hym whose life will be my death, and whose death will be the preseruacion of my lyfe?"). This is reminiscent of Henry II's rhetorical musings that instigate the murder of Becket, as recorded by Holinshed:[31]

> [*Margin*: The occasion of the kings words that cost bish. Becket his life.] The king giuing eare to theire complaint, was so displeased in his mind against archbishop Thomas, that in open audience of his lords, knights, and gentlemen, he said these or the like words: "In what miser-able state am I, that can not be in rest within mine owne realme, by rea-son of one onelie preest? Neither is there any of my folkes that will helpe to deliuer me out of such troubles."
>
> There were some that stood about the king, which gessed by these words, that his mind was to signifie how he would haue some man to dispatch the archbishop out of the waie.[32]

The physical circumstances of the two deaths are also similar in Holinshed:

1) Both victims are assailed by a group of armed men.
2) Like Richard, Becket offers some resistance, albeit nonlethal: "And herewith taking on other of the knights by the habergeon, he floong him from him with such violence, that he had almost throwne him downe to the ground."[33]
3) Both receive their deathblows on their heads, which had been anointed.
4) The murderer(s) are subsequently spurned by their kings: "King Henrie [II] gaue them so litle thankes for their presumptuous act, sounding to the euill example of other in breach of his lawes, that they despairing vtterlie of pardon, fled one into one place, and another into another" (Ellis, 1807-8, 2: 136).
5) Both kings deny complicity in murder: when Henry II finally purges himself he vows "that he neither willed, nor commanded the archbishop Thomas to be murthered, and that when he heard of it, he was sorie for it" (2: 143).
6) Each king receives a penance for the murder: one of the articles of Henry II's penance is that within three years "he should take vpon him the crosse, and personallie passe to the holie land" (2: 143). (The comment in the margin is "O vile subiection vnbeseeming a king!")

Other parallels existed also. Like Henry IV, Henry II had a namesake son who was riotous in his youth (2: 130-31). Both Richard, in French chronicles and in Shakespeare, and Becket, in hagiographic accounts, are compared with Christ and parallels are drawn between their deaths and the Passion.[34]

In the late sixteenth century any reminiscences of Thomas Becket's murder would have been highly charged politically and in terms of the characters of Bolingbroke and Richard. From the time of the Reformation, Becket was officially persona non grata, declared by royal proclamation in 1538 "a rebel and traitor to his prince,"[35] and his shrine in Canterbury Cathedral was destroyed, as were those of other "counterfeated Sainctes."[36] Tudor and Elizabethan antiquarians were assiduous in scratching out of manuscripts that had been in monastic hands the words "pope" (occasionally substituting "bishop of Rome") and "saint" as a title of Becket (in favor of "bishop"). Chronicles such as Fabyan's, originally published before 1538 and reprinted after that date, were carefully edited and their history altered to show Becket in a vile light.[37]

Nevertheless, the murders of Richard II (Exton version) and Thomas Becket were similar, and there were other links between these two and Henry IV that were probably known to Shakespeare and his audience, in particular the story attached to the consecration oil used to anoint Henry IV. John Capgrave describes Henry's coronation:

> Thus was he crowned on Seynt Edward day and anoynted with þat holy oyle þat was take to Seynt Thomas of Cauntirbury be oure Lady, and he lefte it in Frauns. This oyle was closed in a egel of gold and þat egil put in a crowet of ston, and be reualacion Herry, þe first duke of Lancastir fond it, and brout it hom to Ynglond, and gaue it to þe Prince Edward [the Black Prince], to þis effect, þat aftir his faderes deces he schuld be anoynted with þe same. And aftir þe princes deth it was left in þe kyngis tresory, and neuyr man tok kep þerto til, a litil before þat þe king [Richard] exiled þe Bischop Thomas [Arundel], þis relik was found, and certayn writing þeron, as Thomas of Cauntirbury left it. Than was Kyng Richard glad, and desired of þe bischop to be anoynted new, but he wold not. But for al þat þe kyng bare it with him into Yrland, and whan he was take in his coming ageyn, he dylyuered it to Thomas Arundel, and soo was Herry crowned with þe same.[38]

Capgrave's account is a shortened adaptation of a popular story given by Thomas Walsingham, who recounts that Richard came across the eagle and ampulla while rummaging around in his ancestors' relics in the Tower of London and that the writing attached to these was a prophecy of Thomas Becket.[39] The underlying prophecy, the so-called "Vision at Sens" or "The Ampulla Prophecy," survives in Latin in many manuscripts and chronicles.[40] It was translated into French by Jean Bouchet in the *Annals of Aquitaine*, which were known to Edward Hall.[41] In the late fifteenth century the compiler of Lambeth MS 84 made an English translation of the prophecy, which he found prefixed to a manuscript of the Latin *Polychronicon*, and inserted it into his account of Becket. The following text has not been printed before:

> [Lambeth MS 84, fol. 93] [*Margin*: A Prophesi.] Also it is red in Policronicon a prophese, wryttyn in Latyn in þe begynnyng of þe booke, þat seyth thus:
> Whan I Thomas, Archebisshop of Cauntirbury, was exilid & fled in to Fraunce, & so went to Rome to Pope [*erased*] Alexandre, then beyng olde, to telle hym þe evyl & malicius customys & abusiouns þat þe kyng of Engelond wolde haue brouht in to þe cherche.
> And on a nyhte, as I was in þe cherche of Seint Columbe in my prayours, praying vnto þe queen of heuyn þat she woolde geve vnto þe kyng

of Engelond & to his ayeres ful purpose & wyl to amende ther trans-
gressis doon vnto þe cherche, and at Crist of His mercy & beneuolence
myhte make them to love þe cherche.

And anon þe blessyd virgin Marie apperyd vnto me, hauyng afore
her breste an egil of golde hangyng, & helde in her hande a lytil cruet
of stone; she, takyng þe egil from her brest, & put þe cruet into þe egle
& shet it fast. And then she toke it me in myn hand, seyng to me thes
woordis be ordyr: "This oynement shal serve to annoynte with þe kyngis
of Engelond, but nat he þat now regneth nor hereaftyr shal regne, for-
whi they ar wykkyd & of evyl disposicioun & yewse moche synne & shal
yewse. But ther ar [fol. 93v] kyngis hereaftyr to come þat shal be herewith anoyntyd, & they shal be blessedful & gret subportyrs of
holichirche; they shal pesibile recouer þe land lost by her auncestours.
There is a kyng of England to come þat shal be first anoyntyd with this
oynement, þat shal wynne þe lande lost by his fadyrs afore, that is to
sey, Normandy & Aquitaney, withoute resistyng. This kyng shal be
grettest of al kyngis, & he shal edifie many chirchis in þe holy lande &
wyn þe cite of Babilone, in þe whiche he shal bylde many chirchis. And
in what batayle þat þe kyng bere þe egil on his brest, he shal haue þe
victorie of his enemyes & evyr augment his kyngdom. And thow art a
martir to come."

And then I besouhte of þe blessidful virgin Marie þat she woolde
shew me where þat I myht kepe suche a precius holi relique as þat was.
Then she answeryd to me & sayde, "Ther is a man in this cete callid
William, whiche is a monke of Seint Ciprian in Pictauensis, & he is
vnryhtfully expulsid oute of his place by his abbot. And thow shalt go
vnto þe pope [*erased*] & byd hym to compelle his abbot to resseyue hym
ageyne in to his abbey. And take hym þe egil with þe cruet, to bere
them into þe cite of Pictauensis & in þe chirche of Seint Gregore, þat is
nyh þe cherche of Seint Hillarie, & þere to hide them in þe west ende
of þe cherche vndir a grete stone, there to be founde in tyme to come.
And be þe hede of a pagan they shal be founde"—and ther she depar-
tyd away.

Then I closid this egil in a vessel of lede & toke it to þe monke, bid-
dyng hym do as I was comandyd.

Although the "Ampulla Prophecy" may have been composed earlier, it was readily applied for political purposes to Henry IV, the first
king anointed with Becket's sacred unction, and was but one of a
number of prophecies whose interpretation strengthened Henry's
claim to legitimacy. The sacred oil continued to be used at corona-
tions throughout the fifteenth century.[42] Given the emphasis placed
on the fact of anointment by Richard and other characters in the play

(see 1.2.38, 2.1.98, 2.3.95, 3.2.55, 4.1.127, 4.1.206), it may have had significant resonances for Shakespeare and his audience.

The "Ampulla Prophecy" also indicates the general associative context in which to view Henry's expiatory intention to liberate Jerusalem and his desire in his will, duly honored, to be buried in Canterbury Cathedral, where his tomb stands on one side of the site of Becket's shrine (destroyed in 1538), while that of the Black Prince, Richard's father, stands on the other.[43]

The golden eagle-shaped ampulla continues to be used in the coronation ceremony; in its present form it dates from the time of Henry IV (perhaps replacing Richard's pendant-sized one), elaborated and reshaped for Charles II.[44] Mary Tudor felt that the efficacy of the unction had been tainted by its use in the crowning of her Protestant half-brother Edward VI and sent to the pope for new consecrated oil, but Elizabeth returned to Becket's unction for her coronation.[45] One should not push the possible analogies too far however. If the staunchly Protestant Hall intended any parallels between Richard and Becket, then he would have intended them to be drawn to the detriment of Richard.

• • •

Behind Shakespeare's account of the murder of Richard II by Pierce de Exton, the beginning of the "continuall discension for the croune of this noble realme" (Hall, 1550, title page), lies a tradition that stretches back through Holinshed, Hall, Fabyan, and Caxton to "diuers other Pamphlettes, the names of whom are to moste men vnknowen" (Hall). Variously described as "our English Chronicles . . . rustie brasse, and worme-eaten bookes" in Nashe's *Pierce Penilesse* (86) or as "the leaues of a dog-hay, leaues of a worme eaten Chronicle" in *Every Woman in Her Humor* (2.1.197-98),[46] the late medieval chronicles nevertheless provide the background against which to measure the dramatist's handling of received historical knowledge and attitudes—the mental clutter of fact, falsehood, conjecture, rationalization, legend, myth, prejudice, opinion, and moral judgment that forms a nation's sense of itself, its past, and its place in the world—which Shakespeare shared with his audience.

Notes

1. Derek Traversi, *Shakespeare from "Richard II" to "Henry V"* (Stanford: Stanford University Press, 1957), 48.
2. The text quoted is that of *The Pelican Shakespeare*, ed. Matthew W. Black, rev. ed. (Baltimore: Penguin, 1970), with scene locations added.
3. Charles Lethbridge Kingsford, *English Historical Literature in the Fifteenth Century* (Oxford: Clarendon Press, 1913), 271-74; Geoffrey Bullough, *Earlier English History Plays: Henry VI, Richard III, Richard II*, vol. 3 of *Narrative and Dramatic Sources of Shakespeare* (London: Routledge; New York: Columbia University Press, 1966), 3:13-14, 362-63.
4. See Graham Pollard, "The Bibliographical History of Hall's Chronicle," *Bulletin of the Institute of Historical Research* 10 (1933): 12-17.
5. Bullough, *Narrative and Dramatic Sources of Shakespeare*, 3:362.
6. Cf. Gordon W. Zeeveld, "The Influence of Hall on Shakespeare's Historical Plays," *ELH* 3 (1936): 317-53.
7. Here and elsewhere below in quotations from manuscripts and early printed books, the punctuation, capitalization, and division into paragraphs have been modernized. Corrections and minor errors in the texts have been emended silently. Textual variants, variant readings, folio numbers, and editorial comments are enclosed in square brackets.
8. *The Union of the Two Noble Families of Lancaster and York, 1550* (Menston, Yorkshire: Scolar Press, 1970) (a facsimile of Richard Grafton's second edition of 1550). The 1548 edition is printed in Henry Ellis, ed., *Hall's Chronicle* (London: J. Johnson, F. C. and J. Rivington, 1809).
9. R. S. Wallace and Alma Hansen, eds., *Holinshed's Chronicles: Richard II, 1398-1400, Henry IV, and Henry V* (Oxford: Clarendon Press, 1923), 24-26.
10. See Lister M. Matheson, "Historical Prose," in *Middle English Prose: A Critical Guide to Major Authors and Genres*, ed. A. S. G. Edwards (New Brunswick: Rutgers University Press, 1984), 210-14; Donald Edward Kennedy, "Chronicles and Other Historical Writing," in *A Manual of the Writings in Middle English, 1050-1500*, ed. Albert E. Hartung, vol. 8 (New Haven: Archon Books, for The Connecticut Academy of Arts and Sciences, 1989), 2629-37.
11. Lister M. Matheson, "The Middle English Prose *Brut*: A Location List of the Manuscripts and Early Printed Editions," *Analytical and Enumerative Bibliography* 3 (1979): 265.
12. Friedrich D. Brie, ed., *The Brut or The Chronicles of England*, 2 vols., EETS 131, 136 (Part I: Oxford: Oxford University Press, [1906] 1960; Part II: Millwood, N.J.: Kraus Reprint, [1908] 1987).
13. A. S. G. Edwards, "John Trevisa," in *Middle English Prose: A Critical Guide to Major Authors and Genres*, ed. A. S. G. Edwards (New Brunswick: Rutgers University Press, 1984), 143.
14. J. R. Lumby, ed., *Polychronicon Ranulphi Higden Monachi Cestrensis* (London: Rolls Series, 1882), 8: 522-87 (the text of Caxton's *Liber ultimus*). See Lister M. Matheson, "Printer and Scribe: Caxton, the Polychronicon, and the *Brut*," *Speculum* 60 (1985): 601-7.

15. Matheson, "Printer and Scribe," 607-9.

16. See Benjamin Williams, ed., *Chronicque de la Traïson et Mort de Richart Deux, Roy Dengleterre* (Vaduz: Kraus Reprint, [1846] 1964), lxxxiii-xcii.

17. The full *Liber ultimus* is printed in Lumby. The relevant text from Lambeth MS 84 is edited in Brie 2:590/22-592/21. The present text and collation are reedited from the originals.

18. For Fabyan, see Kingsford, *English Historical Literature*, 261-65; Louisa D. Duls, *Richard II in the Early Chronicles* (The Hague and Paris: Mouton, 1975), 181-82, 187-88, 246-47; Antonia Gransden, *Historical Literature in England, II: c. 1307 to the Early Sixteenth Century* (Ithaca: Cornell University Press, 1982), 245-48; Kennedy, "Chronicles and Other Historical Writing," 2654-55.

19. Robert Fabyan, *The New Chronicles of England and France*, ed. Henry Ellis (London: F. C. and J. Rivington [etc.], 1811), 568-69.

20. For an overview see Bullough, *Narrative and Dramatic Sources*, 354, 369-72; Kenneth Muir, *The Sources of Shakespeare's Plays* (New Haven: Yale University Press, 1978), 46-51.

21. Peter Ure, "Shakespeare's Play and the French Sources of Holinshed's and Stow's Account of Richard II," *N&Q* 198 (1953): 426-29. For Stow's translation, see Williams, *Chronicque de la Traïson et Mort de Richart Deux, Roy Dengleterre*, vi-vii.

22. See Williams, *Chronicque de la Traïson et Mort de Richart Deux, Roy Dengleterre*, vii; Matheson, "Printer and Scribe," 605.

23. Williams, *Chronicque de la Traïson et Mort de Richart Deux, Roy Dengleterre*, vi; cf. Wallace and Hansen, *Holinshed's Chronicles*, 7.

24. Wallace and Hansen, *Holinshed's Chronicles*, 15, 21, 26; Williams, *Chronicque de la Traïson et Mort de Richart Deux, Roy Dengleterre*, vii.

25. Matthew W. Black, ed., *Richard II, The Pelican Shakespeare*, rev. ed. (Baltimore: Penguin, 1970), 17; for an argument that the scene is a late addition, however, see David M. Bergeron, "The Deposition Scene in *Richard II*," *Renaissance Papers* (1974): 31-37.

26. Lily B. Campbell, *Shakespeare's "Histories": Mirrors of Elizabethan Policy*, 3rd ed. (London: Methuen, 1964), 173, 191, 196-97; C. A. Greer, "The Deposition Scene of *Richard II*," *N&Q* 197 (1952): 492-93.

27. William Poel, *Shakespeare in the Theatre* (New York: Benjamin Blom, [1913] 1968), 112.

28. See Campbell, *Shakespeare's "Histories*," 162, quoting J. E. Neale's *Queen Elizabeth* (New York, 1936), 279.

29. Campbell, *Shakespeare's "Histories*," 176.

30. *A Myrroure for Magistrates* in Bullough, *Narrative and Dramatic Sources*, 422; Daniel, in Bullough, *Narrative and Dramatic Sources*, 457; [John Hayward], *The First Part of the Life and Raigne of King Henrie the iiii, extending to the End of the First Yeare of His Raigne* (London: John Wolfe, 1599), 132.

31. Theodore A. Stroud, "Shakespeare's Richard II as a Saint Manqué in a Compounded Tragedy," *Iowa State Journal of Research* 53 (1979): 203.

32. *Holinshed's Chronicles of England, Scotland, and Ireland*, ed. Henry Ellis, 6 vols. (London: Johnson, and Rivington, [etc.], 1807-8), 2:134.

33. Ibid.; Becket's slight resistance undercuts Stroud's argument that by resisting Richard fails to become a "Becket-like martyr" ("Shakespeare's Richard II," 203-4). It is, however, in accord with Karl F. Thompson's contention that Richard follows the pattern of martyrdom presented in John Foxe's *Actes and Monuments*, where the faithful die heroically in action; see Thompson, "Richard II, Martyr," *ShQ* 8 (1957): 159-66.

34. Muir, *The Sources of Shakespeare's Plays*, 50; Paul N. Siegel, *Shakespeare's English and Roman History Plays: A Marxist Approach* (London and Toronto: Associated University Presses, 1986), 38-39; Paul Alonzo Brown, *The Development of the Legend of Thomas Becket* (Philadelphia: n.p., 1930), 134-37.

35. Arthur Penrhyn Stanley, *Historical Memorials of Canterbury*, (Philadelphia: George W. Jacobs, 1899), 296.

36. Ellis, *Hall's Chronicle*, 826.

37. Francis Thynne, however, in his *Liues of the Archbishops of Canturburie* (1568), incorporated in the 1587 edition of Holinshed, describes Becket as "a good souldior both for the church and the kingdome" (Ellis 4: 689). Holinshed himself speaks of "that Romish rakehels ambitious and traitorous heart" (Ellis, *Hall's Chronicle*, 2:147).

38. John Capgrave, *Abbreuiacion of Cronicles*, ed. Peter J. Lucas, EETS 285 (Oxford: Oxford University Press, 1983), 214 (line 27)-215 (line 10).

39. *Historia Anglicana*, ed. Henry Thomas Riley, 2 vols. (London: Rolls Series, 1863-64), 2:239-240. A similar account, in English, is found in certain texts of the Peculiar Versions of the prose *Brut* and the related text of "Davies's" *Chronicle*; for the latter, see John Silvester Davies, ed., *An English Chronicle of the Reigns of Richard II., Henry IV., Henry V., and Henry VI.*, Camden Society 64 (London: J. B. Nichols, 1865), 14.

40. Brown, *The Development of the Legend of Thomas Becket*, 226n6, 227. Latin texts of the prophecy are printed in *PL* 190: 391-94; as part of a collection of assorted legends in the *Eulogium Historiarum Sive Temporis*, ed. Frank Scott Haydon, 3 vols. (London: Rolls Series, 1858-63), 1:406-7; and, with the ampulla's later history, in Walsingham's *Annales Ricardi Secundi et Henrici Quarti*, a continuation of John de Trokelowe and Henry de Blaneford, *Chronica et Annales*, ed. Henry Thomas Riley (London: Rolls Series, 1865), 297-300 (see also Chris Given-Wilson, trans. and ed., *Chronicles of the Revolution, 1397-1400: The Reign of Richard II* [Manchester and New York: Manchester University Press, 1993], 201).

41. Bouchet's French text is printed in John Webb, ed., "Translation of a French Metrical History of the Deposition of King Richard the Second," *Archaeologia* 20 (1824): 266-67 (also contains the French text of Jean Creton's *Histoire du Roy d'Angleterre Richard*).

42. Percy E. Schramm, *A History of the English Coronation*, trans. Leopold G. Wickham Legg (Oxford: Clarendon Press, 1937), 131-33, 137-38; J. W. McKenna, "The Coronation Oil of the Yorkist Kings," *EHR* 82 (1967): 102-4.

43. J. A. Nichols, *Collection of all the Wills . . . of the Kings and Queens of England [etc.]* (New York: Kraus Reprint and AMS Press, [1780] 1969), 203; Stanley, *Historical Memorials*, 176.

44. Brian Barker, *The Symbols of Sovereignty* (Newton Abbot, Devon: Westbridge Books; North Pomfret, Vermont: David and Charles, 1979), 80-82 and plate opposite 84; Tessa Rose, *The Coronation Ceremony of the Kings and Queens of England and the Crown Jewels* (London: HMSO, 1992), 94 (plate) and cf. 97-99.

45. Rose, *The Coronation Ceremony*, 98. Elizabeth complained of the rank smell. The last of the original unction was used at the coronation of James I (Barker, *The Symbols of Sovereignty*, 82).

46. Thomas Nashe, *Pierce Penilesse, His Svpplication to the Divell (1592)*, ed. G. B. Harrison (New York: Barnes and Noble, [1924] 1966); *Every Woman in Her Humor* (Anon, 1609), ed. Archie Mervin Tyson (New York and London: Garland, 1980).

Family by Death: Stage Images in Titus Andronicus and The Winter's Tale

Randal Robinson

Trained by productions and informed by dreams, we can find, in the images of Shakespeare's stage, emphases, patterns, and connections that reside deeper than words. Reading the stage images of *Titus Andronicus* and *The Winter's Tale*, for example, we realize that these plays are strange but not distant relations, works born of the selfsame psychic issues. Consider, first, these visual patterns.

In *Titus Andronicus*, act 4, scene 2, a black man and two white men relax onstage, laughing. To them enters a nurse with an infant. The nurse, a woman alone among men, shows the infant's face to the black man, with loathing. The black man touches the infant tenderly, but the white men move against the infant, and one draws his sword. The black man, protecting the infant, draws a scimitar, takes the infant from the nurse, forces the nurse and the white men to sit, and suddenly stabs the nurse, delighting as she collapses. Moments later the black man sends the white men away and, alone onstage, he cradles the infant lovingly.

In *The Winter's Tale*, act 2, scene 3, a king sits apart onstage, talking. He summons and dismisses an attendant. Then enters a lone woman with an infant. Male protectors try to shield the king from the woman, but the woman moves to the king and presents the infant affectionately. The king looks at the infant with loathing. The woman defiantly puts the infant down, and the king angrily motions that it be taken away. When the king's supporters move, the woman threatens them, goes to the infant, and shows its face. She looks from the infant's face to the king's, as if comparing them. The king rages. The attending men pressure the woman to leave, and she reluctantly disappears. The king makes threatening motions against the infant and gestures to his chief supporter to remove it. The man, after hesitating, takes up the infant and leaves. The king orders the remaining men away, and they depart through one upstage door as the king, alone, exits through the other.

In *Titus Andronicus*, in the final scene, an emperor and a middle-aged woman enter. Then an old man in cook's dress appears and, with him, a woman whose face is curtained by a veil. The old man presents a dish of food to the emperor and middle-aged woman, and as the guests eat, others onstage are still. Then the old man and the veiled woman, collaborating, orchestrate the removal of her veil and the penetration of her body by his sword. As they harmonize their movements, they resemble each other onstage. The old man is missing one of his hands, and the woman, now seen to be young, is missing both of hers. After the old man and young woman have finished their movements, the old man stabs the middle-aged woman furiously, only to be stabbed in turn by the emperor. Moments later, after a controlling figure has gestured toward an infant that is either dead or under threat of death, a young boy kisses the corpse of the old man. Others then place the old man and young woman together in death, as if preparing their bodies for a common grave. The body of the middle-aged woman lies apart and alone. Attendants treat it roughly, with disrespect. No woman remains alive onstage.

In *The Winter's Tale*, in the final scene, a king and a young woman enter together, directed by an older woman. Onstage, hidden behind a curtain, is a third woman, in statue form. The older woman draws the curtain and shows the statue. In their responses to this statue, the king and young woman resemble one another. Each of them, strongly impassioned, starts to touch the statue, and the older woman prevents each of them from doing so. The older woman then moves nearer the statue and all others stand still. Under the older woman's direction, the statue moves with life, descends, embraces the king, and then embraces the young woman. The king joins the hand of the older woman and the hand of an older man, making a marriage. Three women remain alive onstage. The movements of the men harmonize with those of the women as all leave in unity.

These visual sequences show that *Titus Andronicus* and *The Winter's Tale* have much in common. So do other visual similarities. For example, each play contains a flirtatious pregnant woman. *The Winter's Tale*, like *Titus Andronicus*, includes a visually significant, sometimes powerfully silent, young boy (Mamillius in the one play, young Lucius in the other). In each play an older man behaves in destructive ways, onstage, toward a younger male (Leontes has his son Mamillius violently removed from his loving mother and so causes the son's death, and Titus kills his youngest son, Mutius, after Mutius supports the loving union of Lavinia and Bassianus). Each play presents at least one destructive figure in striking stage disguise (Tamora, Demetrius, and Chiron, though eager to ruin Titus's life, present themselves as his helpers—Revenge, Murder, and Rape—and Polixenes, though malevolent toward the love of Florizel and Perdita, appears to them in the guise of a friendly stranger). Also, each play includes discovery of hidden gold, displays of action-provoking documents, and a weakened, much-changed figure opposed by an unsympathetic judge or judges (Titus pleads to the Tribunes, who pass him by, and Hermione pleads before the hostile Leontes).

Significant messages wait in such visual links between *Titus Andronicus* and *The Winter's Tale*: messages about Shakespeare as playwright and as person over the years. If Shakespeare changed much from the time he wrote his early tragedy (sometime before 1594) and the near-end of his career in 1610 or 1611, he also remained much the same. Early as well as late he was concerned with the emotionally charged fantasies that these two plays visually proclaim: fantasies of killing the infant and setting the infant free. And early as well as late, Shakespeare enjoyed dramatizing his interests in primitive issues by primitive visualizations of bodies in motion onstage, bodies making significant patterns, as bodies commonly do in the nocturnal playworlds of our dreams.

The Winter's Tale is easier to read than *Titus Andronicus*, and we can use that popular and respected play to understand the force of the earlier, sometimes ridiculed drama.[1] *The Winter's Tale* presents a king, Leontes, who fears the infant inside him. Provoked to experience a primitive hunger for love by the image and activities of his pregnant wife, Hermione, Leontes separates himself from her. He says the one who feels illicit attraction to this pregnant woman is his boyhood friend, Polixenes, and he gives orders to have Polixenes killed. He also identifies with his five-year-old son Mamillius, persuading himself that the boy has no need of mothering, and he separates the boy from the queen. Hermione, he says, can "sport herself / With that she's big with. . ." (2.1.60-61).[2] Then, after the infant is delivered and set free of prison, Leontes becomes increasingly determined to believe "This brat is none of mine. . ." (2.3.92). The infant is all the more a disgraceful weakling for being a girl, and Leontes cannot consciously perceive his likeness to it, even though Paulina shows that he and the infant have similar physical features.

The behavior of Leontes is at odds with the principles of the universe, as the universe appears in *The Winter's Tale*. Mamillius, deprived of his mother, dies. Hermione, thought dead, disappears. Oppressed by loneliness, Leontes gives himself to a motherly figure, Paulina, as Mamillius gave himself to Hermione in act 2, scene 1. Under

Paulina's tutoring, Leontes comes to accept his desire for the lost Hermione, and he lovingly associates himself with the daughter who has developed out of the infant he once tried to kill. Before the statue of Hermione, Leontes corresponds with Perdita emotionally and moves as Perdita moves. When Hermione comes to life again, having heard that the lost infant is found, Leontes responds to her warmly, and he himself becomes a maker of marriage as he joins Camillo and Paulina, hand in hand.

The hero of *The Winter's Tale*, then, makes a kind of progress that modern therapists would associate with health. It resembles progress imagined for patients by such object-relations theorists as Ronald Fairbairn, for example, and Harry Guntrip.[3] For Fairbairn, a neo-Freudian theorist, the chief repressible drive of the human psyche is a drive for intimate, tender, and lasting relationships with real people. A person can oppose and repress this drive and in the process divide into three contending egos. The chief operating ego becomes an ego looking for tolerance and approval—for honor and esteem—instead of love. Under the surface, however, lies a libidinal ego, which preserves the hunger for truly good relationships, and a fierce anti-libidinal ego that hates all dependency and persecutes especially wishes for love. A person like Leontes, who is frightened by uncontrollable fantasies of disgrace when circumstances make him intensely libidinal, can become fanatical in his efforts to drive the libidinal self out of his world—to perceive that libidinal self as It, not I, as Other, not Self. But a person can also make progress toward the acceptance and development of his libidinal ego—can come to express in mature ways his drive for good relationships. In *The Winter's Tale*, Leontes seems to make such progress.

In *Titus Andronicus*, on the other hand, we find a hero similar only to the early Leontes.[4] Though Titus goes mad and becomes a rebel against the administrators of the state, he makes no essential changes in goals or values. The beginning of Titus prefigures his end, and there is little that is joyful in either. He is always in struggle, and perhaps any actor who tries to assume his personality must become, as I did quite unknowingly while performing in an adaptation of *Titus Andronicus*, "fraught with anxiety," as one reviewer wrote, "and suffused with a male angst."[5] Yet Titus lives in a playworld that presents us values far different from those dominant in *The Winter's Tale*, and Titus is much preferable to the libidinal figures who invade and violate his life.

Titus is all Roman manhood. He has buried all but a few of his five and twenty valiant sons in a tomb 500 years old. This tomb, which he has "sumptuously re-edified" (1.1.354), serves as the visual focus for the opening scene and as the destination for Titus and his remaining sons as they enter. The attraction Titus demonstrates toward this tomb emphasizes his desire for honor and name, not love. He calls the tomb the "sacred receptacle of my joys, / Sweet cell of virtue and nobility" (1.1.95-96), and he is steadfast in his reverence for it and those buried in it even though his reverence puts him in conflict with Tamora, thus with "A mother's tears in passion for her son" (1.1.109). Fearful of being untrue to the worthy dead and of having his world haunted by their unappeased spirits, Titus makes it piety to authorize the sacrifice of Alarbus, Tamora's eldest son. Perhaps Titus even watches (he does, for example, in Jane Howell's BBC production of 1985) as Lucius places some of the "entrails" of Alarbus in a small burning dish onstage, to "feed the sacrificing fire, / Whose smoke like incense doth perfume the sky" (1.1.147-48).

Titus has raised his daughter, Lavinia, as well as his sons, to seek public respect. Lavinia, a young marriageable woman, is her father's chief pupil. She is young and feminine. Hunger for love in her could be intense, and she could provoke in others, as well as express, strong libidinal impulses. In her first speech, however, Lavinia suggests that she is too well trained to become such a disgraceful creature and so suggests that Titus has willed control generally—in her as in himself. This is how Lavinia commends herself:

> In peace and honor live Lord Titus long;
> My noble lord and father, live in fame.
> Lo, at this tomb my tributary tears
> I render for my brethren's obsequies,
> And at thy feet I kneel, with tears of joy
> Shed on this earth for thy return to Rome.
> O, bless me here with thy victorious hand,
> Whose fortunes Rome's best citizens applaud. (1.1.160-67)

This Lavinia, and this Lavinia only, is the one Titus perceives as "The cordial of mine age to glad my heart" (1.1.169). Only thus can she "live; outlive thy father's days, / And fame's eternal date, for virtue's praise" (1.1.170-71).

Because Titus has trained his daughter so well, and by implication, thus trained his own self, he is the most admired person in the state, and he could, if he wished, be candidate for emperor. His brother Marcus, just after Lavinia's first speech, offers Titus the "palliament of white and spotless hue" (1.1.185). Titus, however, needs a parental figure to bestow approval on him, and so chooses rather to name an emperor than be one. So he chooses Saturninus, and being thus the emperor's benefactor, he expects to be esteemed for life. Titus is now at his peak. He will descend, then rise again.

The descent of Titus follows a change in Lavinia. Betrothed to Bassianus, Lavinia obediently allows her father to bestow her on Saturninus. So far so good for Titus. But Lavinia is not as well trained as her father supposes, and within minutes she acquiesces in a rebellion against her father. Without protesting at all, Lavinia lets herself be taken away and married by her beloved, Bassianus, as his "lawful promised love" (1.1.301). She subordinates her father's wishes and expresses, in body if not in speech, a desire to have her own chosen spouse. In this way she somewhat resembles the love-inspired Florizel of *The Winter's Tale*.

The reaction from Titus shows the panic he experiences when threatened with disgrace by amatory forces. Feeling himself dishonored by the situation to which Lavinia has contributed, Titus kills his youngest son, Mutius, when Mutius supports Lavinia and Bassianus in their flight. Thus, Titus resembles the early Leontes and also the Polixenes of the sheep-shearing scene. Feeling himself undermined by a deviant woman, Titus does injury to a son who is close to that woman in order to free himself from suspicion of taint. For Titus, nothing can be right unless Lavinia exists under the control of social, not personal, forces. He insists that Lucius "restore Lavinia to the emperor" (1.1.299), and when Titus weakens to accept the burial of Mutius in the family tomb, he feels himself as good as lost: "Well, bury him, and bury me the next" (1.1.389).

The relationship of Titus to Lavinia now changes too. Titus does not again speak to Lavinia or even recognize her presence so long as she retains her initial visual form. Thus, he does not speak to her or about her in the latter part of the opening scene, when they are together onstage for almost 100 lines, or in act 2, scene 2, in which he welcomes Saturninus and Tamora, but not her, to the hunt. Only after other figures in the playworld become the chief releasers of libidinal forces, and Lavinia herself becomes a victim of libidinal forces, can Titus renew his connection with her.[6]

The libidinal forces to which Titus becomes opponent swell in power during the central part of the play. These forces are not, as in *The Winter's Tale*, associates of flowers, summertime light, and a harmonious dance of shepherds and shepherdesses. In this playworld libidinal forces are ugly, frightening, and grotesque associates of dark and secret spaces. They have, as in *The Winter's Tale*, their chief sign in an infant, but an infant far different from the one in the later play. In *The Winter's Tale* the infant is the true creation of the "good goddess Nature" (2.3.103) and a cause for joy and love:

> Behold, my lords.
> Although the print be little, the whole matter
> And copy of the father—eye, nose, lip,
> The trick of's frown, his forehead, nay, the valley,
> The pretty dimples of his chin and cheek, his smiles,
> The very mould and frame of hand, nail, finger. (2.3.97-102)

In *Titus Andronicus,* where libidinal forces threaten to take all identity from the hero, the infant is a horror. The Nurse, her vision of ugliness informed by a malevolent Elizabethan racism, presents the infant as "A devil," "A joyless, dismal, black, and sorrowful issue!" (4.2.63, 66).[7] "Here is the babe," she says,

> as loathsome as a toad
> Amongst the fair-faced breeders of our clime.
> The empress sends it thee, thy stamp, thy seal,
> And bids thee christen it with thy dagger's point. (4.2.67-70)

The infant, a devil to her, truly comes from forces this play connects with a netherworld. In addition the chief releasers of the primitive forces for which the infant is reminder and sign are the infant's own parents, the two outsiders from the land of the enemy Goths, against whom Titus has long done heroic and eminent battle.

Of these two parents, Tamora is the more significant. She expresses libidinal desires that characters elsewhere, as in *The Winter's Tale,* can perceive as good. Tamora's seductive efforts toward Aaron in the woods, when her body is swelling with maternity, resemble the flirtations of Hermione toward Leontes in act 1, scene 2 of *The Winter's Tale* and those of Perdita toward Florizel in act 4, scene 4. And Tamora is conscious that her desires are infantlike in character. She wants to sit down with Aaron in the shadows of the woods and listen to the hounds' "yellowing noise":

> And after conflict such as was supposed
> The wand'ring prince and Dido once enjoyed,
> When with a happy storm they were surprised,
> And curtained with a counsel-keeping cave,
> We may, each wreathèd in the other's arms,
> Our pastimes done, possess a golden slumber,
> Whiles hounds and horns and sweet melodious birds
> Be unto us as is a nurse's song
> Of lullaby to bring her babe asleep. (2.3.20-29)

In this playworld, however, desires such as Tamora's are illicit. She expresses them toward a male forbidden her as an empress, and she expresses them overtly only in this concealing shade, apart from the civilization of urban Rome. The desires are dark, like the infant that grows inside her. They cause Tamora's evil, and she cannot renounce them. She can want their visible representation, the infant, buried from the perceptions of her scrutinizing world, but only because she fears losses of power and freedom. In conscience, she accepts the libidinal desires with ease.

Aaron, unlike Tamora, is infantlike chiefly in a hostility to codes accepted in the civilized adult world, not in erotic urges.

> Madam, though Venus govern your desires,
> Saturn is dominator over mine. . . .
> Vengeance is in my heart, death in my hand,
> Blood and revenge are hammering in my head. (2.3.30-31, 38-39)

Aaron ridicules Lucius for having "a thing within thee callèd conscience" (5.1.75), and he revels in forbidden cruelties that set him apart from ordinary human beings:

> Even now I curse the day, and yet I think
> Few come within the compass of my curse,
> Wherein I did not some notorious ill. . . . (5.1.125-27)

Though Aaron cannot associate his sociopathic inclinations with infancy ("I am no baby, I, that with base prayers / I should repent the evils I have done" [5.3.185-86]), he does feel a deep kinship with the infant, and he is determined to protect the child and persuade someone "to nourish and bring him up" (5.1.84).

These two parents of the infant, Aaron and Tamora, supersede Lavinia as a threat to Titus, and Tamora especially becomes the identity that Titus must engage as counterforce. Tamora overwhelms. In act 1 she is able to turn the chief Roman praise-giver into an infantlike disciple, promising Saturninus that "She will a handmaid be to his desires, / A loving nurse, a mother to his youth" (1.1.334-35). In her presence, Lavinia unexpectedly changes. Oppressed by her influence, Titus becomes a man with few opportunities to express the identity he has been shaping since youth. At one point, abandoned onstage, he wonders that he must "walk alone" (1.1.342), and he loses eminence as a speaker as Tamora's eminence swells. For the most part, after the burial of Mutius, Titus as speaker merely reacts to others—to Saturninus, to Tamora, to the Tribunes—in postures of respect. Only with the return of Lavinia in act 3, scene 1, in a form that marks her as once again radically different from Tamora, does Titus again promote his own identity in action and in word.

Formerly Lavinia has been, like Tamora, the desired of Saturninus, a stranger to her father's will, an affectionate beloved, and a woman of striking beauty. When she appears to her father now, in act 3, scene 1, Lavinia is a grotesque, deflowered woman who trembles like an aspen's leaf. She lacks her hands, "those sweet ornaments / Whose circling shadows kings have sought to sleep in" (2.4.18-19). As her sometimes bleeding mouth proclaims, she lacks a tongue, and as her walk, perhaps, and her posture indicate, she has also suffered injuries in unseen parts of her body. Raped and mutilated, she cannot be the erotic woman she was before. In her, a creature so transformed, desire for honor must prevail. Lavinia is once again her father's daughter, and Titus, rejected by the governors of Rome, finds in Lavinia new inspiration:

> I am the sea; hark how her sighs doth flow!
> She is the weeping welkin, I the earth:
> Then must my sea be movèd with her sighs;
> Then must my earth with her continual tears
> Become a deluge, overflowed and drowned. . . . (3.1.225-29)

Titus also finds in Lavinia a cause, as he does in the two sons whose severed heads the libidinal Aaron has had delivered. Speaking to his brother and to the children he has trained and seen go unrewarded—to the severed heads of Martius and Quintus, to Lucius, and to Lavinia—Titus vows to struggle again for the principles that give him purpose.

> You heavy people, circle me about,
> That I may turn me to each one of you
> And swear unto my soul to right your wrongs. (3.1.276-78)

Titus intends to restore again a family bound together by pursuit of honor and by opposition to libidinal powers. He starts moving himself and Lavinia toward the family tomb.

In *The Winter's Tale* the end envisioned by the chief playwright within the play is reunion in life. Paulina looks forward to a drama that joins together lives saved, renewed, and rediscovered; and life, Paulina knows, depends on the will to love. As Florizel says to Perdita, "I cannot be / Mine own, nor anything to any, if / I be not thine" (4.4.43-45).

In *Titus Andronicus* the goal envisioned by the chief playwright within the play is reunion in death. Titus has glorified such reunion from the start. Putting his sons in the tomb in the opening scene, he says:

> In peace and honor rest you here, my sons;
> Rome's readiest champions, repose you here in rest,
> Secure from worldly chances and mishaps.
> Here lurks no treason, here no envy swells,
> Here grows no damnèd drugs, here are no storms,
> No noise, but silence and eternal sleep.
> In peace and honor rest you here, my sons. (1.1.153-59)

We learn after his death that Titus has expressed toward his grandson, young Lucius, strong impulses for an intimate, caring union like that the loving mother enjoys with an infant. Says Lucius the father: "Many a time he danced thee on his knee, / Sung thee asleep, his loving breast thy pillow" (5.3.162-63). But Titus has subordinated his concern for mother-infant connections and left his grandson only the lips of the dead to touch. Marcus instructs young Lucius:

> O, now, sweet boy, give them their latest kiss.
> Bid him farewell; commit him to the grave;
> Do them that kindness, and take leave of them.
> (5.3.169-71)

Where libidinal forces threaten to make a man a dark child, a Tamora, or an Aaron, the escape from danger and pain is residence with one's family in the tomb. When Titus and Marcus carry the severed heads of Martius and Quintus offstage, Titus may (as he did in the Stratford, Ontario production of 1978) slowly bring his one son's head upward, to put the son's cheek against his own. Tenderly. And in hope of peace.

In the final scene of *Titus Andronicus* the fusion with family members in death is the final good. The libidinal figures—Tamora, Aaron, and the infant—all suffer isolated ends. The infant, dead or alive, lies apart from his parents. Aaron will be set "breast-deep in earth" and famished: "There let him stand and rave and cry for food" (5.3.179-80). Tamora, who has fused with family members in a traumatizing, not peaceful, way by eating the flesh of her bled, mutilated, ground, and cooked boys is not to be buried as a parent within a familial group but simply discarded as a "ravenous tiger" (5.3.195):

throw her forth to beasts and birds to prey.
Her life was beastly and devoid of pity,
And being dead, let birds on her take pity! (5.3.198-200)

Countering the fates of the libidinal Tamora, the sociopathic Aaron, and the hated infant are the fates of Titus and Lavinia. In death, mutilated but at peace, the father and daughter join as family. Says Lucius: "My father and Lavinia shall forthwith / Be closèd in our household's monument" (5.3.193-94). At play's end Lavinia and Titus are moving toward the tomb with which our experience of Rome began. Titus has heroically prevented significant changes, and Rome's new governor will be Titus's son.

Compared with its close relation, *The Winter's Tale, Titus Andronicus* is nightmare. It reveals signs of pathology we do not like to own, in ourselves or Shakespeare. Yet the play appeals, especially by its visual design, as its recent production history reveals.[8] Through this tragedy Shakespeare gives us primitive, symbolic drama about infantlike desires we value and hate, embrace and renounce. Desires that make life a burden and thoughts of death relief from daily struggles. Desires we can mutilate to receive proper social rewards. Slaughtered infants displayed in their coffins. Young boys dead. Lavinias butchered and resting in the family tomb. As in nocturnal visions, when we too become playwrights and dramatize the deepest issues of our lives. What's more, Shakespeare gives the advantage of seeing these all in public, not alone. He helps us move our fears to a shared space and frees us from isolation, making our nightmares communal. *Titus Andronicus* is a brutal and morbid drama, but it is, in truth, all our own.

Notes

1. Psychoanalytic critics agree that the patterns of *The Winter's Tale* develop from profound psychological issues, and Murray M. Schwartz is especially illuminating in his two essays: "Leontes' Jealously in *The Winter's Tale*," *American Imago* 30 (1973): 250-73, and *"The Winter's Tale*: Loss and Transformation," *American Imago* 32 (1975): 145-99. Using ideas taken from classical psychoanalytic theory, Schwartz argues that Leontes's pathology forces us to concentrate on "the deepest level of oral anxieties. At that level the infant craves love as nourishment and dreads the possibility of maternal malevolence" ("Leontes' Jealousy in *The Winter's Tale*," 267). Leontes "desires and fears maternal presence," and he has an "ambivalent desire for feminine powers" (*"The Winter's Tale*: Loss and Transformation," 146, 198-99). Also valuable are the discussions by C. L. Barber, "'Thou that beget'st him that did thee beget': Transformation in

Pericles and *The Winter's Tale*," *Shakespeare Survey* 22 (1969): 59-67; Stephen Reid, "*The Winter's Tale*," *American Imago* 27 (1970): 263-78, and Richard P. Wheeler, *Shakespeare's Development and the Problem Comedies: Turn and Counter-Turn* (Berkeley: University of California Press, 1981), especially 217-21.

2. My texts for *The Winter's Tale* and *Titus Andronicus* come from the Pelican edition: *William Shakespeare: The Complete Works*, ed. Alfred Harbage (Baltimore: Penguin, 1969).

3. I provide a summary of Fairbairn's ideas on endopsychic splitting in "The Identity and Temptations of Shakespeare's Richard III," *Psychoanalysis and Psychotherapy* 11, no. 1 (1994): 56-66. Most of Fairbairn's important essays appear in *An Object-Relations Theory of the Personality* (New York: Basic Books, 1954). Guntrip discusses Fairbairn's work and adds his own theoretical contributions, as well as ideas on therapeutic goals and methods, in *Personality Structure and Human Interaction* (New York: International Universities Press, 1961) and *Schizoid Phenomena, Object-Relations and the Self* (New York: International Universities Press, 1969).

4. The most helpful essay on the psychological issues dominant in *Titus Andronicus* is David Willbern's "Rape and Revenge in *Titus Andronicus*," *ELR* 8 (1978): 159-82. In Willbern's view, the play presents an "unconscious equation of marriage and rape, sexuality and violence. . ." (163). The drama expresses an ambivalent fantasy in which rescues of women oppose hostile attacks on women, and the hostile attacks develop from a primitive fear of the "catastrophically perceived preoedipal mother, who threatens total dismemberment and destruction (the devouring mother)" (171). Also especially valuable are Cynthia Marshall's "'I can interpret all her martyr'd signs': *Titus Andronicus*, Feminism, and the Limits of Interpretation," *Sexuality and Politics in Renaissance Drama*, ed. Carole Levin and Karen Robertson (Lewiston, New York: Mellen, 1991), 193-213, and the chapter on *Titus Andronicus* in C. L. Barber and Richard P. Wheeler, *The Whole Journey: Shakespeare's Power of Development* (Berkeley: University of California Press, 1986) 125-57.

5. The review from which I quote, by Philip Van Vleck, appeared in the Durham, N.C. *Herald-Sun*, 14 August 1993.

6. Cynthia Marshall perceives a pattern in Shakespeare's treatment of Lavinia similar to the one I here describe. Lavinia, she argues, "is in effect punished, by rape, for her nascent sexuality and independent voice. . . .[T]he rape achieves the goal of ensuring that Lavinia will not be powerful, but will be frozen in a posture of dependence and humiliation" (194). Concerning the place of women in the playworld of *Titus Andronicus*, see also Marion Wynne-Davies, "'The Swallowing Womb': Consumed and Consuming Women in *Titus Andronicus*," *The Matter of Difference: Materialist Feminist Criticism of Shakespeare*, ed. Valerie Wayne (Ithaca: Cornell University Press, 1991), 129-51, and Douglas E. Green, "Interpreting 'her martyr'd signs': Gender and Tragedy in *Titus Andronicus*," *ShQ* 40 (1989): 317-26.

7. That the infant, as well as Aaron, has the appearance of a Moor to the onstage observers is significant. As Emily C. Bartels points out in "Making More of the Moor: Aaron, Othello, and Renaissance Refashionings of Race," *ShQ* 41 (1990): 433-54, the racist attitudes of the period produced the commonplace designation of the Moor, in particular, as Other. This play uses references to the child's darkness to encourage designations of the infant-in-general as Other.

8. Alan C. Dessen discusses the play's stage history in his work for the Shakespeare in Performance series: *Titus Andronicus* (Manchester: Manchester University Press, 1989).

Bearing "A Wary Eye": Ludic Vengeance and Doubtful Suicide in Hamlet

Philip C. McGuire

Immediately before the start of fencing competition during which *Hamlet* will receive the wound that kills him, Claudius commands, "And you, the judges, bear a wary eye" (5.2.277).[1] "The judges" to whom he speaks are onstage, but the call to "bear a wary eye" applies also, in ways I intend to explore in this essay, to those who as members of theater audiences or as readers—as students, critics, teachers, scholars, or devotees of Shakespeare—find themselves engaged in judging and interpreting *Hamlet, Prince of Denmark*.

These days it does not take an unusually "wary eye" to ascertain that *Hamlet* is the preeminent example of the Renaissance revenge tragedy. What may be more difficult to discern is that Hamlet kills Claudius as part of a sequence of events that set *Hamlet* apart from the typical revenging protagonist, who commonly kills the villain by means of actions undertaken as part of a cunningly devised, deftly executed strategy. For example, in Cyril Tourneur's *Revenger's Tragedy*, written and first performed approximately four years after *Hamlet*, Vindice uses the skull of his beloved Gloriana, which he carries during the play's opening soliloquy, to take vengeance on the lecherous old duke who had her murdered for refusing his advances. Employing the cosmetic arts, including face-painting, Vindice makes her skull so alluring that, roused to blinding lust, the duke takes it for the face of a beautiful woman and proceeds to kiss it. With that kiss he falls victim to the deadly poison that Vindice had placed where Gloriana's lips once hung. In *The Spanish Tragedy*, written by Thomas Kyd and first performed perhaps as much as a decade prior to *Hamlet*, the protagonist Hieronimo persuades the two men who have murdered his son to take roles in a play. The plot of the play, written by Hieronimo during his student days years before, calls for the characters they agree to play to die, and Hieronimo casts himself and his son's beloved Bel-Imperia as the characters who are to slay them. During the performance of the play, he and she proceed to kill not just the characters the two villains are playing but the villains themselves.

At the conclusion of *Hamlet*, however, cunning and plotting of the kind displayed by Vindice and Hieronimo are the tools not of Hamlet but of his adversaries, Claudius and Laertes. They employ what Hamlet calls "<god-like reason>" (4.4.39)[2] as they plot his death, "<looking before and after>" in time in an effort to foresee and pre-pare for every contingency. The point of Laertes's sword will not be blunted, so that, capitalizing on his superior swordsmanship, he can stab Hamlet. On the chance that the wound Hamlet receives will not be mortal, Laertes resolves to annoint his sword with a poison so potent that the slightest scratch will be fatal. Claudius, anticipating the possibility that Laertes will not wound Hamlet at all, decides that a poisoned chalice should be prepared for Hamlet, "whereon but sip-ping, / If he by chance may escape your venomed stuck / Our pur-pose may hold there" (4.7.161-63).

Hamlet's killing of Claudius, unlike the killings done by Vindice and Hieronimo, is improvised rather than plotted. It arises sponta-neously, independently of any planning on Hamlet's part, from a fencing competition that he and others refer to as "play." Claudius prepares Laertes to agree to the plot to kill Hamlet by explaining how the French horseman Lamord's[3] "masterly report" of Laertes's skill with a rapier so impressed Hamlet "That he could nothing do but wish and beg / Your sudden coming o'er to play with you" (4.7.97, 105-6). The unnamed lord whom Claudius sends (in the Second Quarto only) to confirm Hamlet's willingness to test his swordsman-ship against Laertes asks "<if your pleasure hold to play with Laertes>" (5.2.196-97). That same lord also conveys the Queen's wish that Hamlet "use some gentle entertainment to Laertes before you fall to play" (5.2. 204-5). Hamlet himself speaks of the competition in which he and Laertes are about to engage as play. Before the assembled court of Denmark, he declares that he "will this brothers' wager frankly play," and after scoring the first hit, he declines to drink from the cup Claudius offers: "I'll play this bout first," he says, "Set <it> by a while" (5.2. 251, 286).

Hamlet's actions and attitudes as he prepares for and then engages in (what he takes to be) swordplay with Laertes are extremely com-plex, and one facet of that complexity is a quality that I shall call ludic. That quality, easily and often overlooked, begins to come into focus if one considers the definition of play offered by J. Huizinga in *Homo Ludens*: "Play is a voluntary activity or occupation executed within certain fixed limits of time and space, according to rules freely accepted but absolutely binding, having its aim in itself and accompanied by a feeling of tension, joy, and the consciousness that it is 'different' from 'ordinary life.'"[4] Hamlet's decision to participate in the fencing match is free and voluntary. In fact, it is a decision made and carried through despite the anxiety that he discloses to Horatio as they await the arrival of the Danish court and the start of the competition: "Thou wouldst not think how ill all's here about my heart; but it is no matter" (5.2. 210-11). Like play as Huizinga defines it, the match between Hamlet and Laertes is a temporary activity of fixed, agreed-upon duration—"a dozen passes" (5.2. 163-64). Hamlet undertakes it with a sense that it is distinct from the realm of tasks and obligations that he summarizes directly before learning of the proposed wager:

> He that hath killed my king and whor'd my mother,
> Popp'd in between th'election and my hopes,
> Thrown out his angle for my proper life
> And with such cozenage—is't not perfect conscience
> ^To quit him with this arm? And is't not to be damned
> To let this canker of our nature come
> In further evil?^ (5.2. 64-70)

For Hamlet, testing his skill with (supposedly) blunted rapiers against Laertes's is autonomous activity to be engaged in and enjoyed during the "^short^" period—while "^the interim is mine^" (73)—before Claudius learns from England what has happened to Rosencrantz and Guildenstern.

How Claudius and Laertes "play" during the fencing match further defines the ludic quality of Hamlet's participation. For them, the competition has an ulterior and practical purpose, the killing of Hamlet, and they feel, as Hamlet does not, an urgency to act now, to "put the matter to the present push" (5.1.298). As the match unfolds, each of them plays in the sense that Hamlet used the term when he dismissed outward manifestions of grief—"all forms, moods, shapes[5] of grief" as "actions that a man might play" (1.2.82, 84). Laertes's deadly intentions and actions belie the pledge that he makes to Hamlet immediately before they take up the foils: "I do receive your offered love like love, / And will not wrong it" (5.2.249-50). Claudius's toast to Hamlet's health and his command that cannon should sound in celebration. "If Hamlet give the first or second hit, or quit in answer of the third exchange" (5.2. 266-67) are playing of the same kind, involving feigning, dissembling.[6]

Not only does Hamlet have no plan for killing Claudius as he takes up the foils, but as the final scene begins he has also developed

a radically different perspective on the processes of plot and coun-
terplot in which he had earlier proved himself so adept (e.g., the
play-within-the-play) and from which he has taken delight:

> <For 'tis the sport to have the engineer
> Hoist with his own petard, and 't shall go hard
> But I will delve one yard below their mines
> And blow them to the moon. O, 'tis most sweet
> When in one line two crafts directly meet.> (3.4.213-17)

The final scene opens with Hamlet recounting what happened on the
ship carrying him and Rosencrantz and Guildenstern to England. At
precisely the moment when he starts telling of leaving his cabin and
beginning to take action, he breaks off and says to Horatio:

> let us know
> Our indiscretion sometimes serves us well
> When our deep plots do pall; and that should learn us
> There's a divinity that shapes our ends,
> Rough-hew them how we will. (5.2.7-11)

A few moments later Hamlet receives and accepts the invitation to
engage in swordplay. As he awaits the arrival of Laertes and the
Danish court, he responds to Horatio's suggestion that the match be
canceled by declaring, "Not a whit, we defy augury," in effect dismissing the capability of "<looking before and after>" that Claudius and
Laertes, in concocting the strategem of the swordplay, so conspicuously demonstrate. "There is," Hamlet goes on to say,

> ^a^ special providence in the fall of a sparrow.
> If it be ^now^, 'tis not to come; if it be not to come,
> it will be now; if it be not now, yet it will come.
> The readiness is all. (5.2.217-20)

Rejecting efforts to decipher and shape the future, Hamlet
embraces what he now regards as the single certainty with which
he must square his actions: in time he and Claudius will die—if
not "now," then at some future instant. Hamlet's capacity to
engage in play that has a ludic quality sets him apart not only from
his adversaries within the play, Claudius and Laertes, but also from
Vindice and Hieronimo, his fellow revengers. He is, as they are
not, a ludic avenger—a feature of how *Hamlet* concludes that dis-
tinguishes it from other Renaissance revenge tragedies. Exploring

the implications of that feature requires consideration of what happens during and after the swordplay.

•   •   •

As the fencing match begins, Hamlet is a clear underdog. The wager, after all, is not on whether he will win or lose but on whether Laertes will or will not outscore him by three or more touches. Hamlet assures Horatio that, having "been in continual practice," "I shall win at the odds" (5.2.209), but even that assurance, with its key phrase "at the odds," acknowledges Laertes's superior swordsmanship. Once the competition is under way, however, Hamlet does more than beat the odds. He scores the first two hits and holds his own in the third exchange, which ends with Osric declaring, "Nothing neither way" (5.2.304). It is conceivable that Laertes lets Hamlet score the first two touches as part of his strategem, or that his sense of guilt inhibits his fencing skills. It is equally possible, however, and far more easily played, that Hamlet in the first several exchanges is fencing at a level of dexterity beyond what he had estimated himself capable of. If so, then those exchanges are moments when Hamlet's fencing skills are at their zenith, when he is most nearly the fencer he is capable of being at his best, when he achieves a level of excellence that today's athletes call "the zone." They are also the moments when Hamlet's play is most fully ludic.[7]

In his directions to the players, Hamlet calls upon them to "Suit the action to the word, the word to the action" (3.2.17-18). The ludic quality of his swordplaying has a bearing on the issue—of recurring concern to Hamlet and to commentators on the play—of whether he manages to make his actions and his words "suit" one another and, if so, when. Before beginning the competition with Laertes, Hamlet is capable of articulating his new understanding of humankind's limited power to shape "our ends," but his capacity to transform those thoughts into actions that accord with such limit is conveyed by what he in fact does. During those moments when his swordplay, in contrast to Laertes's, possesses a ludic quality—when he comes closest to engaging in play for its own sake—Hamlet succeeds in suiting his words to his actions and his actions to his words.

The ludic quality drains from Hamlet's swordsmanship at the moment that Laertes's blade opens a wound in his flesh, thereby beginning the process by which Hamlet and all the onstage spectators except Claudius come to understand that what they took to be playful competition was also a deadly duel. Neither the Second Quarto nor the Folio version of *Hamlet* specifies with any precision how Laertes wounds Hamlet. The former reads:

> <*Ostr.* Nothing neither way.
> *Laer.* Have at you now.
> *King.* Part them, they are incenst.
> *Ham.* Nay, come againe.
> *Ostr.* Looke to the Queene there howe.
> *Hora.* They bleed on both sides, how is it my Lord?> (5.2.305-7)

The Folio offers essentially the same dialogue, changing "howe" to "hoa," but after "Haue at you now" it provides a stage direction that is inconclusive: "^*In scuffling they change Rapiers^*." In performance, on the other hand, an overwhelmingly monolithic tradition calls for Laertes to wound Hamlet not in a fair exchange but sneakily. In *The Masks of "Hamlet"* Marvin Rosenberg provides an extensive account of the various ways in which Laertes has wounded Hamlet in productions across the centuries.[8] Often, he strikes during a pause between exchanges, while Hamlet's back is turned, or he is catching his breath, or he is distracted by, perhaps even responding to, Gertrude's first cry of pain. Rosenberg's discussion, the fullest available, makes no mention of any production in which Laertes wounds Hamlet in a manner that does not violate the codes governing fencing, which correspond to those "rules freely accepted but absolutely binding" that Huizinga mentions as characteristic of play. The performance tradition of which Rosenberg's book offers such compelling evidence both magnifies Hamlet's fencing skills and heightens the villainy of Laertes. Nothing in either the Second Quarto or the First Folio contradicts that practice, but by the same token, nothing in either version mandates it. Both allow at least one other option: Laertes wounds Hamlet in a fair exchange as the superiority that even Hamlet acknowledges finally makes itself (almost literally) felt.[9]

However Laertes comes to hit Hamlet, the wound he inflicts ensures the success of his and Claudius's scheme: Hamlet does die. Their success, however, is part of a larger ordering of events they had not anticipated. Gertrude drinks the poisoned wine prepared for Hamlet, and Hamlet, after being wounded, gains possession of the venom-tipped sword and uses it to kill first Laertes, then Claudius. The way in which events outrun the ability of Claudius and Laertes to foresee them is anticipated in Claudius's account of the equestrian skills of the Norman Lamord. His riding, Cladius asserts,

> Had witchcraft in't; he grew unto his seat,
> And to such wondrous doing brought his horse
> As he had been incorpsed and demi-natured
> With the brave beast. So far he topped my thought

That I in forgery of shapes and tricks
Came short of what he did. (4.7.86-91)

The passage draws upon the iconographic tradition of signifying the relationship between reason and passion in terms of that between a horse and its rider.[10] Conventionally, the horseman astride the animal struggles to master and restrain its energies, just as reason should rule passion, but Claudius's account alters that convention. The relation between Lamord and his horse is one of fusion and integration, not restraint and suppression. Lamord "grew into his seat," seemingly "incorpsed and demi-natured / With the brave beast."

The merging of horse and rider suggests an integration of reason and passion that manifests itself in physical actions. Such integration is consistent with Hamlet's directions to the players, whom he calls upon for actions and acting that avoid the excesses of passion:

Nor do not saw the air too much with
your hand, thus, but use all gently; for in the
very torrent, tempest, and, as I may say, ^the^
whirlwind of your passion, you must acquire and
beget a temperance that may give it smoothness. (3.2.4-8)

At the same time, he warns them against actions and acting devoid of passion: "Be not too tame neither, but let your own discretion be your tutor" (3.2.16-17). Such integration is also consistent with the terms in which Hamlet praises Horatio as one of those

Whose blood and judgment are so well <commedled>[11]
That they are not a pipe for Fortune's finger
To sound what stop she please. (3.2. 68-70)

"Give me that man," he continues,

That is not passion's slave, and I will wear him
In my heart's core, ay, in my heart of heart,
As I do thee. (3.2.70-73)

During the final scene of Hamlet, Claudius is once again a spectator to a display of another of the skills expected of a courtier—fencing. That display is also, like Lamord's riding, part of a sequence of actions that dwarf his powers of thought. Just as Lamord's feats on horseback "topped" what Claudius imagined to be possible then and what he can conceive of now "in forgery of shapes and tricks," so

Hamlet's actions while engaged in swordplay that for him has a ludic component and then after he is wounded surpass Laertes's and Claudius's power to anticipate them.

The swordplay in *Hamlet* illustrates an essential difference between experiencing a play in performance and reading the words that make up its play-text(s)—differences pointed toward in Claudius's account of how the feats of horsemanship performed by Lamord "topped my thought," surpassing what he could conceive by "forgery of shapes and tricks." Reading *Hamlet* requires that one either disregard the actions constituting the swordplay or turn to "forgery" equivalent to Claudius's in an effort to envision—in what Hamlet himself calls the "mind's eye" (1.2.185)—the actions involved. In contrast, audiences watching *Hamlet* performed witness what the actors playing those characters do as they speak and move in fact, in deed, not in thought. Reading empties the swordplay of its physical content, flattening and reducing—abstracting and decorporealizing—the movements of actors' bodies into bland stage directions like those the Folio provides: "^*They play*^" and "^*Play*^."[12] Only those who watch *Hamlet* being performed see the particular physical movements that constitute the swordplay; only they have an opportunity to "bear a wary eye." It is just such actions—bodily, corporeal—that most conspicuously distinguish drama as a medium from purely verbal arts.

If, as I argued earlier, the moments when Hamlet's swordplay has a ludic quality can be moments of fullness and success, there remains the question of whether, and to what extent, his acts of killing Laertes and Claudius are a continuation or a falling off. That question cannot be answered without reference to specific performances, to specific occasions when *Hamlet* is played rather than read and a given actor (player) performs Hamlet's actions. It is clear from the play-text(s) that Hamlet stabs Laertes and Claudius with the rapier they prepared in order to kill him, but nothing is specified about how he does so. A stage diretion unique to the Folio says of Laertes and Hamlet, "^*In scuffling, they change Rapiers*^." "Scuffling" suggests actions less stylized than fencing, but it leaves open the question of how Laertes and Hamlet act once they have changed rapiers.[13]

Does Hamlet—as in Laurence Olivier's 1948 film—wound Laertes by a thrust put home with the grace and agility with which he scores his earlier touches? Or does the fencing degenerate, once Hamlet is wounded, into a brawl, the equivalent of a street fight with rapiers and daggers—as in Peter Hall's 1965 production for the Royal Shakespeare Company and in Zeffirelli's film, when Mel Gibson, seeing his own blood, dropped his weapon, then rushed Laertes and staggered him with a right cross. The dialogue and (in the Folio only) the stage direction provided for the moment when Hamlet stabs Claudius allow for at least two radically incompatible possibilities: "The point envenomed too? Then, venom, to thy work. ^*Hurts the King*^" (5.2.324). Hamlet may stab coolly, calmly, rationally—in a physically graceful action that mirrors his movements while at play and shows him balancing his blood and judgment, tempering passion by discretion. Or he may run Claudius through (stabbing once, twice, how often? and where? in the genitals? the chest? the stomach?) in actions that mark a falling off from the grace with which audiences saw him play and that make him, for those moments at least, what he had earlier praised Horatio for not being, "passion's slave."

A further complication is that Hamlet need not stab both men in the same fashion. In addition, how(ever) Hamlet stabs Claudius may, or may not, be how he forces him to drink from the poisoned cup that has killed Gertrude:

> Here, thou incestuous, murderous, damnèd Dane,
> Drink ^off^ this potion. Is thy ^union^[14] here?
> Follow my mother. ^*King Dyes*^ (5.2.327-29)

Does Hamlet in fact *force* him to drink? Traditionally he does but not always. In Trevor Nunn's 1970 production for the Royal Shakespeare Company, Claudius accepted the cup from Hamlet and drank of his own volition. A third possibility—enacted in Hall's 1965 Royal Shakespeare Company production—is that Hamlet pours the poisoned potion into the ear of Claudius, thus reenacting both how his father was killed and how, during Hamlet's device of the play-within-the-play, the nephew kills his uncle.

How, having taken vengeance upon Claudius, does Hamlet himself die? Formulating an answer is made more difficult by differences between the Second Quarto and the Folio versions of *Hamlet*. In the former, Hamlet, as he dies, says, "The rest is silence" (5.2.360), and he expires without uttering another sound. How he dies fits how he says he will die—in silence. The Second Quarto, then, gives a Hamlet who, during the moments of his dying (as during the moments when his swordplay had a ludic quality), is able to "suit the action to the word, the word to the action." He succeeds, during his final moments on the stage of the world, in acting as he called upon the players to act on the theatrical stage. The Folio, however, disrupts the symmetry between Hamlet's words and actions. The Hamlet of the Folio speaks a final sentence identical to that of his counterpart in the Second Quarto: "The rest is silence." To that sentence, however, the Folio adds four utterances: "^O, o, o, o^." They may convey (to cite some of the most obvious possibilities) physical agony as the poison completes its work, despair, grief, fear, resistance to death, and resignation to it as well as a mixture of them. Whatever those utterances may convey when a given actor playing Hamlet sounds them, perhaps as moans, they ensure that "the rest is" not "silence," that there is no final (and thus in some sense definitive) fit between Hamlet's words and actions. Instead, in contrast to the Second Quarto, the final words and final actions of the Folio Hamlet are at odds.

After Hamlet expires, Horatio, in both the Folio and the Second Quarto, speaks his moving farewell: "Now cracks a noble heart. Good night, sweet prince, / And flights of angels sing thee to thy rest" (5.2.361-62). A notable feature of the stage history of *Hamlet* is that virtually every production from the Restoration until late in the nineteenth century concluded at this point. So have numerous twentieth-century productions including, most prominently, the Olivier, Richardson, and Zeffirelli films, which stand among the most widely seen productions of *Hamlet* in history. There is, then, ample evidence that Hamlet's dying and Horatio's words can function as a satisfactory conclusion to the play, yet neither the Second Quarto nor the Folio calls for the play to conclude there. Both continue for nearly fifty more lines before ending.

The moments from Horatio's farewell to the end of the play take up the issue of political and social order in Denmark but, equally important, they do so in a way that draws attention to the connection between such order and the processes of interpreting and judging what has happened. That connection is anticipated in how the Danish court reacts when Hamlet "^*Hurts the King*^." Both The Second Quarto and the Folio specify that "*All*" cry, "Treason, treason" (5.2.325). Who is it court members are proclaiming to be a traitor, Hamlet or Claudius? Nothing in either playtext allows one to answer that question with certainty, although individual productions can construct an answer by, for example, having "*All*" point to either Hamlet or Claudius. What cannot be disputed, however, is that the words "Treason, treason" arise from and give voice to an interpretation of what "*All*" the Danish court has just seen. That interpretation also constitutes a judgment—a judgment framed, it is crucial to note, in political terms.

In both the Second Quarto and the Folio, the final words spoken in the play are Fortinbras's directions for removing Hamlet's corpse:

> Let four captains
> Bear Hamlet, like a soldier, to the stage,
> For he was likely, had he been put on,
> To have proved most royal; and for his passage,
> The soldiers' music and the rite of war
> Speak loudly for him.
> Take up the ^body^.[15] Such a sight as this
> Becomes the field, but here shows much amiss.
> Go bid the soldiers shoot. (5.2.397-405)

When Ophelia lamented what she judged to be Hamlet's fall into madness, she praised him in terms that stressed the range of his gifts: "O, what a noble mind is here o'erthrown! The courtier's, soldier's, scholar's, eye, tongue, sword" (3.1.153-54). Fortinbras's directions, on the other hand, focus exclusively, perhaps even reductively, on Hamlet's soldierly qualities. The command to provide "The soldiers' music and the rite of war" for Hamlet both arises from and contributes to a process by which Fortinbras interprets Hamlet and the events culminating in his death and then seeks to impose that interpretation on Denmark as part of the process by which he converts his claim to the Danish throne into a political fact. By characterizing Hamlet as a royal warrior killed before his soldierly potential could be fulfilled, Fortinbras is shaping the Danes' assessment of him as their king, encouraging them to see him as the embodiment of what Hamlet never had the chance to become: a royal warrior.

Horatio, too, offers an interpretation of what has happened when, in obedience to Hamlet's dying charge that he remain alive "To tell my story," he outlines what he will say when he speaks "to th'yet unknowing world":

> So shall you hear
> Of carnal, bloody, and unnatural acts,
> Of accidental judgments, casual slaughters,
> Of deaths put on by cunning and forced cause,[16]
> And in this upshot, purposes mistook
> Fall'n on th'inventors heads. All this can I
> Truly deliver. (5.2.351, 381, 382-88)

In formulating and delivering that "story," Horatio will both find meaning in and create meaning from the events audiences have just witnessed, and he will do so for reasons that are at least partly political. By reducing Denmark's stunned incomprehension, the "story" will help, he hopes, to avoid social and political disorder: "But let this same be presently performed, / Even while men's minds are wild, lest more mischance / On plots and errors happen" (5.2. 395-97).

Horatio's "story" of Hamlet will bear the same relationship to what has happened that "The Murder of Gonzago" bears to the Ghost's narrative of how he died at Claudius's hands and that all versions of the *Hamlet*(s) owned by the acting company for which Shakespeare provided scripts bear to earlier written versions of the Hamlet story that go back to Saxo's *Historia Danicae*, written late in the twelfth century. In fact, the processes of selecting, shaping, arranging, interpreting, and judging that Horatio will employ as he fashions his "story" and that Fortinbras employs to cast Hamlet as a "soldier" are those that actors and directors also use each time Hamlet is produced and performed. From among the array of performance possibilities, they select, arrange, and shape those that they will perform, determining, for example, such matters as how Laertes wounds Hamlet and how Hamlet stabs Claudius.

By ending not with its protagonist's death but with Horatio's and Fortinbras's acts of interpretation and judgment, *Hamlet* does more than hold up a mirror in which those who experience the play—in performance or on the page—can see the processes of interpretation and judgment in which they are themselves engaged. The ending of *Hamlet* also anticipates and accommodates the diversity of interpretation and judgment that is, as Rosenberg has demonstrated, such a conspicuous feature of performances and commentary over the centuries. Horatio and Fortinbras offer differing, perhaps even conflicting interpretations of *Hamlet*—as Buzz Goodbody's 1976 production for the Royal Shakespeare Company emphasized by having Horatio register dismay at Fortinbras's command that Hamlet's corpse be carried off "like a soldier." Horatio calls upon "flights of angels" to "sing" Hamlet to his rest, while Fortinbras calls for "four captains" to bear him off to the sound of cannon fire: "Go bid the soldiers shoot." The Folio ends with a stage direction that, in contrast to the "*<Exeunt>*" in the Second Quarto, ensures that audiences hear the guns firing: "*^Exeunt Marching: after the which, a Peale of Ordenance are shot off^.*"[17] Does Horatio, perhaps yielding to the power that Fortinbras is gathering to himself, join in that "*^Marching^*," or do audiences, bearing a "wary eye," see him resist that power by walking rather than marching as he exits?

Fortinbras's act of selecting one from among Hamlet's attributes—his (potential) capacity as a royal warrior—and using it to shape his assessment of Hamlet mirrors what has long been the most common strategy of interpreting and judging him and the play: the attempt to identify a tragic flaw in Hamlet. Those who employ that strategy sometimes justify it by citing Hamlet's account to Horatio—found only in the Second Quarto—of how "<oft it chances>" that an individual

> <Carrying, I say, the stamp of one defect
> Being Nature's livery or Fortune's star,
> His virtues else, be they as pure as grace,
> As infinite as man may may undergo,
> Shall in the general censure take corruption
> From that particular fault.> (1.4.23, 31-36)

Spoken voice-over while the words were displayed on the screen, Hamlet's observation served as a prologue for Olivier's film, which proceeded to identify Hamlet's tragic flaw by adding the comment: "This is the tragedy of a man who could not make up his mind."

Note, however, that Hamlet says it is "the general censure" that accepts the idea that "one defect," a single "particular fault," can corrupt all the "virtues," no matter how pure or numerous, a person also possesses. Hamlet is describing how most people weigh the relationship between an individual's flaws and virtues, but he is not endorsing that process or the judgments it yields. Hamlet's directions to the players make clear his own opinion of the validity of "the general censure." "The censure" of "one" person who is "judicious" "must," he tells them, "o'erweigh a whole theater of others" (3.2.26-28). The processes and norms that the mass of people, the general public, use when forming a judgment are not, Hamlet insists, those best suited to assessing a man's actions on the stage or in life.

The dialogue between the gravediggers takes up the issue of how a person's final actions are judged:

FIRST CLOWN:
   Is she to be buried in Christian burial, <when she> willfully[18] seeks her own salvation?
SECOND CLOWN:
   I tell thee she is; therefore make her grave straight. The crowner hath sat on her, and finds it Christian burial.
FIRST CLOWN:
   How can that be, unless she drowned herself in her own defense?
SECOND CLOWN:
   Why, 'tis found so.
FIRST CLOWN:
   It must be *se offendendo*, it cannot be else. For here lies the point:if I drown myself wittingly, it argues an act, and an act hath three

branches <— it is to act, to do, and to perform.>[19] Argal, she
drowned herself wittingly. (5.1.1-13)

This exchange sets the First Clown's judgment that Ophelia's drowning is an act of suicide against the official, legally authoritative judgment of the coroner ("crowner") that she is entitled to the Christian
burial denied to those who kill themselves. Whose judgment is correct?

Any effort to answer that question brings one face-to-face with the
fact that Gertrude's account is the only information that the play provides about the circumstances of Ophelia's death, and that account
contains contradictory information. Gertrude reports that Ophelia
fell into the stream accidentally when "an envious sliver broke"
(4.7.174)—a detail incompatible with a judgment of suicide—but
Gertrude also reports that Ophelia did not try to save herself. Once in
the water, she did nothing, Gertrude says, but chant "snatches of old
<lauds>,"[20] acting as if she were "incapable of [comprehending] her
own distress, / Or like a creature native and endued / Unto that element" (4.7.178-81). The priest officiating at Ophelia's burial declares
that "Her death was doubtful" (5.1.227)—a judgment consistent with
the conflicting details of Gertrude's report.

Compounding that sense of doubt are the conflicting assessments
of Ophelia's "obsequies" (5.1.226) offered by various characters.
Hamlet, observing the "maimèd rites" being extended to the corpse
he does not yet know is Ophelia's, comments, "This doth betoken /
The corpse they follow did with desperate hand / Fordo its own life"
(5.1. 219-221). Laertes seems to concur, asking in anguished grief,
"What ceremony else?" and "Must there no more be done?" (5.1. 225,
235). The priest has no doubts, however, that Ophelia is receiving
burial rites "enlarged" beyond what is fitting:

> but that great command o'ersways the order
> She should in ground unsanctified <been> lodged[21]
> Till the last trumpet. For charitable prayers,
> ^Shards^, flints, and pebbles should be thrown on her.
> (5.1. 226, 228-31)

His sentiments echo those of the Second Clown, who asserts that if
Ophelia "had not been a gentlewoman, she should have been buried
out o'Christian burial" (5.1. 23-25).

The attention that characters in *Hamlet* give to how Ophelia dies
and is buried highlights the tendency, not uncommon among
Shakespearean scholars and critics, to impose certainty of judgment

on what is "doubtful." Those in authority—the coroner and "great command"—determine that Ophelia will receive a certain kind of burial, however "doubtful" her death. As if in response to that judgment, competing judgments of the rites as "maimèd" on the one hand or "enlarged" on the other are formulated and voiced. Laertes calls for "more" to "be done," while the two clowns and the priest judge that Ophelia does not deserve the rites she does receive. All the judgments are arbitrary in that each rests on certainty that has been fashioned from what is "doubtful."

Any judgments audiences reach regarding Ophelia's death are made inescapably "doubtful" by a factor easily overlooked in reading: the play does not allow its audiences to see how she dies. They do not see her death performed. Like readers, they must envision it in the "mind's eye," by the "forgery of shapes and tricks" like that which left Claudius "short" of Lamord's equestrian feats. By placing Ophelia's death offstage, the play ensures that it eludes even the most "wary eye."[22] *Hamlet* uses Ophelia's death and the conflicting judgments it generates as a mirror that illuminates efforts to understand and assess the actions and the acting that culminate in the deaths—enacted before the audience's eyes—of Laertes, Gertrude, Claudius and, especially, Hamlet. To look into that mirror is to face both the limits within which judgment operates and the need to make judgments within those limits as one strives to be that single "judicious" spectator whose "censure" is to be prized more than "a whole theatre of others."

Any judgment of Hamlet or of *Hamlet* based exclusively on reading its play-text(s) rests—as does any judgment about Ophelia's death—on words alone. Such a judgment does not take into account what actors and the characters they portray do—the specific acts that they perform and their audiences see. Because it does not, every judgment of that kind, whatever its specific content, cannot escape being as "doubtful" as any assessment of Ophelia's death. Perhaps right, perhaps persuasive, perhaps compelling, but always and necessarily "doubtful" at its core. In fact, the more authority such a judgment claims, acquires, or is given—the more it takes on force and effectiveness equivalent to that of the judgment of the coroner and of "great command"—the more likely it is to provoke counter-judgments analagous to those that the two clowns and the priest reach regarding Ophelia.

Judgments based on what actors and the characters they play do during performances of *Hamlet* have not been and will not be unanimous. Those actions, including the act of speaking words aloud, vary from era to era, production to production, even performance to performance as shifts in theatrical conditions and conventions and in the more general culture make it possible over time to perceive and enact possibilities from among those allowed by the Folio and the Second Quarto, which are themselves different. In addition, members of the same audience will differ in how they assess the actions and the acting they see and hear, much as Ophelia, Polonius, and Claudius do after witnessing Hamlet's behavior during the "nunnery" scene. *Hamlet* itself anticipates and allows for such diversity in the different judgments of Ophelia's death and in the different assessments of Hamlet voiced by Horatio and Fortinbras as the play ends. For Hamlet, it is "playing," not play wri(gh)ting or play reading, that holds "the mirror up to nature" (3.2.22), and it is "the play"—what the actors will do and say—that, by catching "the conscience of the King" (2.2.605-6), will enable Hamlet to judge the veracity of the ghost and Claudius's guilt. *Hamlet* is profoundly concerned with the specific judgments and interpretations one comes to, but it is also concerned, at least equally, with the processes by which they are reached. It asks that those processes arise from and be rooted not in the "forgery of shapes and tricks" but in the playing of *Hamlet*. It asks that the play as performed—the actions and the acting, not simply the printed texts—be "the thing" to which, *our* consciences caught, we respond, bearing "a wary eye."

Notes

1. In quoting from *Hamlet*, I follow David Bevington's edition, unless noted otherwise: *Complete Works of Shakespeare* (New York: HarperCollins, 1992). An early version of this essay was presented at the 1990 meeting of the Shakespeare Association of America as part of a seminar on "Ludic Elements in the Plays of Shakespeare and His Contemporaries" led by Douglas L. Peterson. I am grateful to him and the other members of that seminar for their help, especially Cynthia Marshall, who provided a detailed written response to that seminar paper upon which I drew frequently in composing this essay.

2. These words appear in the Second Quarto (1604) of *Hamlet* but not the Folio (1623). Words present in Q2 but not in F are enclosed within horizontal carets when quoted: <. . .>. Those present in F but not in Q2 are enclosed in vertical carets: ^. . .^. For discussions of the implications—for performance, analysis, and editorial practice—of differences in the three versions of *Hamlet*, including the First Quarto (1603), published during or shortly after Shakespeare's lifetime, see Paul Werstine, "The Textual Mystery of *Hamlet*," *ShQ* 39 (1988): 1-26, and Philip C. McGuire, "Which Fortinbras, Which *Hamlet*?" *The "Hamlet" First Published (Q1, 1603): Origins, Form, Intertextualities*, ed. Thomas Clayton (Newark: University of Delaware Press, 1992), 151-78. In quoting from F, Q2, and Q1, I follow Paul Bertram and Bernice W. Kliman, eds., *The Three-Text "Hamlet":*

Parallel Texts of the First and Second Quartos and First Folio (New York: AMS, 1991).

3. In F, his name is Lamound.

4. *Homo Ludens: A Study of the Play Element in Culture,* trans. R. F. C. Hull (London: Routledge, 1949), 28. This definition is useful for my purposes, but it has flaws, foremost among them the claim that "play" has "its aim in itself." It seems to me that "play" can have aims or purposes outside itself. A child at play, for example, may have no aim other than the activity itself, but that playing can serve the larger purpose of contributing to the child's physical, emotional, and psychic development. The concept of play as recreation traced by Glending Olson and Douglas L. Peterson demonstrates the existence, during the Middle Ages and into the sixteenth century, of a species of play that has purposes outside itself; it contributes to the health and longevity of those who engage in it. See Olson, *Literature as Recreation in the Later Middle Ages* (Ithaca: Cornell University Press, 1982), and Peterson, "Lyly, Greene, and Shakespeare and the Recreation of Princes," *Shakespeare Studies* 20 (1988): 67-88. Hamlet himself speaks of "the purpose of playing" (3.2. 20), and two persuasive accounts of the purpose(s) of that kind of playing in early modern England have been offered by Louis Adrian Montrose, "The Purpose of Playing: Reflections on a Shakepearean Anthropology," *Helios* n.s. 7 (1980): 51-74, and Stephen Greenblatt, *Shakespearean Negotiations: The Circulation of Social Energy in Renaissance England* (Berkeley: University of California Press, 1988). For a critique of Huizinga's conception of play, see Roger Callois, *Man, Play, and Games,* trans. Meyer Barash (Glencoe, Illinois: Free Press, 1961).

5. In F, "shewes."

6. For a full discussion of this aspect of the playing that occurs during the final scene, see Maynard Mack, "The World of *Hamlet,*" *Shakespeare: Modern Essays in Criticism,* ed. Leonard F. Dean, rev. ed. (London: Oxford University Press, 1967), 242-62.

7. One way of conveying that ludic quality in performance is to have Hamlet indulge in some mischievous, boyish pranks. In the 1969 movie directed by Tony Richardson, Nicol Williamson, drawing on a stage practice that goes back at least to Edwin Booth, reached behind his back with his sword and scored the second hit by smacking Laertes on his backside, then grinned, shrugging in almost sheepish self-delight at his naughtiness. For his 1990 film, Franco Zeffirelli had Hamlet and Laertes use two-handed swords for the second exchange. Mel Gibson's Hamlet pretended that his sword was too heavy, drawing laughter from the assembled court as he staggered while trying to hold it before him, then winking at Gertrude.

Eugen Fink notes that during ludic play at its most intense, "time is experienced not as a precipitate rush of successive moments, but rather as the one full moment that is, so to speak, a glimpse of eternity"—"The Oasis of Happiness: Towards an Ontology of Play," *Game, Play, Literature,* ed. Jacques Ehrmann (Boston: Beacon, 1971), 21. If that is so, it is singularly appropriate that Hamlet is engaged in play that has a ludic quality when he receives the wound that confirms his participation in the passage that, Gertrude tells him, everyone makes: "all that lives must die, / Passing through nature to eternity" (1.3. 72-73).

8. Marvin Rosenberg, *The Masks of "Hamlet"* (Newark: University of Delaware Press; London and Toronto: Associated University Presses, 1992).

9. The First Quarto (1603) includes a stage direction that points toward that possibility: "*They catch one anothers Rapiers, and both are wounded, Laertes falles downe, the Queene falles downe and dies.*" Because most Shakespeareans continue to regard Q1, the so-called "bad" quarto, as a version of *Hamlet* that is neither legitimate nor authoritative, it customarily receives very little attention. I do not agree with that practice, for reasons set out in "Which Fortinbras, Which *Hamlet*," but in this essay I concentrate on differences between Q2 and F, both of which are accepted as legitimate and authoritative. I have done so for tactical reasons, preferring to avoid triggering a controversy about the status of Q1 that might deflect attention from the points I am trying to make in this essay.

10. For additional discussion of this passage, see Margaret W. Ferguson, "*Hamlet*: Letters and Spirits," in *Shakespeare and the Question of Theory*, ed. Patricia Parker and Geoffrey Hartman (New York and London: Methuen, 1985), 292-309, and Harry Levin, *The Question of Hamlet* (London: Oxford University Press, 1959).

11. In F, "co-mingled."

12. The corresponding stage directions in Q1 are "*Heere they play*" and "*They play againe*"; Q2 gives no stage directions.

13. For a recent discussion of how the exchange of weapons occurs, see James L. Jackson, "'They Catch One Another's Rapiers': The Exchange of Weapons in *Hamlet*," *ShQ* 41 (1990): 281-98.

14. In Q2, "the Onixe."

15. In Q2, "bodies." For a discussion of this difference, see Margarida G. Rauen, "*Hamlet*'s Bodies," *ShQ* 41 (1990): 490.

16. In Q2, "for no cause."

17. Q1 ends without a final stage direction.

18. In F, "that wilfully."

19. In F, "and an Act hath three branches. It is an Act to doe and to performe."

20. In F, "tunes."

21. In F, "have lodged."

22. Interestingly, both the Olivier and the Zeffirelli films of *Hamlet* show their audiences moments from Ophelia's death. The Olivier presentation is deeply influenced by John Everett Millais's 1852 painting of Ophelia floating in the stream. That painting is both an example of and a contributor to what Elaine Showalter terms an "obsession in later nineteenth-century painting" with Ophelia; "The English Pre-Raphaelites painted her again and again, choosing the drowning which is only

described in the play, and where no actress's image had preceded them or interfered with their imaginative supremacy" ("Representing Ophelia: Women, Madness, and the Responsibilities of Feminist Criticism," in *Shakespeare and the Question of Theory,* ed. Parker and Hartman, 84). Showalter also directs attention to Delacroix's 1843 lithograph *La Mort d'Ophélie,* which shows Ophelia "half-suspended in the stream as her dress slips from her body" (84). The existence of such graphic and filmic representations across a century and half attests to the power of the desire to see that the play as scripted in F and Q2 (as well as Q1) both arouses in its audiences and then frustrates.

Contributors

John A. Alford (Michigan State University) has written extensively on such medieval figures as Chaucer, Langland, and Rolle. His books include (ed.) *A Companion to Piers Plowman* (University of California Press), *Piers Plowman: A Glossary of Legal Diction* (Brewer), *Literature and Law in the Middle Ages: A Bibliography of Scholarship* (Garland), and (co-editor) *Literature and Religion in the Later Middle Ages* (MRTS).

David Bevington (University of Chicago) is the author of *From "Mankind" to Marlowe, Tudor Drama and Politics,* and *Action Is Eloquence: Shakespeare's Language of Gesture* (all by Harvard University Press). He has also edited *Medieval Drama* for Houghton Mifflin (the standard anthology) and the *Complete Works of Shakespeare (Bantam* and *HarperCollins)*, as well as *The Macro Plays* and numerous individual plays for Penguin, Oxford, Cambridge, and the Revels series.

T. P. Dolan (University College, Dublin) has directed and produced medieval plays both in this country and abroad. He revised T. P. Dunning's *Piers Plowman: An Interpretation of the A Text* for Oxford University Press. He is now completing an edition of Richard Fitzralph's Latin sermons, an edition begun by Arnold Williams.

John R. Elliott, Jr. (Syracuse University) is the author of *Playing God: Medieval Mysteries on the Modern Stage* (University of Toronto Press) as well as numerous articles on medieval and Renaissance drama. He has also directed productions of early English plays both in North America and in England.

John B. Friedman (University of Illinois) has published *The Monstrous Races in Medieval Art and Thought* (Harvard), *Orpheus in the Middle Ages* (Harvard), *John de Foxton's Liber Cosmographiae (1408): An Edition and Codicological Study* (Brill), and *Northern English Books, Owners and Makers in the Late Middle Ages* (Syracuse University). He has just completed *An Annotated and Discursive Bibliography of Medieval Iconography* for Garland Publishers. Arnold Williams directed his Ph.D. dissertation.

Alexandra Johnston (University of Toronto) is the founder and present director of the Records of Early English Drama (REED), published by the University of Toronto Press. She has co-edited the *Records of Early English Drama: York* (2 vols.), and published numerous articles on medieval drama, especially on the York cycle. She has also directed, or acted in, several productions of medieval plays.

William G. Marx (Michigan State University) has directed six productions of medieval plays, including *Mankind*, the *Second Shepherds' Play*, the *Wakefield Last Judgment*, and the *Chester Noah's Flood*. His production of the *Second Shepherds' Play* was videotaped, with an introduction by Arnold Williams, for commercial distribution. His essay here is part of a book in progress on modern production of medieval drama.

Lister M. Matheson (Michigan State University) is the general editor of a collection of scientific treatises in Middle English, *Popular and Practical Science of Medieval England* (Colleagues Press) and is a former associate editor of the *Middle English Dictionary*. He has published many articles on such subjects as the medieval romance, historiography, William Caxton, and manuscripts. His graduate courses in medieval drama have often culminated in public performances.

Philip C. McGuire (Michigan State University) is the author of *Speechless Dialect: Shakespeare's Open Silences* (University of California Press), and *Shakespeare: The Jacobean Plays* (Macmillan and St. Martin's Press). He is also co-editor of *Shakespeare: The Theatrical Dimension* (AMS Press) and serves on the Advisory Board of the Shakespeare Education and Shakespeare Interactive Archive projects at Massachusetts Institute of Technology.

David Mills (University of Liverpool) is co-editor of the standard edition of the *Chester Mystery Cycle* (EETS), and editor of the same cycle in a modernized spelling version (Colleagues Press). He is also co-author of *The Chester Mystery Cycle: Essays and Documents* (University of

North Carolina Press), and "The Drama of Religious Ceremonial" in the *Revels History of Drama in the England Language.* He is currently co-editing the Cheshire records for the Records of Early English Drama.

Randal Robinson (Michigan State University) is the author of *Unlocking Shakespeare's Language: Help for the Teacher and Student* (National Council of Teachers of English), as well as *"Hamlet" in the 1950s: An Annotated Bibliography* (Garland). He has appeared in university and professional theatrical productions, and with Peter Holben Wehr he has developed a computer program on Shakespeare's language.

Martin Stevens (City University of New York) is the author of *Four Middle English Mystery Cycles* (Princeton) and many articles on a range of medieval literary subjects. He co-edited *The Towneley Plays* for the Early English Text Society. He is co-General Editor of the Early English Drama in Translation Series (SUNY Press) and co-editor of The New Ellesmere Facsimile Project (Huntington Library Press). Arnold Williams was his dissertation adviser.

Index

The index includes the names of authors, works, and historical persons; it does not include *dramatis personae* or endnote documentation.

A

Abraham (Dublin), 114
Aelred of Rievaulx, *Speculum Charitatis*, 15
Aeschylus, 51
Alba, 189
Albion Knight, 151
Alford, John A., 6, 10, 151-77
Altman, Joel, 157, 158, 170
Amalarius of Metz, 3, 9, 15, 17, 22; *De Officiis Libri IV*, 15
Aquinas, Thomas, 2
Aristophanes, *The Clouds*, 51
Arundel, Thomas, bishop, 213
Augustine of Hippo, 2; *City of God*, 113
Aureus de universo, 204

B

Bale, John, *King John*, 168
Barnes, Barnabe, *The Devil's Charter*, 78
Beaumont, Francis, 52; *Thierry and Theodoret*, 80; and John Fletcher, *The Maid's Tragedy*, 74, 78
Becket, Thomas, 211, 212, 215

Benediktbeuern Christmas play, 56; Passion Play, 56, 59
Bereblock, John, 185, 186
Berger, Sidney, 108
Berkeley, Thomas, 52; *The Lost Lady*, 83
Bernard, Samuel, 182
Bevington, David, 4, 10, 14, 51-83, 128
Bible: Genesis 9:20, 118; John 11:11, 58; Luke 23:24, 57; Luke 24, 15; Matt. 2:12, 56; Matt. 25:1-13, 93; Matt. 25:10-13, 57; Matt. 26:40-45, 57; Matt. 27:63, 60; Song of Songs, 94
Bloch, Howard, 112
Bodkin, Maud, 2
Bonhomme, Pasquier, 204
Bouchet, Jean, *Annals of Aquitaine*, 213
Brewer, Anthony, 52; *The Lovesick King*, 79
Brome, Richard, 52; *The Antipodes*, 83; *The Queen's Exchange*, 74; and Thomas Heywood, *The Late Lancashire Witches*, 74

259

Brooke, Tucker, 1, 151
Brown, John Russell, 108
Brut, 202-4, 206, 208-9. *See also*
    Caxton, William, *Chronicles of*
    England
Bryden, William, 107
Buckeridge, John, 184
Bullough, Geoffrey, *Narrative and*
    Dramatic Sources of Shakespeare, 198
Burghley, Lord, 186, 210
Burns, Edward, 108
Burton, Robert, 181; co-author of
    Alba, 189

C

Calfhill, James, 181; *Progne*, 186
Campbell, Josie P., 116, 117, 121
Capellanus, Andreas, *The Art of*
    Courtly Love, 111
Capgrave, John, 213
Carew, George, 186
Carew, Peter, 187
Carey, Millicent, 113, 115, 118
Cartwright, William, 181; *The Royal*
    Slave, 182, 190, 191
Castle of Perseverance, The, 4, 28, 35,
    36, 39, 41, 52, 56, 133, 159
Cavendish, William, 52; and James
    Shirley, *The Country Captain*
    (*Captain Underwit*), 83
Cawley, A. C., 127
Caxton, William, 202-4, 208, 209,
    215; *Chronicles of England*, 204;
    Liber ultimus, 204, 206, 207, 209.
    See also Brut
Chambers, E. K., 14
Chapman, George, 52
Charles I, 182, 185, 190
Charles II, 215
Chaucer, Geoffrey, 110; *The Book of*
    the Duchess, 164; *The Friar's Tale*,
    35; *The Knight's Tale*, 26, 186; *The*
    Miller's Tale, 163
Chekhov, Anton, *Uncle Vanya*, 51

Chester cycle, 87, 110; *Doomsday*, 136;
    Massacre of the Innocents, 4, 103,
    104, 105; *Noah* (the Flood), 109-
    26, 135; *Purification*, 136
Chettle, Henry, 52, 67; and Anthony
    Munday, *The Death of Robert, Earl of*
    Huntington, 74; *Downfall of Robert*
    Earl of Huntington, 67; *The Trial of*
    Chivalry, 67
Christmas Prince, The, 7, 183
Chronicque de la traïson et mort de
    Richart Deux, 204, 207, 209
Clanchy, M. T., 19
Coletti, Teresa, 85
Conflict of Conscience, The, 152
Contention between Liberality and
    Prodigality, The, 10, 156, 157, 165
Conversion of St. Paul, The (Fleury), 58
Cornish Creation, 110
Cornish Ordinalia, 107
Cowling, Douglas, 135
Creton, Jean, *Histoire du Roy*
    d'Angleterre Richard II, 209
Cysat, Renward, 39-41

D

Dalaper, John, 186, 187
Dan Jeremy, *Lay Folks Mass-Book*, 19
Daniel, Samuel, *Arcadia Reformed* (*The*
    Queen's Arcadia), 189; *Civil Wars*,
    211
Daniel (Beauvais play), 1
Davenant, William, 52; *Albovine, King*
    of the Lombards, 81; *The Cruel*
    Brother, 81; *The Platonic Lovers*, 82
Davenport, Robert, *The City Nightcap*,
    81
Davenport, Tony, 108, 137, 138
de Meun, Jean, 112
de Vocht, Henry, 127
Dee, John, 209
Dekker, Thomas, 52; and Thomas
    Middleton, *The Honest Whore*, 74
Denny, Neville, 107, 113

Digby Conversion of St. Paul, 59

Digby Mary Magdalene, 58

Dolan, T. P., 3, 9, 13-24

Duffy, Eamon, 18

E

Earl of Leicester, chancellor of
Oxford University, 180

Ebstorf map, 3, 28, 30, 42

Edes, Richard, 181

Edward, the Black Prince, 213

Edward VI, 187, 202, 215

Edwards, Richard, 186, 187

Elckerlijc, 127-29, 131, 135, 148

Elizabeth I, queen, 7, 10, 26, 63, 185,
186, 188, 189, 210

Elliott, John R., Jr., 7, 10, 107, 113,
116, 179-94

Enough Is as Good as a Feast. See
Wager, William

Every Woman in Her Humor, 215

Everyman, 5, 6, 9, 10, 52, 85, 127-49,
154

Exton, Sir Piers de, 8, 195, 199, 201,
204, 207, 209, 211, 215

F

Fabyan, Robert, 202, 207, 208, 215;
*New Chronicles of England and
France,* 206

Fairbairn, Ronald, 224

Faithful Friends, The, 79

Fasciculus temporum, 204

Fergusson, Francis, 53

Fisher, Jasper, 182

Flanigan, Clifford, 108

Fleming, Abraham, 201, 207

Fletcher, Alan J., 127

Fletcher, John, 52; *Love's Pilgrimage,*
79; *Monsieur Thomas,* 79; *The
Wandering Lovers, or The Lovers'
Progress,* 80; *The Wild Goose Chase,*
80; *The Woman's Prize, or The Tamer*

Tamed, 79; and Francis Beaumont,
The Maid's Tragedy, 74, 78; and
Philip Massinger, *Sir John van
Olden Barnavelt,* 80; *The Spanish
Curate,* 80; *Thierry and Theodoret,*
80

Fleury playbook: *Conversion of St.
Paul,* 58; *Herod,* 4; *Ordo ad
Repraesentandum Herodem (The
Service for Representing Herod),* 54;
The Slaughter of the Innocents, 58;
Tres Clerici (The Three Scholars),
57

Ford, John, 52; *The Lover's Melancholy,*
81

Freud, Sigmund, 2

Friedman, John B., 4, 9, 99-108

Froissart, Jean, 202

G

Gager, William, 180, 181; *Rivales,* 188

Gibson, Gail McMurray, 86, 90, 96,
97

Gibson, Mel, 242

Gilbert, P. J. P., 97

Ginzberg, Louis, 112, 118

Goffe, Thomas, 181; *Raging Turk
(Bajazet II),* 74

Goodbody, Buzz, 246

Gosson, Stephen, 180

Grammaticus, Saxo, *Historia Danicae,*
246

Grandes chroniques de France, 204

Grantley, Darryll, 108

Graves, Robert, 2, 112

Greene, Robert, *Friar Bacon and Friar
Bungay,* 52, 66

Gregory the Great, Pope, 16, 152,
159, 169, 170; *Moralia in Iob,* 152;
Pastoral Care, 152

Grimald, Nicholas, 181

Guntrip, Harry, 224

Gwinne, Matthew, 182; *Vertumnus,*
189, 190

H

Hall, Edward, 7, 195, 198, 200-4, 208, 210, 211, 215; *Vnion of the Two Noble and Illustre Famelies of Lancastre and Yorke*, 198
Hall, Peter, 8, 242
Hardison, O. B., Jr., 14, 44
Hardy, Thomas, 13
Harling, Anne, 96
Hayward, John, *King Henry the IV*, 211
Henricus de Frimaria, *Tractatus de occultatione vitiorum sub specie virtutum*, 153
Henry II, 211, 212
Henry IV, 195, 198, 202, 209, 212, 214, 215
Henry V, 200, 208
Henry VIII, 198
Hereford map, 3, 28-29, 31, 32, 33, 34-36, 42
Herod (Fleury), 4
Heylin, Peter (chaplain to Charles I), 182, 184
Heywood, Thomas, 67; *If You Know Not Me You Know Nobody* (*The Troubles of Queen Elizabeth*), 74; *Love's Mistress, or The Queen's Masque* (*Cupid and Psyche, or Cupid's Mistress*), 82; *Trial of Chivalry*, 67; and Richard Brome, *The Late Lancashire Witches*, 74
Hickscorner, 138
Higden, Ranulph, *Polychronicon*, 204, 207, 209, 213
Hilarius, *Suscitatio Lazari* (*The Raising of Lazarus*), 58
Hippolytus, 180
Holiday, Barten, 181
Holinshed, Raphael, 7, 195, 200, 209-11, 215; *Chronicles*, 198
Holkham Picture Bible Book, 113
Horace, 110
Howell, Jane, 225
Huizinga, J., *Homo Ludens*, 236, 237

Hutten, Leonard, 181; *Bellum Grammaticale*, 188

I

Irenaeus, 2

J

Jambeck, Thomas J., 127, 142
James I, king, 7, 184, 188-90
James VI of Scotland, 210
Johnston, Alexandra F., 4, 9, 85-98
Jones, Inigo, 189, 190
Jonson, Ben, 52, 182; *Volpone*, 78
Julian of Norwich, 96
Juvenal, 110

K

Kempe, Margery, 96; *The Book of Margery Kempe*, 96
Kennedy, George, 1
Killigrew, Henry, 52; *The Conspiracy* (*Pallantus and Eudora*), 82
Killigrew, Thomas, *The Princess, or, Love at First Sight*, 82
King Leir, 67
Kolve, V. A., 110, 113, 121, 163
Korzybski, Alfred, *Science and Sanity*, 28
Kupfer, Marcia, 32
Kyd, Thomas, 65, 68; *The Spanish Tragedy*, 52, 63, 66, 235

L

La Seinte Resureccion (*The Holy Resurrection*), 57
Lancashire, Ian, 138
Langland, William, 110; see also *Piers Plowman*
Lateware, Matthew, 182
Laud, William, Archbishop, 183, 185
Lawes, Henry, 191

Lawes, William, 191
Lay Folks Mass-Book, 3, 18, 19, 22
Legenda Aurea, 91, 92
Lewis, C. S., 169
Leyerle, John, 2, 85
Like Will to Like, 51, 61, 157
Lindenbaum, Sheila, 107
Llewellyn, Martin, 179, 181
Ludus Coventriae (N-Town cycle),
   100, 110, 111, 114-15, 153. *See also*
   N-Town cycle
Luzerner Osterspiel, 39
Lydgate, John, 65
Lyly, John, 68; *Endymion*, 52, 60, 62,
   63; *Sappho and Phao*, 51, 63

M

MacKenzie, Roy, 157
Maid's Metamorphosis, The, 74
Mankind, 2, 51, 61, 136, 165, 168
Markham, Gervase, 52; *Herod and
   Antipater*, 74
Marlowe, Christopher, 65; *Doctor
   Faustus*, 52, 65, 66; *Edward II*, 52,
   66; *The Jew of Malta*, 65; and
   Thomas Nashe, *Dido Queen of
   Carthage*, 52
Marx, Karl, 2
Marx, William G., 5, 9, 109-126
Mary I, queen (Mary Tudor), 187,
   215
Mary, Queen of Scots, 187, 210
Mary Magdalene (Digby), 61, 153
Massinger, Philip, 52; and John
   Fletcher, *Sir John van Olden
   Barnavelt*, 80; *The Spanish Curate*,
   80; *Thierry and Theodoret*, 80; *A
   Very Woman, or The Prince of
   Tarent*, 82
Matheson, Lister M., 7, 8, 195-219
Mathew, Toby, 181; *Marcus Geminus*,
   186
May, Charles, 182
Mayne, Jasper, 52; *The City Match*, 83

McGuire, Philip C., 8, 9, 235-53
Mead, Robert, 181
Meditationes vitae Christi, 96
Medwall, Henry, *Fulgens and Lucrece*,
   1, 10, 137, 138, 171, 172; *Nature*, 6,
   7, 151-77
Memlinc, Hans, *The Passion of Christ*,
   37, 38
Merbury, Francis, *Marriage between
   Wit and Wisdom*, 1, 152
Meredith, Peter, 85, 107
Meres, Francis, 180
Middleton, Thomas, 52; and
   Thomas Dekker, *The Honest
   Whore*, 74; *The Revenger's Tragedy*,
   74, 78, 235
Mills, David, 5, 6, 9, 10, 127-49
Milton, John, 106; *Comus*, 67
Missale Romanum, 17
Moran, Dennis V., 134
Morton, John, Archbishop of
   Canterbury, 159
Munday, Anthony, 52. *See also*
   Chettle, Henry
Munsen, William, 141
Myrroure for Magistrates, 211

N

N-Town cycle, 4, 27, 60, 85-98, 137,
   153; *Assumption*, 91; *Death and
   Burial*, 87. *See also Ludus Coventriae*
Nabbes, Thomas, 52; *Totenham Court*,
   81
Nashe, Thomas, *Pierce Penilesse*, 215;
   and Christopher Marlowe, *Dido
   Queen of Carthage*, 52
Nelson, Alan, 108, 115, 179
Neuss, Paula, ed., *Aspects of Early
   English Drama*, 107
New Custom, 152, 164
Newcastle fragments, 110, 111, 112
Nice Wanton, 139
Nunn, Trevor, 8

O

Occupation and Idleness, 61
Olivier, Laurence, 8, 155, 242, 244,
  247
Ordo ad Repraesentandum Herodem
  (*The Service for Representing Herod*)
  (Fleury), 54
Ordo Repraesentationis Adae, 56
Palamon and Arcyte, 186, 187
Orrell, John, 189

P

Palmer, Barbara, 111
Patai, Raphael, 112
Peele, George, 65, 68; *The Battle of
  Alcazar*, 66; *The Old Wife's Tale*, 52,
  64
Piers Plowman, 141, 153, 160, 169. *See
  also* Langland, William
Pius V, Pope, 17
Plautus, 180
Poel, Edward, 127
Propertius, 110
Prudentius, *Psychomachia*, 6, 152,
  169

R

Rainolds, John, 180, 187
*Rare Triumphs of Love and Fortune,
  The*, 51
Rastell, Richard, 107
Records of Early English Drama
  (REED), 179
Redford John, *Wit and Science*, 51, 61
Respublica, 152
Revenger's Tragedy, The, 74, 78, 235
Richard II, 200, 209, 210, 212
Richard III, 186
Richardson, Tony, 244
Rider, W., 52; *The Twins*, 82
Riggio, Milla, 107
Robinson, Randal, 8, 221-33

Rose, Martial, *Wakefield Mystery Plays*,
  100
Rosenberg, Marvin, 240, 246
Ross, Laurence, 108
Rossiter, A. P., 110, 152

S

Sandsbury, John, 182
Schell, Edgar, 107
*Second Part of the Seven Deadly Sins,
  The*, 64-65
Seneca, 180
Shakespeare, William, 1, 10, 25, 42,
  43, 65, 71, 74, 204, 209; *As You
  Like It*, 3, 43, 154; *Cymbeline*, 52,
  72, 73, 74; *Hamlet*, 9, 52, 53, 69,
  235-53; *Henry IV, Part 1, 68; Henry
  IV, Part 2*, 44, 52, 53, 68; *Henry V*,
  44-45; *Henry VI, Part 1*, 67; *Henry
  VI, Part II*, 67; *Henry VIII*, 74; *Julius
  Caesar*, 52, 69; *King Lear*, 52, 70,
  71; *Macbeth*, 71, 72; *Merchant of
  Venice*, 43; *A Midsummer Night's
  Dream*, 52, 53, 62, 64, 68; *Othello*,
  52, 70; *Pericles*, 52, 71, 73; *The Rape
  of Lucrece*, 52; *Richard II*, 7, 8, 195-
  219; *Richard III*, 52, 67, 69; *Romeo
  and Juliet*, 52, 69, 74; *The Taming of
  the Shrew*, 52, 65, 68, 79; *The
  Tempest*, 52, 69, 72; *Titus
  Andronicus*, 8, 221-33; *The Winter's
  Tale*, 8, 221-33
Shirley, James, 52; and William
  Cavendish, *The Country Captain*
  (*Captain Underwit*), 83
Sir Gawain and the Green Knight, 164
Skelton, John, *Magnificence*, 168
Slaughter of the Innocents, The (Fleury),
  58
Sophocles, *Ajax*, 184, 185, 189
Spector, Stephen, 90
Speed, John, 182
Spenser, Edmund, *Faerie Queene*, 153
Spivack, Bernard, 152, 164, 172

Sponsus play (Saint Martial at Limoges), 57
Stanislavski, Constantin, 9
Stevens, Martin, 3, 10, 25-49, 85, 107
Stock, Brian, 26
Stow, John, 209
Stringer, Philip, 188
Strode, William, 181; *Floating Island*, 190
Suckling, John, 52; *Brennoralt, or The Discontented Colonel*, 83

T

Taylor, Jerome, 108
Taylor, Joseph, 191
Tertullian, 2
Thierry and Theodoret (Francis Beaumont?), 80
Thomas of Woodstock (*1 Richard II*) 67
Tigg, E. R., 128
Tourneur, Cyril (or Thomas Middleton), *The Revenger's Tragedy*, 74, 78, 235
Towneley Cycle, 99-108, 110, 119; *Creation*, 58; *Killing of Abel*, 103, 104, 105; *Noah*, 5, 100, 103, 106; *Offering of the Magi*, 59; *Resurrection*, 60; *Second Shepherds' Play*, 2, 59, 103, 105, 114
Transitus Mariae, 91
Traversi, Derek, 7, 195
Tres Clerici (*The Three Scholars*), 57
Tres Sibyllae, 188
Treveris, Peter, 204
Trevisa, John, 204
Trial of Chivalry, The, 67
Trial of Treasure, The, 10, 155-57
True Chronicle History of King Leir, 67
Tucker, Thomas, 183
Turner, Victor, 27
Two Noble Ladies and the Converted Conjurer, The, 80

Twycross, Meg, 107
Twyne, Brian, 190
Tydeman, William, *English Medieval Theatre, 1400-1500*, 107

U

Ulysses Redux, 180
Ure, Peter, 209

V

Valiant Welshman, The, 79
van Diest, Peter, 128
Veldener, Johan, 204
Vitruvius, 189

W

Wager, William, *Enough Is as Good as a Feast*, 152; *The Longer Thou Livest the More Fool Thou*, 152, 171
Wakefield cycle, 99-108; see also Towneley cycle
Walsh, Martin W., 107
Walsingham, Thomas, 201, 213
Wars of Cyrus, 67
Watson, Edward, 179, 181
Webster, John, 52
Wickham, Glynne, 25, 137, 168
Wilde, George, 182; *Love's Hospital*, 184, 190
Wilde, Oscar, *Importance of Being Ernest, The*, 1
Williams, Arnold, frontispiece (photo), 1-3, 5, 9, 85, 99, 100, 107, 110, 119, 127, 179
Williams, Tennessee, *Streetcar Named Desire*, 1
Wilson, Arthur, 52; *The Inconstant Lady, or Better Late Than Never*, 81
Wilson, F. P., 171
Windsor, Miles, 185-88
Wisdom, 107, 153
Wood, Anthony, 188

Woolf, Rosemary, 90, 111, 114, 121
Worde, Wynkyn de, 204
Wortham, C. J., 128
Wright, Abraham, 182

Y

York cycle, 37, 86, 87, 91, 110;
   Coronation of the Virgin, 91; *Death*

of the Virgin, 91, 92; the "Fergus" play,
   91; *Flight into Egypt*, 60
Young, Karl, 14
Youth, 138
Yuletide, 183

Z

Zeffirelli, Franco, 8, 242, 244

DATE DUE